Truth & DARE

one year of dynamic devotions for girls

ann-margret HOVSEPIAN

David C Cook®

transforming lives together

TRUTH AND DARE
Published by David C Cook
4050 Lee Vance View
Colorado Springs, CO 80918 U.S.A.

David C Cook Distribution Canada
55 Woodslee Avenue, Paris, Ontario, Canada N3L 3E5

David C Cook U.K., Kingsway Communications
Eastbourne, East Sussex BN23 6NT, England

David C Cook and the graphic circle C logo
are registered trademarks of Cook Communications Ministries.

LCCN 2011934831
ISBN 978-1-4347-0208-1
eISBN 978-0-7814-0671-0

© 2011 Ann-Margret Hovsepian
Published in association with the literary agency of Credo
Communications LLC, Grand Rapids, Michigan

The Team: Susan Tjaden, Amy Konyndyk, Nick Lee, Renada Arens, and Karen Athen
Cover and interior design: Luke Flowers
Drawing in "A Strange Answer to Prayer" courtesy of Joni Eareckson Tada

Printed in the United States of America

First Edition 2011

1 2 3 4 5 6 7 8 9 10

073111

To Alexis and Melissa, my lovely nieces:
May you always seek God's truth and dare to live for Him

Introduction

Have you ever been to a party or a sleepover where someone said, "Hey, I have an idea! Let's play Truth or Dare!" Depending on who was in that group, the game could have been fun … or very, very embarrassing and awkward.

In Truth or Dare, the basic idea is that when your turn comes around, you get to choose if you want to tell the truth about something (without knowing what you might be asked) or take a dare (without knowing what you might be challenged to do). It's a risky game because you might have to answer a very personal question, or you might have to do something gross, scary, or embarrassing. Either way, both "truth" and "dare" in this game can end up feeling like negative, stressful words.

But knowing the truth and being daring—God's way, the way the Bible talks about—are awesome, positive experiences!

In this devotional, *Truth and Dare*, you will discover hundreds of amazing truths in God's Word. Each day, you'll look up and read the Bible verses at the top of the page. When you first read them, a lot of the Bible verses might seem hard to understand and even harder to live out, but as you keep reading, you'll see that the Bible is a perfect fit for you and that you don't have to wait until you're an adult to "get" it.

At the end of each day's devo, you'll also be challenged to apply what you've learned to your everyday life … in a way that's not gross, scary, or embarrassing. (Whew!) The more "dares" you take as you go through this book, the stronger and braver you'll grow in your faith and the more you'll know the awesome God who created and loves you!

If you've ever thought that being a Christian is tough or boring, *Truth and Dare* will help you see that it can be exciting and full of blessings. The *truth* in the Bible can help you *dare* to do great things for God.

Okay, then … I *dare* you to get started! Each day, flip to the next page and look up and read the Bible verse listed before reading the Truth and Dare sections for that day. It's a good idea to pray before and after you do each day's devotion, asking God to help you focus on and understand what He wants to teach you through His Word. Also, take time to answer the journaling questions (you're allowed to write in this book!) or to jot down whatever thoughts come to mind as you work on the devotion.

Here we go!

Ann-Margret Hovsepian

Don't you just love fresh, new things? Bright white gym socks, a pretty new journal, a great new backpack ... There's something cheery about using something for the first time and enjoying it while it's still clean and beautiful.

New Year's Day is a bit like that. You've got twelve months ahead of you that haven't been lived yet, and they're full of chances for fun new beginnings. How exciting!

For a lot of people, New Year's is a time to make *resolutions*—promises to themselves or to God about things they want to change and improve in their lives. For example ...

- I will lose ten pounds.
- I will practice my flute every day.
- I will stop biting my nails.
- I will floss my teeth more often.
- I will keep my room clean.

Even if you're starting this book on a different date from January 1, think about the next twelve months and what *your* resolutions will be for the year ahead.

- _____
- _____
- _____
- _____
- _____

We've got two resolution suggestions that will make this a great year for you:

1 Take fifteen minutes every morning to work on your *Truth and Dare* devo. (Read the tips in the introduction to get the most out of your devos.)

2 Take fifteen minutes every night to review the devo, think about what you learned during the day, and pray.

When you take time out for God each day, you'll be amazed at how He helps you take care of all the other important things in your life!

Got More Time?

In the space below, write out a prayer asking God to help you stick to a regular routine of doing your devos. Tell Him about any other changes in your life you need help with. Finish off by telling Him what you're looking forward to this year.

Journaling

Dear Jesus, thank you for being the truth.
Help me to dare to live for you. Amen.

1 John 2:24

Remain in Him

Truth
If you keep God's Word inside you, you will remain in God.

It may seem obvious, but the most important thing to know if you own a goldfish is that it always needs to be inside its tank or bowl. It would be pretty silly to keep your goldfish in a birdcage or doghouse, wouldn't it? The fish needs water to survive!

As a Christian, you need the truth of God to live and grow … not just once in a while but all the time. You can't ignore the things you read in the Bible or learn at church and expect to have a strong and healthy relationship with God.

That's why studying the Bible—and doing devotions like the ones in this book— is important. The more you fill yourself with the things God is teaching you now, the easier it will be for you to follow Him later in life.

DARE Don't let go of anything God teaches you.

TRIPLE-DOG DARE!

1. Get a cute notebook or journal and use it to write down all the important things you learn about God and being a Christian.

2. Every Sunday, take some time to reread and think about the notes you wrote during the week before.

3. Draw a picture of what you learned today.

Journaling How did it go? What did you learn?

Mmm ...Tastes Good!

Truth When you "taste" god's goodness, everything else seems yucky.

People go on diets for different reasons. Some might need to lose weight to avoid heart problems. Others might have a sickness that could be made worse by certain foods (for example, people with diabetes shouldn't have too much sugar, and people with high blood pressure shouldn't have too much salt). And some people have allergies to things like nuts, milk, or wheat.

When you're on a diet, it's hard at first to say no to foods you used to enjoy. But after a while, your taste starts to change, and you start enjoying new kinds of food—food that's better for you!

New Christians have to go through a change in their "diets" too. Instead of lying, getting angry, feeling jealous, or spreading gossip—which are like spiritual "junk food"—you start to crave the good spiritual food that God gives.

DARE Make sure your spiritual food is good for you!

TRIPLE-DOG DARE!

1 List five bad habits or attitudes you know God wants you to change. Next to each one, write its opposite and ask God to help you change your "taste" from bad to good.

2 For the next week, give yourself one point every time you do something from the "good" side of your list. Take off a point whenever you go back to the bad habit or attitude. See how you did after a week.

3 Make a small sign with the words of 1 Peter 2:2–3 and put it up on the fridge or your bulletin board.

Journaling How did it go? What did you learn?

Day and Night

Truth
The secret to true success is studying God's Word.

What topic interests you more than anything else? For some girls it might be dolphins; for others it might be fashion design, music, basketball, chess, babysitting, or painting.

Whatever your favorite thing is, you probably spend as much time as you can on it … reading about it, practicing it, buying "stuff" that relates to it, talking about it, and daydreaming about it. Of course, the more time you spend studying something, the more you learn about it, and you can become a bit of an expert after a while! That's how people become successful in their careers: by enthusiastically learning about something.

Imagine if you applied the same enthusiasm and energy to your relationship with God and studying the Bible. Not only would you have more peace and joy in your life because you'd feel close to God all the time, but you would also feel less confused or worried in tough situations because you'd have extra wisdom from the Bible to help you deal with them.

DARE Make God's Word your favorite subject!

TRIPLE-DOG DARE!

1 Ask your parents if you can have a Bible quiz book (or see if your church library has one). Quiz yourself often to help you remember Bible facts.

2 Whenever you pray before a meal, take an extra minute to review what you learned in that day's devotions.

3 Before you do each day's devotions, see if you can remember the dare from the day before (without peeking!).

Journaling — How did it go? What did you learn?

Tough Times ...Good Times

Truth
Difficult situations can help you grow spiritually.

What's your first thought when something bad happens to you or to your family, such as a sickness, an accident, fighting, or some other kind of stress? Do you thank God? Do you jump for joy? Do you feel good inside?

Like most people, you probably feel confused, scared, and maybe even angry.

The Bible tells us to be glad when we go through hard times because those difficulties can make us stronger and more mature if we put our trust in God.

Caterpillars struggle in cocoons before they become beautiful butterflies. Pearls start off as grains of sand that irritate an oyster. Diamonds start out as coal that is put under a lot of pressure. Flowers were tiny seeds that pushed through lots of dirt before they bloomed. And gold has to go through incredibly hot fire before it's pure.

Don't be afraid of tough situations. Through them, God can turn your life into something amazing.

DARE Thank God even for the tough days.

TRIPLE-DOG DARE!

1. During a rough time, don't ask God to change the situation. Instead, ask Him to give you peace about it.
2. Are you having a tough day? Thank God for at least ten blessings in your life.
3. Pray for the person who is making you feel bad.

Journaling How did it go? What did you learn?

_____

_____

_____

_____

_____

_____

_____

Invisible Beauty

Truth *Your problems won't last forever, but heaven will!*

Let's start with a challenge: Stare at the air! Not at the things around you ... just the air.

What? You can't see it? But you know it's there, right? You breathe it in and out all the time without even thinking about it.

What else can't you see but know it exists because of your other senses? There's the wind (touch), music (sound), the *smell* of cinnamon, and even better, the *taste* of the apple pie the cinnamon is in.

Some of the most important things in life are things that none of your senses can detect but that you know in your heart are real: God, love, faith, and heaven, to name a few.

The Bible says to focus on—or look at—spiritual things instead of things in the world. When you do, you'll be able to handle the temporary problems of life on earth.

DARE   Keep your eyes on what's invisible.

TRIPLE-DOG DARE!

1 List ten things you can't see that make you happy. Take time to thank God for them.

2 Make a list of a few things you're worried about right now. Will they still be problems in a month? In a year? In heaven? Trust God to get you through your problems.

3 Do you know someone going through a hard time? Write today's verses in a blank card and add a note that you're praying for her. Don't forget to pray before you give her the card!

Journaling   How did it go? What did you learn?

This book is all about the importance of both *knowing* and *living* the Word of God. Knowing the Bible is great, but it's kind of pointless if you don't practice what you learn in your daily life. And you can't obey God and live for Him if you don't know your Bible.

Take this quiz to see how you rate on the Truth and Dare scale.

1 One day you overhear a boy in your class telling his friends that the world was created by a big explosion and that humans evolved from monkeys. You …
  a. listen curiously. You didn't know that!
  b. feel sad that he doesn't know the truth, but you don't get involved.
  c. start making fun of him for believing the way he does and tell him, a little rudely, that God created the earth.
  d. ask him and his friends if they'd like to hear what you believe and then tell them about God and creation without getting upset when some of them laugh at you.

2 You're at the mall with your friend who isn't a Christian, and she asks you to sneak a T-shirt into your bag because it's bigger than hers. You …
  a. do it and grab one for yourself. Hey, they were only $5 each. Does it matter?
  b. do it, telling yourself she's the one stealing, not you.
  c. call her a thief and tell her that God is going to punish her.
  d. offer to buy the T-shirt for her since stealing is wrong. Explain that, besides the risk of getting in trouble, stealing will make her feel awful.

3 You really want the part of Dorothy in your school's production of *The Wizard of Oz*, but it is given instead to a popular girl who always seems to get what she wants. You …
  a. secretly hope that she gets sick or somehow messes up her part.
  b. tell yourself you don't really care.
  c. tell your drama teacher that you feel it's unfair that you didn't get the part just because you aren't as popular as the other girl.
  d. congratulate the other girl and try out for another part in the play.

If you answered ...

- **mostly A,** you don't seem to know some of the basic lessons the Bible teaches. Start reading your Bible.... And work on your Truth and Dare devotional every day!
- **mostly B,** you have some knowledge of what's right and wrong but don't really know how to live out the truth in everyday situations.
- **mostly C,** you understand the basics of what the Bible teaches, and you have the courage to act on it. But you don't always use wisdom, which can create problems in your Christian life.
- **mostly D,** you are learning to apply the truths of the Bible in a daring but mature way. Keep it up!

Got More Time?

Ask your mom or another mature Christian woman to pray with you that, as you read the Bible and work on these devotionals, God will help you to learn more about Him and live courageously for Him. Ask her to check with you once in a while to see how you're growing in your faith. (And be ready to answer her honestly when she does!)

Journaling

"Today you are you, that is truer than true.
There is no one alive who is youer than you!"

—Dr. Seuss

Take Out the Trash!

Truth *God wants you to have a pure heart ... and mouth.*

Have you ever seen those TV shows where an organizing expert visits a family and helps them get rid of all the clutter and junk they don't need, clean up and redecorate their house, and then develop new habits to keep their house nice and neat?

Maybe you've done a "clean sweep" of your own room. Didn't it feel great?

When you ask Jesus to become your Savior and forgive you for your sins, His Holy Spirit comes to live in your heart and does a clean sweep. Do you think He'd feel very welcome or comfortable if you started filling up your heart again with anger, mean thoughts, or bad words?

If you don't let wrong thoughts into your heart and mind, they won't come out of your mouth either.

DARE Get rid of any spiritual "garbage" in your life.

TRIPLE-DOG DARE!

1 Ask God to help you get rid of any angry feelings that might tempt you to say mean things to someone.

2 Do you use words that God probably doesn't like? Work on "deleting" them from your vocabulary. Ask a friend to remind you whenever you use those words.

3 Take time to clean up your room and get rid of clutter, asking God to forgive you for your sins (be specific) while you work.

Journaling How did it go? What did you learn?

Colossians 3:12

The Best Outfit Ever

Truth *Your inward "clothes" can make you more beautiful than your outward ones.*

Fashion can be a big deal for most girls, whether they're five years old or fifty or even ninety-five! Designers and owners of clothing stores know that girls enjoy shopping for new outfits, accessories, shoes, and jewelry because they like to look nice. Girls also usually notice what other girls are wearing.

Maybe that's not you. Maybe you don't care about new styles or looking "girly." Still, you probably give at least a little bit of thought to what you wear each day. But how much do you think about your spiritual appearance … the part of you people see when they watch your behavior and character?

The Bible says to "wear" compassion, kindness, humility, gentleness, and patience. When you make those qualities a priority, people will notice them even more than they'd notice the best clothes you could ever wear.

DARE Dress like a child of God … inside and out!

TRIPLE-DOG DARE!

1. For each of the five qualities listed, think of someone you know who "models" that characteristic and ask God to help you "wear" it too.

2. Make a pretty sign with the words of this verse and hang it inside your closet as a daily reminder.

3. Play designer and sketch a cool outfit. Next to your drawing, write about one of the qualities you want to "wear" this week.

Journaling How did it go? What did you learn?

Don't Stay Angry

Truth — *god wants you to deal with anger quickly.*

Often when there's a terrible accident or natural disaster, such as a tornado or earthquake, you'll hear people talk about how sorry they feel that they didn't say "I love you" the last time they saw a family member who died in that incident. Some will say that they wish they hadn't gone to bed still feeling angry about something the night before.

Those are feelings of *regret,* and God knows how much they hurt us. But anger that isn't taken care of right away can also hurt the people we love—even if they're still with us the next day.

Today's verse is good advice to make peace with anyone you're feeling angry at before the end of each day. Not only will you sleep better, but you'll have no regrets the next day.

(As a bonus, the more you do this, you'll probably find that you don't get angry at others as easily because forgiving becomes a good habit.)

DARE   Let go of your anger!

TRIPLE-DOG DARE!

1. Is someone angry at you (for example, your parents) for something you did? Ask for forgiveness as soon as possible.

2. If you can't make up with someone before bedtime, make a plan to do it as soon as you can and then pray for that person.

3. Are you angry at someone but he or she doesn't know about it? Ask God to help you forgive him or her, remembering how God has forgiven *your* sins.

journaling   How did it go? What did you learn?

Move That Mountain!

Truth — *You don't need giant-sized faith to experience God's power.*

In Joshua 10:1–15 (you'll read that story as one of your dares today), something very unusual happened for the first and only time in the history of the world!

During a terrible war between God's people (Israel) and their enemies (the Amorites), Joshua realized the Israelite army was running out of time, so he desperately prayed that God would stop the sun from setting. God accepted Joshua's prayer, and His people were able to continue fighting by daylight. The sun didn't go down until the people of Israel won the battle—almost a full day later!

Today's verses don't promise that you can make the sun stop or make a mountain jump into the ocean just by saying so. The point is that when you truly trust God with your difficulties, He will amaze you with His power.

You might never see a tree move into the sea, but you may see two people forgive each other, a sickness healed, or a fear disappear. If God would make the sun stand still, why wouldn't He help you with your problems? He loves you!

DARE — Exercise your faith!

TRIPLE-DOG DARE!

1. Read Joshua 10:1–15.

2. In your journal, write about a problem you are worried will never be solved. Tell God you believe He can take care of it and ask Him to give you peace about it.

3. Search an encyclopedia or on the Internet with your parents to find out how small mustard seeds are. Next time you have some mustard, remind yourself to trust God.

Journaling — How did it go? What did you learn?

Delicious Words

Truth
When you take time to season your words, they can "taste" great!

You probably already know that you shouldn't use too much salt, but do you know why? Too much salt can cause high blood pressure (when your blood is trying too hard to push through your arteries), heart disease, kidney stones, and edema (when parts of your body swell up because of too much fluid).

Still, there are times when just a little pinch of salt can make the difference between "yuck" and "yum." If you don't regularly use a lot of salt, its flavor comes out a lot more when there's just a bit of it in your food.

The Bible talks about seasoning your words with "salt." That means being thoughtful and kind whenever you speak and bringing out the best in others. As a result, when people ask you about your faith in God, they'll want to listen because they'll know they can respect and trust what you say.

DARE Make your words delicious.

TRIPLE-DOG DARE!

1 For the next day or two, try to cut back on salt as much as possible and notice how different your food tastes. Ask God to help you season your words with just the right amount of His "salt."

2 Try this: Taste just one little grain of salt and pay attention to how much flavor it has. Then think about how you can be salt in someone's life. Dab a tiny spot on this page with a glue stick and then place a few grains of salt as a reminder.

3 Do you know someone who feels bad about herself? Write her a note that will let her see God's love in you.

Journaling How did it go? What did you learn?

Read Matthew 5:3 and John 3:16.

For the next eight weekends, we're going to look at the Beatitudes in Matthew 5. *Beatitudes* is another word for *blessings*. During one of His sermons to the large crowds that used to follow Him, Jesus talked about eight types of people who would be blessed or happy … people you wouldn't really *expect* to feel blessed or happy.

As the first blessing, Jesus said, "Blessed are the poor in spirit, for theirs is the kingdom of heaven."

You know what it means to be poor, but what did Jesus mean by "poor in spirit"? Another way of thinking about this verse is to think of *humility*. Some people think that being humble means you believe you're not smart or worth much. They think it means that you consider yourself below everyone else. That's not true humility.

True humility is when you see yourself for exactly who you are. In other words, you know what you're good at, and you know what you need to work on. You don't pretend to be better than you are, and you don't pretend to be worse than you are.

As a Christian, when you understand that everything good in your life is a gift from God, then you are "poor in spirit." That's when you tell God that you need His forgiveness and salvation. And that's when you can receive "the kingdom of heaven," which is the eternal life that Jesus promised in John 3:16.

List twenty things you like about yourself.

_____   _____
_____   _____
_____   _____
_____   _____
_____   _____
_____   _____
_____   _____
_____   _____
_____   _____
_____   _____

Now cross out the ones that are gifts from God or that you couldn't have on your own. What are you left with? Take some time to thank God for all the blessings He has given you and ask Him to help you be "poor in spirit" so that you can truly see and appreciate His gifts.

Journaling

Remember: It's okay if you don't
know everything. (god does!)

Stay Pumped!

Truth
When you're excited about your relationship with God, you can serve Him faithfully.

Have you ever been in the middle of a project or activity and thought, "*Ugh!* I can't finish this. It's too hard. It's taking too long. I give up!" or just lost interest in it and quit?

So many jigsaw puzzles are left unfinished. Paintings are started and then forgotten. Kids ask for piano lessons and then, after a few months, decide they don't want to continue. Even relationships are dropped when one or both of the friends don't want to make an effort anymore.

The Bible warns us not to let that happen in our relationship with God.

DARE   Don't give up on God!

TRIPLE-DOG DARE!

1 List a couple of projects you've set aside or promises you haven't kept yet. Make a plan to finish those things as soon as possible.

2 Ask your parents or best friend to help you finish a difficult project by cheering you on and praying for you.

3 Take time to pray and ask God to help you grow in your love for Him.

Journaling   How did it go? What did you learn?

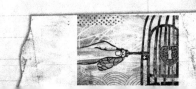

Romans 12:14

Bless Them

Truth
It's not your job to take revenge on those who mistreat you.

A lot of movies, TV shows, and even cartoons have the same message: Get the bad guys! If people hurt you, hurt them back!

The Bible has a different message. As a Christian, you've got a special assignment from God, which is to *bless* the people who persecute you. Persecution is when someone treats you badly because of your faith in Jesus. In North America, we don't face a lot of persecution compared to people in other countries who may be beaten, put in prison, or even killed for their beliefs, but you may have friends who make fun of you for going to church. You may even have teachers who don't respect you for believing in God and creation.

God wants you to show kindness and love to those people, even when it seems unfair. The people who hurt you need God, and the best way for them to find Him is through you. If you patiently forgive them, they will see God's love in you!

DARE Love those who hate you.

TRIPLE-DOG DARE!

1 If someone makes fun of you for your faith, quickly ask God for help. If you can't think of a kind answer, just walk away.... But don't react with anger!

2 Pray for Christians in other countries who suffer for their faith. Ask God to protect them and help them be strong.

3 Think of someone you have trouble liking. Pray for him or her and think of a way to show kindness the next time you meet.

Journaling How did it go? What did you learn?

Damaged but Not Worthless

Truth
god doesn't stop loving someone just because others have.

Have you ever shopped for groceries with your parents and noticed a display marked "Damaged Goods"? Some stores have a shelf with products that have dented or torn packages but are still good on the inside. These items cost less than the regular price because the store owner knows you might end up with broken cookies or, if the label is missing from a can, onion soup instead of chicken noodle.

Good thing food doesn't have feelings or those containers might feel rejected!

Unfortunately, sometimes people reject others just when they really need a friend. For example, if a teenage girl becomes pregnant or if a young boy is caught smoking, they might be judged even if they're very sorry for what they did. Or if your dad lost his job and your family had to start saving money carefully, some kids might have thought you weren't so "cool" anymore.

Today's verse promises that God stays close to those who are hurting. Other people might think they're "damaged," but God still loves them!

DARE
Don't think of yourself—or others— as "damaged goods."

TRIPLE-DOG DARE!

1 Do you feel like you're not worth much? Ask God to help you believe the promise in today's verse.... And thank Him for His love for you.

2 Think of someone who is hurting right now. Share today's verse with her in a cheery card.

3 Ask another Christian to tell you about a time she felt God's love during a tough time.

Journaling
How did it go? What did you learn?

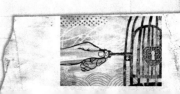

Watch Out for Wolves!

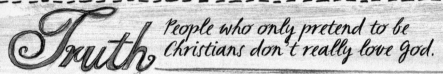

Truth *People who only pretend to be Christians don't really love God.*

In the story of Little Red Riding Hood, the Big Bad Wolf pretends to be Grandma by wearing her nightie and glasses and lying down in her bed with the covers pulled up to his nose. He wants to fool Little Red Riding Hood so that he can eat her!

Of course, this story is a fairy tale, but it does teach a good lesson about looking carefully before trusting people. Little Red Riding Hood knew something wasn't quite right when she noticed big ears, big eyes, and … big teeth!

Jesus warned His disciples—not just the twelve who were with Him while He lived on earth but all His followers including us today—to be careful about people who pretend to follow Him but only want to hurt and confuse true Christians.

The better you know the Bible, the better you'll be able to spot "wolves" who teach things about God or the Bible that aren't true.

DARE Know God's truth so you can recognize the lies.

TRIPLE-DOG DARE!

1. If someone tells you something that doesn't feel right in your heart, pray about it and then check it out in the Bible or with your parents or pastor.

2. Before you trust someone who says she's a Christian, look for proof that she truly loves God and others. Ask God for wisdom too.

3. Make sure that people can see proof of God's love in *your* life by your actions and words.

Journaling How did it go? What did you learn?

Homesick

Truth
We won't really be "at home" until we're in heaven with Jesus.

Isn't it fun to go away sometimes and sleep in a hotel room, in your grandparents' guest room, in a tent, or at a summer cottage? Vacations and sleepovers give us new experiences as we see new places, meet new people, try new foods, and enjoy fun activities.

But, if you're like most girls, you probably feel a little (or a lot!) homesick even when you're having fun. In fact, don't you sort of wish you could be at camp or at your cousin's house *and* be at home at the same time? You miss your parents, your cat, your bed, your *stuff*.

As Christians, we can go through the same feelings of homesickness. We enjoy life on earth and the beautiful things God has blessed us with…. But we also wish we could really be *with* God, face-to-face.

That's why we have to remember not to get too attached to things here on earth. We're just visiting and will be going home to heaven one day!

DARE
Remember that your real home is heaven!

TRIPLE-DOG DARE!

1. Write down at least five ways heaven will be a better home than your earthly home.
2. Write today's truth and verses on a postcard, address it to yourself, add a stamp, and ask a parent or friend to mail it on a random date. It'll be a good reminder on the day you receive it!
3. If you never feel homesick for heaven, ask God to help you be less attached to life here on earth.

Journaling
How did it go? What did you learn?

Read Matthew 5:4 and John 11:1-44.

The second beatitude that Jesus gave was this: "Blessed are those who mourn, for they will be comforted."

In the story of Lazarus, we see a great example of how Jesus comforts those who are sad. Mary and Martha were upset because of their brother's death, so Jesus went to them. He could have told them to stop crying because He already knew He was going to bring Lazarus back to life. Instead, He cried too. He showed that He understood their pain.

Sometimes when you're sad, you may not really want someone to cheer you up. You may just want someone to listen to you, to hug you, and to let you know that she understands, someone who will let you cry and be sad for a while.

God doesn't want you walking around feeling sad, but He understands that sometimes you will go through hard times. The important thing is to never stop trusting Him, to never stop believing that He knows what's going on and that He will get you through your problem. When you trust Him like that, He will comfort you.

This weekend, it's time for a simple art project. Using heavy paper (you can even recycle a cardboard cracker or cereal box or a blank card from a dollar store), make a "comforter" card for someone who is going through a sad time.

Using colorful scraps of fabric or paper cut into small squares (or other shapes, if you're feeling adventurous) and some glue or double-sided tape, design a quilt on the cover of the card. If you recycled a cardboard box, make the entire printed side your quilt, fold the card in half, and use the blank side to write your message. Look for pictures of quilts in catalogs for ideas.

Write the words of Matthew 5:4 on the inside of the card and add a personal message.

Journaling

Get Ready for a New week!

This week will never happen again.
Make the best of it!

Can They See Jesus in You?

Truth

When you're friends with Jesus, people can tell!

Acts 4:1–13 tells the incredible story of how Peter and John were arrested for preaching about Jesus. Even though they were put in jail, about five thousand people they had talked to believed that Jesus had been raised from the dead! The next day, when Peter and John were questioned by many rulers and religious leaders, they answered with confidence and courage because they had the Holy Spirit in them.

The men who listened were amazed by the way Peter spoke because he wasn't an educated leader or teacher like most of them were—Peter had been a fisherman when he met Jesus! But something about Peter's answer told the men that he and John had been with Jesus. They really knew Him and had learned from Him.

When people talk to you, can they tell that you're friends with Jesus? Does your faith in God somehow make you different from others? As you get closer to God, the Holy Spirit can help people see that you have been with Jesus too!

DARE Let people see Jesus in you.

TRIPLE-DOG DARE!

1 Read all of Acts 4.

2 Ask God to tell you if anything in your life doesn't show that you follow Him. If He does, ask Him to help you make some changes.

3 Think of someone who really shows she loves Jesus in the way she lives. Send her a note thanking her for her good example.

Journaling How did it go? What did you learn?

It's All from God

Truth
Whenever you're successful, the thanks should always go to God.

When you've worked hard to finish a project and it turns out great, doesn't it feel good when people notice and tell you that you did a good job? If you receive a reward for making the honor roll, memorizing the most Bible verses, or finishing first in a race, you might be tempted to think, *Wow, I'm good! I really deserve this prize.*

Adults who succeed in their jobs and make a lot of money—or actors, singers, and athletes who become famous—might also be tempted to feel proud of their accomplishments.

What most of us forget is that, even if we've worked hard at something or have natural talents that make us stand out from the crowd, the abilities and intelligence we have come from God. Without the strength and opportunities He gives us, we couldn't do anything!

DARE Give God the glory for everything.

TRIPLE-DOG DARE!

1 List ten things you've done that you're proud of. Then, for each one, write down the ability that God gave you to be able to succeed. Take time to thank God for what *He* did through you.

2 Next time someone says "Good job!" to you, tell him or her how you couldn't have done it without God's help.

3 Do you have a friend who brags a lot about the things she does? Share today's verses with her and encourage her to thank God for the gifts He's given her.

Journaling How did it go? What did you learn?

Don't Harden Your Heart

Truth
A heart that doesn't fear God can't fight temptation.

For today's devotional, you'll need to ask for one raw egg and one hard-boiled egg. (You won't be breaking them so you can just borrow them for a few minutes.) With a marker, make a tiny mark on the boiled egg so you won't get it mixed up with the raw one.

Take the boiled egg and gently spin it on the table like a top. It twirled around quite easily, right? Now, being careful not to drop it, try spinning the raw egg. Did you get the same result? You can't spin a raw egg because it's still liquid inside, but a boiled egg is hard, making it easy to spin.

Our hearts are a little like that. When your heart is "soft" and obedient to God, the Devil can't control you. But when your heart is "hard" and you don't fear (or respect) God and His laws, the Devil can spin you around with the temptations he sends your way.

DARE   Keep your heart soft.

TRIPLE-DOG DARE!

1 Ask your Sunday school teacher if you can show today's lesson to your class one day.

2 Write today's verse on a sticky note and put it on the egg carton in your fridge as a reminder to whoever looks inside! If your parents say it's okay, gently write "soft-hearted" on each egg with a pencil.

3 If you've had trouble saying no to temptation lately, ask God to make your heart soft and obedient again.

Journaling   How did it go? What did you learn?

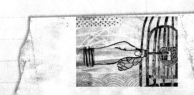

No Doubts

Truth *As you follow Jesus, your doubts will begin to disappear.*

What were you scared of when you were little? The dark? Imaginary monsters under your bed? The sound of thunder? Being left at school by your mom?

Often children—and even adults—feel afraid because they don't understand the new situation they're in. For example, on the first day of preschool a child might think her mom won't come back. But as each day goes by, the little girl learns that her mom always comes to pick her up, and that fear goes away.

You may go through times of confusion or doubt. You might wonder whether God really loves you, if He truly exists, or if your sins are forgiven.

Jesus promised that when you believe in His teaching and follow Him, you will get to know the truth…. And that will set you free from confusion and doubt!

DARE Hang on tight to what you know about Jesus.

TRIPLE-DOG DARE!

1 When you finish your devotions or leave church, take time to think about what you learned before you start something else. That will help you "hold on" to the truth.

2 In your journal, list the things you're worried or confused about. Ask God to help you know the truth. Whenever something becomes clear to you, cross it off the list.

3 Share today's verses with your parents and ask them to tell you about a time the truth "set them free."

Journaling How did it go? What did you learn?

You Can't Hide Sin

Truth   *god sees every sin.*

When I was around eight years old, I stopped at a candy store on my way home from school one day. I bought some candy…. But I also took an extra piece and secretly put it in my pocket. The candy cost only ten cents, but somehow I didn't feel so happy about my "free" candy.

We lived above my dad's radio shop, so I went in there before going upstairs. I tried to sound cheery as I said, "Hi, Dad!" The first thing he said was, "What did you do wrong?"

Whoa … That was freaky! I felt so nervous that I quickly told him the truth, and I had to go right back to the candy shop to pay for what I had stolen. I never stole anything again in my life! Somehow, God had shown my dad that I was guilty about something.

The Bible warns that we can't be sneaky about our sins. One way or another, God will hold us responsible for the wrong things we do, so we'd better not disobey Him in the first place!

DARE   Say no to sin the first time.

TRIPLE-DOG DARE!

1. Is there a sin you've kept secret in your heart without confessing it to God? Ask Him for forgiveness today—not only for the sin, but also for not telling Him about it sooner.
2. If a friend ever asks you to do something wrong, promising that "no one will know," remind her about what you learned in today's devotional.
3. Memorize 1 John 1:9.

Journaling   How did it go? What did you learn?

Meek ...Not Weak

Read Matthew 5:5 and Psalm 37:11.

Imagine that the fastest runner in your class challenged you to a race, just for fun. How would you run? You'd probably push yourself as hard as you possibly could, putting all your strength into that race, hoping to win or at least come close.

Now imagine that a four-year-old said to you, "Race me! Race me!" How would you run this time? Would you run fast to show how easily you could win … or would you slow down a lot to give the younger child a chance to enjoy the race? You might even lose the race on purpose just to make the little girl or boy feel good, right?

That's a good way to understand what meekness is. Some people think that being *meek* is being *weak*. Actually, meekness is when power or strength is controlled. Usually if someone is trying hard to prove how strong or smart or talented she is, that's actually a sign of something weak inside. A truly strong and wise person should be humble enough not to try to prove herself all the time.

Jesus set a good example of meekness many times, such as when He was arrested and then hung on the cross. He could have easily killed everyone who made Him suffer; instead, He held back His power and chose to patiently forgive them.

In the third beatitude, Jesus promised that those who are meek and humble will be rewarded greatly. Remember: There's no reward for those who brag about their strength and act like they're better than everyone else.

This weekend, take time to pray and ask God to help you understand what meekness is. Look for situations where you can show *meekness* instead of *weakness*.

Got More Time?

With your family or a couple of friends, come up with one or two scenarios (imaginary situations) in which someone could practice meekness. Make up a skit about it and have fun acting it out. Afterward, talk about the verses you studied this weekend and what it means to be meek.

Journaling

The best way to _find_ a friend is to _be_ a friend.

Who's Living Your Life?

Truth — Accepting Jesus as your Savior means letting Him live through you.

There are about 31,100 verses in the Bible (there's some cool trivia to remember!). This one definitely isn't the easiest to understand right away. But it's an important verse to start thinking about.

When you believe that Jesus died on the cross to save you from the punishment for your sins, and you give your life to Him, that's called being "born again." It's as if your sins (your old self) were nailed on the cross with Jesus, and your new self came to life when Jesus rose again from the dead.

As a Christian, you have God's Holy Spirit in you, so now you're living for Him and not for your old self. That means making Jesus number one in your life and wanting what He wants more than what you want. That's not always easy, but as you get closer to Jesus, it will become natural!

DARE Give Jesus control of your life!

TRIPLE-DOG DARE!

1. Write down five good qualities you have. Then thank God for being the One to help you grow in those areas.
2. With your parents, look up the lyrics of "Crucified with Christ," a song by the group Phillips, Craig & Dean. Can you make those words your own?
3. Ask an older Christian what this verse means to him or her.

Journaling — How did it go? What did you learn?

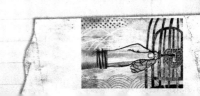

John 20:24-29

Do You Believe It?

Truth — Real faith is when you believe in what you can't see.

Imagine that your friend came to school wearing a red top, and she said to you, "I'm wearing a red top!" Would you believe her? Of course, because you could see with your own eyes that she had a red top on.

What if she told you she had a new blue shirt at home? If your friend usually told you the truth, you'd probably believe her, right? But this time you would be putting your *faith* in what she said because you couldn't actually see the shirt. She might show it to you later, but for now you would simply trust what she said.

Today you read about how Thomas, one of Jesus' disciples, had trouble believing without proof. Jesus said that those who believe in Him without seeing proof will be blessed.

You might sometimes find it hard to believe everything the Bible says about God since you can't see Him with your eyes. But the more you put your faith in Jesus, the more you'll discover that the Bible is really true.... And God will bless you for your faith!

DARE — Take a chance on Jesus!

TRIPLE-DOG DARE!

1. What doubts do you have about God? Take time to pray about them and ask God to help you grow stronger in your faith.
2. List ten things you put your faith in every day. (For example, you trust that your chair will hold you up.) Now list ten things you trust God with.
3. Share today's Bible story with a friend who has doubts about God.

Journaling — How did it go? What did you learn?

The Best Teammate

Truth When god's on your side, you're covered.

Imagine you were playing tug-of-war (the game where two teams pull opposite sides of a heavy rope and try to get the middle point of it over their line) at a picnic, and the opposite team had some tough-looking boys and girls while your team had mostly small, skinny kids. Would you be worried about losing the game? Probably!

What if your dad or another strong adult—let's say a football player!—joined your team? You'd be pretty sure of winning then, right? The opposite team might even seem a lot less scary!

Sometimes life will bring scary and confusing situations your way, and you might worry about how you're going to get through them. Maybe a temptation seems too strong to resist. Maybe kids at school are picking on you.

Today's verse promises that when you're on God's "team," you don't have to feel afraid. He's more powerful than any enemy you might face. He will always take care of you!

DARE Ask Jesus to be on your team.

TRIPLE-DOG DARE!

1 Draw a line down the middle of a blank piece of paper. On one side, list all the things that you feel worried or confused about. On the other side write "GOD" in huge letters and write your name inside the *O*. Take a moment to thank God for His love and protection.

2 If you have a friend who's worried about something, share today's verse with her.

3 Ask your parents to tell you about a time they felt God was on their side.

Journaling How did it go? What did you learn?

Excited about Church?

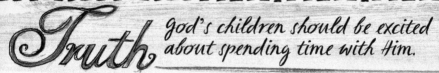

Truth
God's children should be excited about spending time with Him.

How do you react when your mom says, "We're going to grandma's house"? How about when she wakes you up in the morning and says it's time for school? When you're going to your favorite restaurant or mall?

When you love someone and always have a good time with her, you will feel happy whenever you know you're about to see each other. When you enjoy an activity, you will look forward to the next time you get to do it.

Going to church to worship God, learn about Him, and spend time with your Christian family should feel the same way. When you truly love God and want to be with Him, you will react the same way King David did when it was time to go to God's house (the temple where the Israelites worshipped).... You will rejoice!

DARE Get excited about church!

TRIPLE-DOG DARE!

1 Get into the habit of praying the night before church and asking God to make you ready for worship the next day.

2 List ten activities that you look forward to with excitement. If church isn't high on that list, ask God to help you become more joyful about going to church.

3 Pray for Christians around the world who would love to go to church every week but can't because they don't have the freedom to.

Journaling How did it go? What did you learn?

Who Do You Say He Is?

Truth
If you follow Jesus, you have to know who He is.

If someone asked you who Jesus is, would you answer, "Well, my parents say …" or "My pastor says …" or "My Sunday school teacher says …"? Or would you be able to explain who *you* believe Jesus is?

Think of how easily you would describe your mom or your best friend to someone else. You would have no trouble talking about who they are or what they're like because you know them so well. And you know them so well because you spend time with them and talk to them and care about what's happening in their lives.

That's how it should be with Jesus. In today's reading, Peter was able to answer Jesus' question about who He was because he *knew* Jesus.

The more you study your Bible and talk to God through prayer, the more you will know Him too.

DARE   Get to know Jesus!

TRIPLE-DOG DARE!

1 In your journal, describe Jesus as well as you can. If you think you'd have trouble telling someone who He is, ask God to help you get to know Him better.

2 Don't depend on what other people say to help you grow in your relationship with Jesus. Get to know Him yourself, every day.

3 Challenge your best friend to read today's devotion and to do Dares #1 and #2.

Journaling — How did it go? What did you learn?

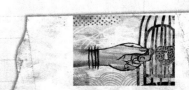

Alexis grew up in a Christian family (in fact, her grandfather was the pastor at her church) and had gone to Sunday school every week since she was little. She read her Bible and prayed every day, but when she was eighteen years old, she had to admit something in her life wasn't right. She was dating a boy who wasn't a Christian. She knew it was wrong not only because her mom and other family members told her so but because the Bible said so. And she couldn't stop thinking about it.

One day, after a good chat with her grandfather, Alexis made up her mind that she wanted to be right with God. Although it was difficult because they had been friends for a long time, she called her boyfriend and told him they couldn't continue dating.

Knowing that she was obeying God gave her the courage to do the right thing. And doing the right thing gave her the courage to go on a one-week mission experience later that month. She was able to help and share her faith with many others, and she also knew that her life could now be a good example to the younger teens who were on the mission trip with her.

Jesus said, "Blessed are those who hunger and thirst for righteousness, for they will be filled" (Matthew 5:6).

When Alexis hungered for God's righteousness instead of her own wants, God filled her with more joy and peace than she had experienced before!

What about you? Are you willing to give up something you know isn't right so that God can replace it with something better? Are you hungry for righteousness?

Look up the definition of *righteous* and write it here: _____
_____
_____

Imagine being "hungry" for righteousness and make up a "recipe" for it. Hint: What ingredients could you add (such as obedience)? What would you do with the ingredients (such as "sprinkle with kind words")?

Journaling

"In prayer, it is better to have a heart without words than words without a heart."

–John Bunyan

Your Best Years

Truth — Following God from a young age will lead to a better life when you're older.

Imagine someone gave you a gift card to your favorite store, but when you went shopping with it, you found out that the expiration date had passed. Or what if someone gave you flowers that were already wilted … or a bottle of pop that had lost its fizz?

You would feel like you didn't really get anything at all, right?

Some young people say, "I'll follow God when I'm older. I just want to have fun now and do whatever I want. I'll become a Christian later." In other words, they want to spend the best years of their life—when they're healthy and energetic and don't have work and family responsibilities—living for themselves instead of God.

That's kind of like eating a big, juicy apple and then giving God the core that's left over at the end.

Right now, you're entering the best years of your life, and you can give them to God as a gift, as thanks for everything He's done for you.… Or you can waste them. What do you choose?

DARE   Give yourself to Jesus … starting now.

TRIPLE-DOG DARE!

1. Think of at least one change you can make in your life to dedicate more of your time to God. Write it down and ask God to help you do it.
2. Make some pretty bookmarks for your friends that say, "Remember your Creator in the days of your youth" (Eccl. 12:1).
3. Ask an older Christian at church to tell you why she thinks it's good to start following Jesus from a young age.

Journaling — How did it go? What did you learn?

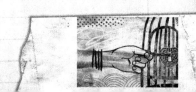

A Bowl of Soup

Truth Sometimes we give up important things for foolish things.

Which would you rather have, if you had to choose between the two:

a. A bag of popcorn now … or your dream party for your thirteenth birthday?
b. A new bike now … or a trip to Disneyland next summer?
c. One hundred dollars to spend however you want now … or your grandparents' house after they die?

It might seem obvious that in each case the second choice is the smart one. But there are people who always want instant gratification—that means they want to have a fun experience right away, even if it means they give up something better in the future. Delayed gratification is when someone waits for something good to happen later.

Esau foolishly chose instant gratification and traded his inheritance for a bowl of soup! It's easy to think you'd never do anything crazy like that, right?

Have you ever skipped reading your Bible to watch TV? Have you ever said you'll pray later so you could talk on the phone? Have you ever given in to temptation and planned on asking God to forgive you later?

Hmmm …

DARE Don't trade spiritual blessings for a moment of pleasure.

TRIPLE-DOG DARE!

1 Read Genesis 27. (You may have to give up some TV time!) Think about the results of Esau's foolish choice and ask God help you make wise choices in life.

2 Think of a few foolish choices you've made lately. Ask God to forgive you.

3 Write down a few ways you can practice delayed gratification, especially in areas where you're used to enjoying something right away.

Journaling How did it go? What did you learn?

490 Times ...or More?

Truth
We should willingly forgive ... again and again and again.

Quick: Think of four things your best friend (or sister) has done to annoy, hurt, or upset you.

It was probably easy to remember 4 things, right? What if you had to list 17 things? It might be harder to think that far back. How about 91 things? Could you think of 490 things?

When Peter asked Jesus how many times we should forgive someone, he probably thought he was being very generous by suggesting seven times. But Jesus answered, "Seventy times seven." Well, if you do the math, you'll know that 70 times 7 is 490.

Did Jesus mean you should keep track of how many times someone sins against you and then, after 490 times, you can stop forgiving him or her? Of course, He knew that most of us would probably lose count long before we reached 490, so what He really meant is that we should forgive every time.

If you think that doesn't sound fair, ask yourself how many times God has forgiven you. Do you think He'll stop after your 490th sin?

DARE Don't keep track of other people's sins.

TRIPLE-DOG DARE!

1 Are you holding a grudge against someone? Ask God to forgive you and to help you forgive that person.

2 Whenever you're tempted not to forgive someone, try to remember how much God has forgiven you.

3 Write "70 x 7" on a sticky note and put it up in your locker at school as a daily reminder to be forgiving.

Journaling How did it go? What did you learn?

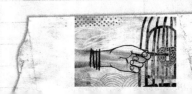

We Imitate What We Worship

Truth *Only God deserves our worship and praise.*

Have you ever noticed that when young people admire celebrities, they sometimes try to look like them? They might dress like them or cut their hair the same way or even talk the same way.

A well-known saying is *imitation is the sincerest form of flattery.* That means that when someone copies you, it's a way of telling you that she likes you and wants to be like you. Of course, sometimes people copy each other just because they're too lazy to come up with their own style or ideas.

If you can tell what kind of music or sports or hobbies someone likes by the way she dresses and behaves, don't you think people should also be able to tell if you follow God? If you really love Him and spend time with Him, you will start becoming more and more like Him! You obviously won't *look* like Him, but people should see His love and goodness in your life.

DARE Let people see you worship God by how you live.

TRIPLE-DOG DARE!

1. List ten things you love about God. Do you have those same qualities in your life? If not, ask God to help you imitate Him.

2. Figure out how much time you spend talking to God each week. Think of how you can add some worship to each day so you can spend more time with Him.

3. Whenever you go to church, focus on connecting with God. He deserves your full attention.

Journaling How did it go? What did you learn?

Bathing in the Mud?

Truth　When we ask God for forgiveness, we have to leave the sin behind!

When you've spent the day playing outside or helping with chores, doesn't it feel good to take a warm bath or shower and scrub all the dirt off you? It's great having clean hair and soft skin again, and for a while you might be careful about getting dirty.

But would you ever take a bath while sitting in a puddle of mud? Would you brush your hair in the middle of a windstorm? Would you put dishes you've just washed back into the dirty sink? Of course not…. There's just no point!

Sometimes that's how people take care of their spiritual "cleaning." They know they have to ask God to forgive their sins, but even as they're praying they're not really sorry for what they've done and can't promise God that they won't do it again. It makes them feel a little better because they think they're being cleaned, but it doesn't actually work. It's like taking a bath in a mud puddle!

DARE　Be sincere when you confess your sins to God.

TRIPLE-DOG DARE!

1. Is there a sin you ask God to forgive you for but then do again and again? Ask Him to help you say no next time you're tempted.

2. Before you confess a sin to God, ask yourself whether you're really sorry for what you did. Remember that God can see your heart.

3. Whenever you wash your face or hands, ask God to make your heart pure too.

Journaling　How did it go? What did you learn?

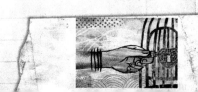

Christiane's childhood was tough. From a young age she and her sisters had to work hard on their father's farm in western Canada. Their dad was strict and sometimes he treated them very badly. When Christiane was sixteen, a neighbor who knew about the situation warned her that she wasn't safe and that she needed to leave her home.

Christiane took her neighbor's advice and went to stay at a shelter for three months until a Christian family invited her to live with them. While she was there, she started going to youth group and learning about the love of Jesus. She also found out that the Bible says to honor your mother and father.

After about a year, Christiane went back to visit her parents, who were sorry for the way they had treated her. Even though she was safe now, it would have been easy for Christiane to stay angry with her dad. But she chose to forgive and share God's love with her family.

Jesus said, "Blessed are the merciful, for they will be shown mercy" (Matthew 5:7).

Christiane showed mercy by going back to her parents and showing forgiveness. Because of that, she now has a good relationship with her whole family and they are learning about God's love through her!

What about you? Are you merciful?

PS: Christiane grew up to become a wife, mother of three children, and leader of a children's ministry at her church. God has blessed her with a good life!

Look up the definition of *merciful* and write it here: _____
_____
_____

Think of someone who has treated you badly. How can you show him or her mercy the way Christiane showed mercy to her family?

Journaling

If you really want to do something, you will find a way. If you don't, you will find an excuse.

James 1:17

Did You Say "Thanks"?

Truth
god gives us wonderful gifts every day that we need to be thankful for.

My family and I live in Montreal, Canada, where we experience all four seasons with different types of weather and even different colors of leaves. The winters can be pretty cold and snowy, which I don't mind, but others find it difficult. For people who live in the north, summers seem too short.

I like to tease my dad because he starts feeling sad that winter is coming ... while it's still summer! I remind him that he should just enjoy summer for as long as it lasts and save his worrying about winter for when it's actually winter.

Summer isn't the only beautiful thing that doesn't last forever. Pretty flowers die, shiny bubbles burst, and brilliant sunsets disappear. If we had them all the time, maybe they wouldn't seem so special, and we wouldn't appreciate them as much.

God blesses you in so many ways each day. What would you rather do: complain about what you don't have or thank God for what you do have?

DARE Thank God for everything!

TRIPLE-DOG DARE!

1 Throughout the day, keep a list of all the things you can thank God for. Don't forget to consider ordinary things.

2 Challenge a friend or sibling to do the first dare with you and compare your lists the next day.

3 Whenever you catch yourself complaining, take a moment to ask God to forgive you and to give you a more grateful attitude.

Journaling How did it go? What did you learn?

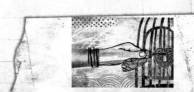

Somebody's Watching

Truth You can't sin in secret. God sees everything.

Have you ever been tempted to keep reading a book after bedtime? Maybe you pulled your covers up over your head and used a flashlight to read so your parents wouldn't catch you.

When we're doing something we're not supposed to, we usually look for ways to hide our actions. A stolen candy bar might be hidden under a bed. A broken DVD might be moved to the back of the shelf. If you forgot to mail a letter for your mom, you might hide it in your backpack to mail it the next day.

What we often forget is that even if we manage to hide our sins from our parents or teachers, we can't hide them from God. He can see everything—not only our actions, but also our bad thoughts and the sins in our hearts.

You don't have to be afraid of God or hide from Him if you always do what's right!

DARE Make sure your actions always honor and please God.

TRIPLE-DOG DARE!

1. Whenever you feel tempted to hide a sin, ask God to give you the courage to be honest about it and to make things right quickly.

2. Play hide-and-seek with your friends. At the end of the game, share today's verses with them and talk about how we can't hide our sins from God.

3. Have you lied to your parents lately? Ask for forgiveness today.

Journaling How did it go? What did you learn?

Sin Is Sin

Truth — *It doesn't matter if a sin is small or big. It's still wrong.*

Let's try a little experiment. Get a piece of scrap paper and crumple it up into a ball. Then find a small but heavy object, such as a battery or an eraser.

You're going to drop them both, but before you do, try to guess which one will hit the floor first. Okay, ready? Hold the crumpled paper and the heavier object straight out in front of you and let them go at the same time. Which one fell the fastest? Not sure? Try again.

Are you surprised? Did you think the heavier object would hit the floor first?

Sometimes we think that there's a difference between "light" sins (such as lying) and "heavy" sins (such as killing), but in God's eyes all sins are serious. Today's verse reminds us that "all wrongdoing is sin."

DARE — Don't make excuses for your "small" sins.

TRIPLE-DOG DARE!

1 Demonstrate today's experiment to your family or friends and then share the Bible lesson with them.

2 Think of some "small" sins in your life that you thought God might not get upset about. Take time today to ask Him to forgive you for them.

3 Tie a string around the crumpled paper and hang it up in your locker at school as a daily reminder of today's verse.

Journaling — **How did it go? What did you learn?**

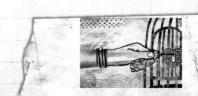

John 8:34-36

Don't Be a Slave to Sin

Truth *Sin can make you a slave.*

For today's devotional you're going to need a helper. See if someone older in your family or a friend has a few minutes to try this experiment. Note: You'll need some thread or thin yarn.

Ask your volunteer to hold her hands out and then tie the string around her wrists just once. Explain that the string is like one sin (for example, a lie). If your volunteer felt sorry for her sin and decided to stop lying, would that be easy to do? Ask her to try to break the string. It should snap easily.

Now wrap the string around her hands about ten times, explaining that each turn of the yarn is a sin she tried to hide. Now ask her to try to break the string. It should be almost impossible.

That's how sin is. The longer you go covering up sin and not asking God for forgiveness, the harder it is to break the habit. It's like being a "slave" to sin. Thankfully, God can free us from sin when we confess to Him!

DARE Break free from sin!

TRIPLE-DOG DARE!

1 Demonstrate today's experiment to some other friends and then share the Bible lesson with them.

2 What sin or temptation do you struggle with most? Ask God to help you break free from it. Carry a piece of string in your pocket—or tie one around your wrist—as a reminder to pray about this often.

3 Think about all the sins God has forgiven you for. Take extra time today to thank Him for His love and patience.

Journaling How did it go? What did you learn?

The Taste Test

Truth — *You'll never know how good God "tastes" until you try for yourself.*

Suppose I showed you a box of chocolates (sorry—we couldn't think of a way to include one with the book!) and asked you if they tasted good. Would you be able to answer yes or no?

Not really! You might say that they *looked* tasty, but you couldn't know for sure that they were good just by looking. You could try smelling them, but even that wouldn't tell you if they tasted good.

If I told you what all the ingredients were, or introduced you to someone who had tasted them and liked them, or ate one myself and told you that they were good, would you know if they really were good? Nope.

Just like you'd have to have one of those chocolates yourself to know how good they tasted, you have to experience God for yourself to know how good He is. You can't just go along with what your parents or Sunday school teacher say.

DARE   Get to know God today!

TRIPLE-DOG DARE!

1 List ten things you know about God. How many of them do you know from experience, and how many from being told? Ask God to help you "taste" Him yourself.

2 Using a cookie or candy bar, share today's lesson with a friend who doesn't know Jesus.

3 Make a pretty sign with today's verse and stick it up on your fridge as a daily reminder.

Journaling — How did it go? What did you learn?

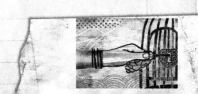

From a young age, JamieLynn wanted to serve God. She wanted to go to South America and help build a church there. When she was sixteen, she started looking for ways to make that dream come true. She got in touch with Canadian Baptist Ministries and found out about a training and missions program she could participate in. She was really excited … especially when she found out there was going to be a mission trip to Bolivia a few months later!

JamieLynn and her dad decided to take the trip together, and JamieLynn started to prepare herself. She spent a lot of time praying and asking God to help her focus less on herself and more on doing what *He* wanted her to do.

In Bolivia, where she helped with different projects and worked with small children, JamieLynn learned a lot! She saw that even though the people there had a very different way of living, they were equally special to God, and the people she met had much stronger faith than a lot of people she knew back at home. JamieLynn also felt like she had led a selfish, spoiled, and greedy life until then. And she wanted to change!

Jesus said, "Blessed are the pure in heart, for they will see God" (Matthew 5:8). JamieLynn saw God in Bolivia, and she sees Him in her everyday life. She doesn't see Him in person, face-to-face, but she sees Him in the amazing things He does in her life and in other people's lives.

To JamieLynn, being pure in heart means following after God's own heart. That doesn't mean never making mistakes but turning around and getting back on the right path. She says, "I try to stay pure in heart by surrounding myself with people who are trying to do the same thing. I look at what I did in a day, and I try to decide if I made good decisions. It's not easy, but if you keep your eyes focused on Jesus and ask for His help, you can do anything!"

What are some ways you can become "pure in heart"?

_____

_____

What are some ways *you* have "seen God"?

_____

_____

Journaling

"Be more than you're expected to be."

–JamieLynn Bagley

Lasting Beauty

Truth

True beauty comes from the inside.

Think of the most beautiful girl or woman you know and describe her in your journal. Include details about her hair, eyes, coloring, size, shape, and so on.

Now think of a woman you look up to because of her kindness and wisdom, someone you trust. Describe the qualities she has that you admire.

How long do you think the beauty of the first person will last? Until she's forty? Sixty? Eighty? Even if she remains pretty in her old age, her looks will change, right?

How long do you think the qualities of the second woman will last? Probably until she dies, right? Inner beauty doesn't go away with age. In fact, it usually gets better, especially when that beauty comes from having a relationship with God.

When you focus more on following Jesus and becoming the girl God created you to be and less on how you look on the outside, people will see and appreciate your inner beauty … now and when you're older, too!

DARE   Don't get caught up with outward appearances.

TRIPLE-DOG DARE!

1. Think of five women you admire for their inner beauty. Write them each a note letting them know how much you appreciate their example.

2. Time yourself as you get ready every morning. See if you can spend more time working on your inner beauty than your outer beauty.

3. Write out today's verse. Now memorize it!

Journaling   How did it go? What did you learn?

Faith on a Tightrope

Truth *True faith means trusting god ... completely!*

Charles Blondin, a French acrobat in the 1800s, was famous for a dangerous tightrope act where he used to walk 160 feet over Niagara Falls on a rope that was over 1,000 feet long! If that wasn't crazy enough, he kept making his act more and more dangerous. In 1860, he walked across the rope … on stilts. Then he did it again, blindfolded. Another time he walked halfway, stopped, cooked an omelet and ate it, and then finished the walk. Then he walked across the tightrope with a wheelbarrow and walked back with a sack of potatoes in the wheelbarrow!

Of course, his audiences were amazed. One day, Blondin asked the Duke of Newcastle if he believed he could carry a man across the tightrope in the wheelbarrow. The duke said he was sure Blondin could do it.… But he would not agree to sit in the wheelbarrow himself.

The duke said he believed in Blondin, but he wasn't willing to trust him with his life.

Some people say they believe in God, but they don't really put their trust in Him. They prefer to go through life trusting themselves instead of God.

DARE Get into God's wheelbarrow!

TRIPLE-DOG DARE!

1. What do you think God might want you to do in the future? Are you willing to obey Him? Talk to Him and ask Him to help you trust Him completely.
2. Make a bookmark with today's verses and memorize them.
3. Share the story of Charles Blondin—and today's lesson!—with a friend.

Journaling How did it go? What did you learn?

The Wheel of Friendship

Truth The closer you get to God, the closer you'll get to your Christian family.

You might not find an ordinary wheel very interesting, but today we'll see how it gives us a good picture of how our relationship with God affects our relationship with people … and the other way around, too!

The center of the wheel (the hub) is connected to the outer circle (the rim) by many spokes. What do you notice about how far the spokes are from each other? The ends that are attached to the hub are close together, but the ends that are attached at the rim are farther apart.

That's how it is with Christians. Think of God as the "hub" and people who love Him as the "spokes." The closer you get to God (through prayer and reading your Bible), the closer you'll get to other Christians. And the closer you get to other Christians, the closer you'll get to God!

That's why going to church and having friends who love God is so important. If you're too far from other people following Him, you won't get the help you need.

DARE Stay close to God's hub!

TRIPLE-DOG DARE!

1 If you don't have any friends who love God (or even if you do!), focus on getting closer to God for now, and pray that He will show you someone you can have a special friendship with.

2 Share the lesson about a wheel's hub and spokes with your family.

3 Make a list of your closest Christian friends. Take extra time to pray for them today.

Journaling How did it go? What did you learn?

You Can't Take It with You

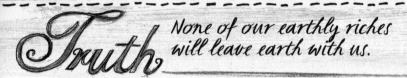

Truth — *None of our earthly riches will leave earth with us.*

There once was a rich man who was dying. He was sad because he had worked hard and wanted to take his money to heaven with him. He prayed that God would let him take some of his wealth, and God told him he was allowed to pack *one* suitcase.

He filled his biggest suitcase with gold bars and went to bed. When he died, he appeared at the gate of heaven. An angel said, "Hold on. You can't bring that in here!" but the man explained that he had special permission.

The angel checked with God and then said, "You're right, but I have to inspect what's inside before letting it in." The angel looked inside the suitcase and laughed. He said to the man, "You brought pavement?"

(It's just a joke!)

Of course, we can't take *anything* to heaven with us, but this story reminds us that the most valuable things on earth are nothing compared to the beauty of heaven. So don't be jealous of rich people. They will leave earth just as empty-handed as you will.

What matters is where you're going, not what you packed!

DARE   Don't admire the riches of others.

TRIPLE-DOG DARE!

1. Impressed by someone else's stuff? Remind yourself that it won't last forever.
2. In your journal list twenty things you're thankful for that don't cost money.
3. Think of someone you know who has a lot of money but doesn't know God. Pray for him or her to believe in Jesus.

Journaling   How did it go? What did you learn?

How's Your Reputation?

Truth
A good reputation is better than riches.

Think of five people you really trust and look up to. What are some of the qualities they have that you admire? List them here:

_____

_____

Did you write, "They're rich" on your list?

If you didn't, it could either be that those people are not rich or that their money is not what makes them special.

So why do you think so many people care more about becoming rich than they do about developing qualities like the ones you listed above?

King Solomon, the writer of today's verse, was one of the wealthiest people who ever lived—but he was also the wisest, and he understood that money is nothing if you don't have a good reputation.

As you think about your goals for the future, ask yourself if you'd rather have "stuff" or the respect and love of the people around you. Go for the second choice and your life will be more joyful!

DARE Choose reputation over riches.

TRIPLE-DOG DARE!

1 Write down five words that you'd like people to use to describe you (for example, *honest* or *kind)*. Ask God to help you develop those qualities.

2 Do you ever put your "stuff" above your relationships? Make a plan to change that habit.

3 Share today's verse with a friend who talks a lot about becoming rich one day and encourage her to develop her inner qualities first.

Journaling How did it go? What did you learn?

Read Matthew 5:9.

To complete this puzzle, look up the verses next to each row of squares, and for each one, find the word describing something that can help make peace between two people who are angry at each other.

(Note: We used the New International Version of the Bible for this puzzle. The answers are at the end of the book.)

James 5:16 — **P**

1 Peter 4:8 — **E**

Colossians 2:6–7 — **A**

Proverbs 19:11 — **C**

2 Samuel 3:12 — **E**

Philippians 2:3 — **M**

Psalm 119:34 — **A**

Colossians 3:12 — **K**

Proverbs 12:26 — **E**

Psalm 130:4 — **R**

Jesus promised that peacemakers would be called sons (and daughters, of course!) of God. Making peace doesn't just mean never fighting or arguing. It also means that when you see people not getting along, you try to help them solve the problem as much as you can … especially people close to you and those you care about.

Sometimes it's easier to just ignore or pretend you don't see a difficult situation between two people. You might think, *It's none of my business!* That's why the first step is to pray. Ask God if there's something you could do to help. When you ask Him, He will give you the wisdom that you need.

This weekend, pray for people you know who are angry at each other. If there are problems between you and others, try to make things right as soon as possible.

Journal about it here.

Journaling

You are loved!

Sweet Words

Truth — *Your kind words can make someone's day!*

Mmm … honey! I like to put a bit of butter and honey on my warm toast and mix them as I spread them. (You should try it sometime!)

Besides being delicious, do you know what other good qualities honey has? Time for a science (and vocabulary) lesson.

1. Honey is *hygroscopic,* which means it absorbs moisture from the air and stays soft instead of drying up. If you put honey on a sore, it would help prevent a scar because the honey would keep your skin moist.

2. Honey is *antibacterial,* which means it keeps bacteria away. Again, if you put honey on a sore, it would protect the sore from becoming infected.

3. Honey contains *antioxidants,* which means honey protects against certain chemicals that could be harmful to your skin or body.

Just like honey makes us feel good physically, a thoughtful and kind message can make someone's heart feel cheery and help her not to give up in a difficult situation.

It doesn't cost anything to share some sweet words with someone else, so why not make a habit of it?

DARE — Add "honey" to your words!

TRIPLE-DOG DARE!

1 Ask God to help you make others feel good today with your pleasant words.

2 Give your mom a note today that lists all the things you love about her.

3 Write today's verse on a sticky note, leaving space to draw a honeycomb pattern around it. Put it on your mirror as a reminder to be sweet every day.

Journaling — How did it go? What did you learn?

Better Than a Magic Eraser

Truth *God's love and forgiveness can wipe out the dirtiest sins.*

Have you ever used one of those "magic eraser" sponges? They're so cool! You wet them with water and they wipe black marks off the wall, water stains off the bathroom sink, or fingerprints off your mirror. Of course, they can't get *every* stain out. If the dirt has gone too deep into a surface, even a "magic eraser" won't clean it.

Some laundry detergents and bleaches are supposed to get any stain out of fabric, but we've probably all had a favorite shirt ruined because we spilled something on it and the stain didn't come out.

Thankfully, God's forgiveness isn't like that. King David had done some pretty bad things that messed up the lives of many people. But when he admitted what he did and asked God to forgive him, God washed away those deep stains in his heart and made him clean again.

When you're truly sorry and ready to change your ways, God will forgive *your* biggest sins too.

DARE Ask God to wipe your sin stains out.

TRIPLE-DOG DARE!

1. Read and memorize Isaiah 1:18. Cut a small heart out of a piece of white felt and put it somewhere you'll see it often. Repeat this verse whenever you see the heart.

2. Whenever you help with cleaning chores, think about how God washes your sins away.… And thank Him for it!

3. Is there a sin you haven't told God about because you think it's too bad? Pray about it right now and trust that He will forgive you.

Journaling How did it go? What did you learn?

Walk Away

Truth *Sin doesn't belong in a Christian's life.*

You know when you're walking and someone comes in the opposite direction and you do this little dance where you both move to your right, then to your left, until one of you finally stands still and lets the other one go by?

I had that experience with a pigeon once. I felt a little playful so I walked straight toward the pigeon, and it walked straight toward me. As we got closer, it started doing that little dance, unsure if it should go left or right. Suddenly, it got nervous, spun around, and quickly walked the other way.

That memory still makes me laugh, but it also makes me think of how we do that little dance with sin. Sometimes temptation surprises us, and we have to think fast.

I wasn't a danger to the pigeon, even if it felt like I was, but the spiritual enemies we face *are* dangerous. With God's help, you can have the wisdom to turn and walk away.

DARE Walk away from temptation.

TRIPLE-DOG DARE!

1 Practice today's lesson with a friend: Walk toward each other, taking turns calling out commands, some that are good and some that are sins. See how fast you can turn and walk away whenever a sin is called out.

2 Do you have any books, magazines, or music that tempt you to sin? Ask God to help you get rid of them.

3 When a friend tells you about something she's tempted to do, help her by coming up with a more God-honoring activity to do together.

Journaling How did it go? What did you learn?

How to Fight Temptation

Truth
Jesus showed us how to say no to the Devil's temptations.

When Jesus lived on earth, He chose to go through the same struggles that we do, even though, as God, He didn't have to. As you read the New Testament, you'll see that Jesus only used His power or did miracles to help others … never for His own good.

Today's verses give us one of the best examples of how Jesus understands what we go through, especially when we're tempted to sin.

There are two important things to notice about Jesus' experience with temptation.

1. The Devil first tempted His body (with bread), then His mind (with the promise of power), and finally His spirit (to dishonor God). The Devil will always try to find your weak spot.

2. Jesus quoted a Bible verse for each temptation He said no to, which means He knew the Bible very well. Knowing God's Word can also help you when you need to say no to sin.

DARE Say no to sin … with confidence!

TRIPLE-DOG DARE!

1 What's your toughest temptation? Use a Bible concordance or ask someone to help you find a verse that can help you say no to it.

2 Write your memory verses in a notebook (or on index cards placed in an envelope) and practice them while brushing your teeth, waiting in line (keep them in your bag), or whenever you have free time.

3 Pray every morning that God will give you strength to resist temptation.

Journaling How did it go? What did you learn?

If You Can't Say Something Nice ...

Truth — *gossip can destroy lives.*

Has your mother ever said, "If you can't say something nice, don't say anything at all!"?

Well, she's right—because the Bible gives us the same advice in many places, especially in the book of Proverbs. Gossip might not seem like a big deal compared to murder or stealing, but it's actually a serious sin that God hates because it can cause a lot of pain.

Gossip is saying things behind someone's back that aren't true or make her look bad. As those words are passed around, her reputation is ruined. Not only that, but your reputation can be damaged because people will feel that you're not kind and you can't be trusted.

Imagine ripping open a feather pillow from the top of a tall building ... and then trying to collect all the feathers again. You can't! Once you gossip, you can never take your words back.... So keep them zipped in.

DARE — Watch what comes out of your mouth.

TRIPLE-DOG DARE!

1. When you're tempted to gossip, think of how you would feel if someone said those things about you.

2. If you've already gossiped about someone, do your best to stop the words from spreading. Apologize if you need to.

3. Spread "un-gossip": Talk to others about how good someone is. She'll feel great if the "un-gossip" reaches her!

Journaling — How did it go? What did you learn?

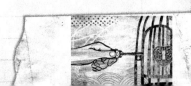

Persecuted but Not Abandoned

Read Matthew 5:10–12 and 2 Corinthians 4:8–9.

Cross out all the letters above odd numbers and then write the rest of the letters in the spaces below to see what 2 Timothy 3:12 says about persecution. (The answer is at the end of the book.)

E	K	G	V	E	H	P	R	Y	O	L	N	E	W	H
2	3	1	8	6	9	7	4	2	4	3	8	6	2	4

O	W	R	A	Y	N	T	M	S	T	O	O	L	U	I
8	6	7	8	1	2	4	7	6	2	9	4	8	3	2

J	V	E	A	H	G	O	J	D	L	Y	B	L	I	P
1	6	4	8	5	2	4	5	2	8	6	7	4	6	3

F	E	D	I	N	C	T	H	Z	R	I	P	S	T	A
6	8	3	2	8	4	3	2	1	8	6	7	2	8	9

J	A	E	S	T	F	U	S	W	I	X	L	O	L	B
2	1	8	4	7	3	2	6	8	4	9	2	7	8	6

Q	E	P	E	R	T	A	S	E	C	U	T	E	Y	D
3	4	6	8	2	1	3	6	4	8	2	2	6	9	4

_ _ _ _ _ _ _ _   _ _ _   _ _ _ _ _   _ _   _ _ _ _   _

_ _ _ _ _   _ _ _ _   _ _   _ _ _ _ _ _   _ _ _ _ _   _ _ _ _

_ _   _ _ _ _ _ _ _ _ _ _ .

Persecution is when someone or a group of people is mistreated, usually because of their color or religion. The Bible warns us that we will be persecuted for our faith in Jesus…. But it also gives us hope:

- God never abandons someone who is suffering because of Him.
- Persecuted believers can look forward to living peacefully in heaven one day.

If you've ever been made fun of because you believe in God, go to church, read your Bible, or pray, you have a little bit of an idea of what persecution feels like. But you may not be able to imagine how people suffer in other parts of the world where it's against the law to talk about God or do any of the things we often take for granted.

In some countries, people who are brave enough to stand up for their beliefs are beaten up, arrested, put in jail, and even killed. If these believers are willing to risk their lives by not hiding the fact that they believe in Jesus…. they must *really* believe in Him, right?

Do you trust God that much? Or do you get nervous about showing you're a Christian?

In the list below, check off the things you're scared, shy, or embarrassed to do:

- ○ Pray out loud at church.
- ○ Pray before eating when you're in public (in a way that people might notice).
- ○ Invite a friend to church.
- ○ Speak up in class if your teacher or another student says something that's against what the Bible teaches.
- ○ Share your testimony (the story of how you became a Christian) in front of everyone at church, Sunday school, or camp.
- ○ Keep your Bible in an obvious place when non-Christian friends come over.
- ○ Join a Christian club at your school.

If you checked off anything, ask God to give you more courage in showing others that you love Him and to help you trust Him to take care of you.

Got More Time?

Find out if your church knows about the International Day of Prayer for the Persecuted Church (usually in November). If not, volunteer to get information and ask your pastor to think about having the church participate this year. (Your parents can help you find the information on the Internet.)

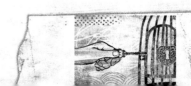

This week, try to notice the beauty
in simple, little things.

Bad Company

Truth Friends who don't love God can have a bad influence on you.

Today we're going to start with a super easy art project. In the space below, use a pencil to write the word FRIENDS in big bubble letters and then color them in, rubbing hard.

When you're done, rub your fingers over the letters.

Do you have black fingers now? (You might want to go wash them off before you continue with the devotional!)

As easily as the lead from the word FRIENDS rubbed off on you, the bad things about the people you hang around with can rub off on you too. If your friends don't love and honor God, if they think sin is fun and nothing serious, if they disrespect their parents and teachers … The closer you get to them, the more you're going to start behaving like them.

To stay pure, make sure you spend time in good company—with others who love and follow Jesus.

DARE Avoid bad company.

TRIPLE-DOG DARE!

1. Do you act differently around your school friends than you do at home or at church? If so, you might be keeping bad company. Ask God to help you find the right kind of friends.
2. Who are some people who encourage you and help you grow spiritually? Think of ways to spend more time with them.
3. Do the "FRIENDS" activity again, on a separate piece of paper, and stick it in your locker. If anyone asks why it's there, tell him or her about today's lesson.

Journaling How did it go? What did you learn?

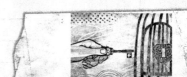

Jeremiah 17:7-8
Deep Roots

Truth — When your faith in Jesus Christ is deep, you don't need to worry about anything.

Whether you live in the country or in a big city, you've probably seen trees that are so big you couldn't wrap your arms around them. The older a tree gets, the taller and wider it grows.

The part of the tree that you *can't* see is what gives it its strength. Beneath the ground are roots that reach deep down. As the tree grows, the roots grow too, spreading themselves down and sideways to "anchor" the tree to the earth and keep it from falling. The roots also send water and nutrients up through the trunk and branches to feed the leaves, flowers, and fruits on the tree.

Trusting God is like growing deep, healthy roots. When trouble or hard times come, you can stand strong through it all because you know deep inside that God will take care of you.

DARE Trust God ... completely!

TRIPLE-DOG DARE!

1 What do you depend on to make you feel good every day? If your faith is in things or other people, ask God to help you switch it over to Him.

2 Draw or print out a picture of a tree with its underground roots and write today's verses somewhere on the page (change "man" to "girl" and "he" to "she"). Then give the picture to a friend who needs cheering up.

3 Do you rush through your devotions every day? Make more time for them so that your "roots" have a chance to sink into God's Word.

Journaling How did it go? What did you learn?

Are You Full?

Truth *Jesus can satisfy your deepest hunger.*

The average robin grows to between seven and eleven inches long, which means you could easily hold one in your hands. Robins aren't huge, but you might be surprised to find out how much they eat!

Robins mainly eat insects and berries, but they also like to snack on earthworms, which are easy for them to find after a rainstorm (or after you mow or water your lawn). How many worms do you think a robin might eat in one day?

Imagine three of your friends lying down in a straight line, head to toe. Now imagine a line of worms that long (about fourteen feet). That's about how many worms a robin will eat. Yeah, kind of gross! Most girls wouldn't even want to touch a worm, but robins seem to like them … to eat!

As a Christian, you need *spiritual* food to grow. Jesus promised that whoever goes to Him will never feel empty in her heart again. The time you spend with Jesus and in His Word will fill you up!

DARE Go to Jesus for your spiritual food.

TRIPLE-DOG DARE!

1 Would you skip eating for a day? Make you sure you don't skip reading your Bible either or you'll get spiritually hungry! Do your devotions every day.

2 Whenever you see a bird (or a worm!) thank God for the gift of His Son, Jesus, and for feeding your heart.

3 At lunchtime, tell your friends about today's devotional. Give them sticky notes with the verse written on them.

Journaling How did it go? What did you learn?

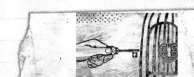

Hebrews 12:1
Travel Light

Truth
We can't run the race of faith if we're loaded down with sin.

Imagine you are about to run in a marathon.

Would you wear your jeans, a turtleneck sweater, rain boots, and a poncho? Would you put on your backpack full of schoolbooks?

That might sound silly because you know that a runner must wear the lightest clothes possible and not carry anything he or she doesn't need. Every little bit of extra weight will slow down a runner.

But did you know Christians also need to travel light—not physically, but spiritually? That means if there's anything that keeps you from growing in your faith or tempts you to sin, you need to get rid of it.

You might have sins you haven't confessed to God yet—those can weigh down your heart. You might have friends who discourage you from obeying God. You might have fears that keep you from doing daring things for God.

With God's help, you can be free of those burdens.

DARE — Get rid of whatever's holding you back.

TRIPLE-DOG DARE!

1. Do your friends tempt you to do things you know are wrong? Ask them to respect your values and your faith in God. If they won't, look for new friends.

2. If your parents say it's okay, write "Hebrews 12:1" with permanent marker on the bottom of your sneakers. Whenever you see it, pray and ask God to help you "travel light" spiritually.

3. Have a "race" with a friend to see who can memorize Hebrews 12:1 first.

Journaling — How did it go? What did you learn?

The Inchworm Lesson

Truth
If we judge others, we will be judged too.

Many years ago, during a church picnic, I spotted the cutest inchworm on our table. It was fun watching him walk! He'd hook himself down with his tail, run forward with his front feet, pull forward the back of his bright green body until he looked like a tiny *omega* (a Greek letter that looks like this: Ω), and then repeat the cycle. He was *fast!*

When I showed him to some of the children, my small niece said, "I can walk faster than that!" It was, of course, silly to compare herself to the tiny worm, but her comment got me thinking.

Sometimes we may look at other people and compare ourselves with them. We may judge them for not loving God as much as we do. We may think we're more mature.

That doesn't please God. He wants us to focus on our own walk with Him and to *encourage* others … not judge them.

DARE Focus on your walk with Jesus.

TRIPLE-DOG DARE!

1. Pray for the spiritual growth of one of your friends today. Later, give her a pretty note telling her you prayed for her.

2. Draw a picture of an inchworm on a sticky note and put it up in your locker or keep it in your planner as a reminder of today's lesson.

3. Have you been judging a friend? Ask God to forgive you and make you more understanding toward her.

Journaling How did it go? What did you learn?

Read Galatians 5:22-23.

If you stood near a big apple tree full of fruit and had enough patience (we're going to be talking about patience in a few weeks!), do you think you could count all the apples on the tree? It might take a while, especially if you lost count sometimes, but you could probably do it.

But could you look at an apple and count how many trees are inside the apple?

Strange question? Maybe, but it's a reminder of how incredibly wise and all-knowing God is. Only He knows how many trees would grow if the seeds inside an apple were planted.

The same God who makes fruit trees grow the fruit we enjoy eating can also grow fruit in you … spiritual "fruit" that grows in your life when God's Holy Spirit lives in you. For the next nine weeks we're going to look at the different qualities listed in these verses, starting with *love*.

How would you describe *love* to someone who had never heard the word before?

_____

_____

Most of us think of love as something you feel, like the "warm fuzzies" you get when you're happy or when you see someone who's really special to you. We often use the word *love* when we mean we *like* someone or something; for example, "I love my math teacher" or "I love my dog" or "I love ice cream."

This weekend, start thinking about how love is something that you *do* and something that you *give*, not just something that you *feel*.

Use this chart to help you work on developing the fruit of love in your life.

Got More Time?

Read and memorize Matthew 22:37–39.

List five people you love.					
Why do you love each one?					
How do you show them love?					
How are you sometimes unloving toward them?					
How will you give them more love this weekend?					

Get Ready for a New Week!

God will not always give you what
you want, but He will always give you
what you need ... when you need it.

Amazing Mysteries

Truth God is greater than we can understand, but we don't have to fear Him.

Do you ever wonder

… who tastes the dog food that is advertised as "great tasting"?

… why they're called *apart*ments when they're stuck together?

… why people park a car on a *driveway* but drive it on a *parkway*?

… why stores that are open twenty-four hours a day have locks on the doors?

… why glue doesn't stick to the inside of the bottle?

… why the alphabet is in that order?

Those are just some fun questions, but you can probably think of more serious questions about life and God—things that confuse you and make you wonder.

Remember this: If we could explain *everything* about God it would mean that either …

1. We are great enough to be able to understand God.

2. God is small enough to be easy to explain.

Also remember that, as you read in today's verses, when you reach out to God and try to stay close to Him, you don't have to feel nervous about the big mysteries of life and God.

DARE Trust God with the things you don't understand.

TRIPLE-DOG DARE!

1 In your journal, write a list of questions you wish you could ask God. Then pray that He'll help you trust Him with the things you don't understand.

2 When a friend asks you a question about God that you can't answer, share the two points from today's devotion.

3 Read all of Job 11.

Journaling How did it go? What did you learn?

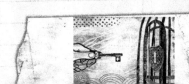

Luke 18:9-14

Praying Mantis ... or Preying Mantis?

Truth *Looking religious is not the same as being righteous.*

Have you ever seen a praying mantis? It's a long bright green insect that looks a little like an overgrown grasshopper. It gets its name from the way it folds its front legs, which makes it look like it's praying.

Although praying mantises look like they're praying, they're actually not very nice creatures. They don't bite humans, but if you ever caught one, it might pinch your finger. When they catch their victims (such as grasshoppers, butterflies, beetles, and even mice and hummingbirds), they bite their necks to paralyze them and then eat them alive!

In today's Bible story, Jesus gave the example of someone who prayed loudly and beautifully but whose heart was not right with God. This man was proud and looked down on other people he thought of as sinners.

Jesus warned His disciples (and us!) that to be right with God on the inside—not just the outside—we have to humble ourselves first.

DARE Pray to God.... Don't "prey" on others!

TRIPLE-DOG DARE!

1. Read Luke 18:18–29 to learn more about the difference between being *religious* and being *righteous*.

2. Do you look down on others because you think they're not as "Christian" as you are? Ask God to forgive you and to give you a more humble attitude.

3. Whenever you pray today, make sure you're not doing it as a duty but because you really want to talk to God.

Journaling How did it go? What did you learn?

"Feed My Sheep"

Truth
If we love Jesus, we have to share Him with others.

Imagine I invited you and your friends to my house for a fun girls' day and told you that I was going to make nachos, burgers, and a delicious chocolate cake. Now imagine you all came over, we hung out together all afternoon, and then when I said it was time to eat, I set the table for one and began eating all the food by myself without offering any of it to you and your friends.

I wouldn't be a very kind and loving friend if I did that, right?

When you decided to follow Jesus, you received many gifts from God: forgiveness for your sins, eternal life, joy, and so much more. Non-Christians around you may see the love of Jesus in you and the peace that you have because you trust Him…. And they may want to experience all that too.

Just as Jesus told Peter, "Feed my sheep," He wants you to share His love with others and give them the spiritual food (the truth taught in the Bible) that they need.

DARE　Feed God's sheep!

TRIPLE-DOG DARE!

1. Do you have friends you've never told about Jesus? Pray for the courage to start talking to them soon.

2. Write "God loves you and so do I" on some sticky notes (add a smiley face!) and sneak them into your friends' planners or lockers.

3. If your best friend is a Christian, come up with some ideas about ways the two of you can share God's love with others.

Journaling　How did it go? What did you learn?

Mark 9:35; Matthew 19:30

First or Last?

Truth — Jesus' followers should think of others before themselves.

Imagine that your teacher came into class one day and said that she had brought a special gift for everyone. As she placed a box full of beautifully wrapped presents on her desk, she asked all the students to get in line to receive the gifts.

From your past experiences, try to imagine where you would end up in the line: near the front, somewhere in the middle, or all the way at the end?

Now imagine that after everyone was lined up, your teacher started giving out the gifts … starting from the *back* of the line! You'd be surprised, right? And if you had rushed to be at the front of the line, you might even feel a little disappointed.

Jesus told His disciples that sometimes those who expect to be first will end up last and those who are last will be first. That means that we shouldn't think our own wants and needs are more important than others'. We should always look out for the good of those around us.

DARE Be willing to go last.

TRIPLE-DOG DARE!

1. Do you always put up your hand to talk in class? Try giving others (who might be more shy than you) a chance.
2. At home, pass food to your family members before you serve yourself.
3. When you feel ignored or like a failure, remember today's verses and how special you are to God!

Journaling How did it go? What did you learn?

Imitate the Original

Truth
You should imitate only God-not others.

Try this fun game with a group of friends later. Sit in a circle and give everyone a piece of paper and a pencil (or you can pass the pencil around). Have the first person copy or trace the picture on this page. The next person has to do the same thing, but she can't use the original drawing in the book; she has to copy or trace the first player's drawing. The third player will copy the second player's drawing and so on until everyone has had a turn. Then compare the last drawing to the original one in the book.

The final result might be quite different from the original picture!

As people who follow Jesus, we should try to be more and more like Him instead of copying others. Of course, if you know someone who loves and obeys God faithfully, it's a good idea to follow his or her example, but our main focus should be on the "original"— God.

DARE Imitate Jesus!

TRIPLE-DOG DARE!

1. After you play the game with your friends, explain today's lesson. If they're not Christians, tell them about Jesus!
2. In your journal, list ten things about your life that *don't* imitate Jesus. Pray for forgiveness and ask God to help you change.
3. Choose one way you will try to be more like Jesus today.

Journaling How did it go? What did you learn?

Read Galatians 5:22; Nehemiah 8:10; and Psalm 28:7.

List ten things that make you happy (for example, eating ice cream or playing with kittens):

1. _____
2. _____
3. _____
4. _____
5. _____
6. _____
7. _____
8. _____
9. _____
10. _____

Now list ten things that make you sad (for example, when a friend moves away or when you're not allowed to do something):

1. _____
2. _____
3. _____
4. _____
5. _____
6. _____
7. _____
8. _____
9. _____
10. _____

Did you know that even in the situations in your second list you can feel joy? You might not feel cheery and smiley because you don't like what's happening, but it doesn't mean you can't have the special joy that comes from God. When you choose to trust and obey God, the fruit of the Spirit creates joy in you even when it doesn't seem to make sense.

Some people think that joy and happiness are the same thing. But they're not quite the same. Happiness is something you feel depending on what's happening around you. Joy is knowing that everything is going to be okay because God is in charge and He loves you. Even in the worst situations, that joy can make you smile on the inside!

- Look at your second list again. For each situation, write down one way you could choose joy.

  1. _____
  2. _____
  3. _____
  4. _____
  5. _____
  6. _____
  7. _____
  8. _____
  9. _____
  10. _____

- Memorize Psalm 28:7.

- Look around for someone who seems discouraged or sad. Help him or her find a way to experience God's joy.

Journaling

Get Ready for a New Week!

"I am who I am today because of
the choices I made yesterday."

–Eleanor Roosevelt

All That Glitters ...

Truth Without God's grace, sin always leads to death.

Imagine you were walking down the street and someone came up to you and offered you a trash can. Not a pretty, empty trash can she just bought at a store … but a smelly trash can full of rotting, disgusting garbage. Would you take it?

What if the person had first sprayed perfume all over the garbage, sprinkled lots of glitter on top, and even put some sparkly stickers on the outside of the can?

Of course, you'd never accept garbage no matter how much someone tried to pretty it up. You wouldn't be fooled that easily! And yet so many people are fooled into thinking that sin is okay. The Devil always pretties up sin so that when you first look at it, you see the glitter and not the garbage. But underneath the glitter, it's still trash!

Lying, stealing, disobeying your parents, and gossiping can be tempting because the Devil tells you you'll feel good. But sin always leads to spiritual death (separation from God). Only obeying God will give you life!

DARE Accept God's gift of life.

TRIPLE-DOG DARE!

1. Think of the last few times you sinned. What tempted you? What was Satan's lie? Decide from now on not to believe the same lies again.

2. Write out today's verse and then memorize it. Repeat it to yourself whenever you toss something in the trash.

3. Do you have a friend who's not a Christian? Share today's devotion with her.

Journaling How did it go? What did you learn?

The Treasure Hunt

Truth *Heaven is the greatest treasure you will ever find.*

Do you enjoy treasure hunts?

In today's Bible verses, Jesus told the stories of two men who found great treasure. One wasn't really looking for treasure, but when he discovered it, he was so excited that he quickly bought the land it was buried in. He went through a lot of trouble and spent a lot of money, but he knew the value of the treasure and did whatever it took so that he could have it.

The second man was looking for a precious pearl, and when he finally found it, he did the same thing the first man did. He gave up everything else he had so that he could buy that pearl!

That's how precious heaven is. It's an awesome, incredible gift from God.... But there's nothing you can do to "buy" your way into heaven, so Jesus paid the price for you by dying on the cross. Your part is to accept His gift and then obey and follow Him. The only things you have to "give up" are your sin and the things in life that are worthless compared to heaven.

DARE Give up anything that gets between you and heaven.

TRIPLE-DOG DARE!

1. List the most valuable things you own. Would you give them up to go to heaven? If not, ask God to help you understand the treasure that heaven is.

2. Look up how pearls are made to get a better idea of why they're so valuable.

3. Read all of Matthew 13.

Journaling How did it go? What did you learn?

The Road Less Traveled

Truth *The road to heaven isn't always easy.*

Robert Frost, a poet who died in 1963, wrote a famous poem called "The Road Not Taken." The last lines of the poem say:

> Two roads diverged in a wood, and I—
> I took the one less traveled by,
> And that has made all the difference.

The poem talks about how, when he was faced with the decision of which way to go, he chose to take the path that seemed less worn-out, not knowing where it would lead.

The Bible also talks about a road that not many people travel on … the road to heaven. Most people, if they have to choose between a small, rough path and a smooth, well-lit road, will take the easy road.

The problem is that the easy road just leads people deeper into sin and farther from God. Sinning is easy. Being selfish and greedy is easy.

The road to *heaven* means giving up sin, trusting Jesus with your life, and following Him no matter what kinds of challenges He leads you through. But it's worth it!

DARE Take the narrow road!

TRIPLE-DOG DARE!

1. What's tempting you today? Ask God for the courage to do the hard—but *right*—thing.
2. Draw a picture that illustrates today's lesson. Include the Bible verses somewhere on your picture.
3. Do you have friends who think they can get to heaven without following Jesus? Share today's lesson with them.

Journaling How did it go? What did you learn?

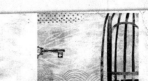

Follow the Right Light

Truth *Jesus' light shows us the way and keeps us safe.*

Have you ever been to a real lighthouse? I visited a beautiful old one at Peggy's Cove in Nova Scotia, Canada. It wasn't very big, but it was neat to think of how many boats it must have kept safe since it was built in 1914.

Lighthouses are not used as much as they used to be, but long ago, before there were more modern ways to guide ships, lighthouses were very important. They helped keep sailors from crashing into cliffs and rocky shores by giving light to a wide area.

Jesus told His disciples that He is the *Light of the world*—not just one shore, but the whole world! Through His words in the Bible, we can know the right way to go and can recognize the dangers put in front of us by the Enemy.

DARE Follow only Jesus' light!

TRIPLE-DOG DARE!

1. Make a colorful bookmark with a drawing of a lighthouse and the words of John 8:12. Give it to a friend!

2. Think of some ways that reading your Bible has helped you in life. Take time today to thank God for His Word.

3. Have you been following the "light" of friends, celebrities, or others? Ask God to help you focus only on Him.

Journaling How did it go? What did you learn?

Speak Up!

Truth
God expects you to stand up for the rights of those who need help.

If you saw a lost kitten or found an injured bird, how would you react? You'd probably want to help it, right? What if one of your classmates started teasing your little sister? Would you protect her?

Most of us would help or rescue a cute animal, family member, or close friend without really thinking about it first. It's an instinct God created us with.

But not all of us react that quickly to help people we don't know, especially if we think we might get picked on or bothered because of our actions.

There are many people in your community who can't help themselves: They might be blind or deaf, disabled, sick, poor, or weak. Unfortunately, they will sometimes receive bad treatment from others. They might be made fun of or ignored or even abused.

God can give you the strength and courage to speak up for them!

DARE   Help someone who's helpless.

TRIPLE-DOG DARE!

1 Whenever you see someone in a wheelchair, don't just walk by. Stop for a moment to see if he or she needs any help.

2 Do you know a child at school who is teased or bullied a lot? Talk to a teacher or the school principal about it.

3 If your friends start making fun of someone, ask them to stop, and explain that God wants us to help others, not be mean to them.

Journaling   How did it go? What did you learn?

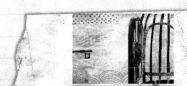

Read Galatians 5:22.

In the space below, draw a picture of what the word *peace* means to you. Don't worry about how well you draw or even if your drawing is "correct." Just try to describe peace with pictures instead of words.

There's an old story about a man who wanted to have the perfect picture of peace, so he looked all over—in art stores and museums and wherever he went—but he couldn't find something that satisfied him. So he held a contest to see if someone could create what he was looking for, and he offered a valuable prize to the winner.

As you can imagine, many artists from far and wide participated in this contest. At last the day came to judge the paintings. One by one they were uncovered while the audience cheered and clapped at the different paintings. Finally they were down to the last two.

When the first one was uncovered, the crowd suddenly became very quiet. It was a picture of a lake that was as smooth as a mirror, surrounded by deep green trees and soft green grass that a few fluffy-looking sheep were grazing on. The sky was painted in the pastels of a beautiful sunset.

The crowd thought that this painting had to be the winner!

Then the man who organized the contest uncovered the final painting, and everyone in the audience reacted with sounds of shock and surprise. In front of them was a picture of a huge waterfall with big waves and splashes of water going over rough and dangerous-looking rocks. The sky was cloudy and there was rain and lightning. The wind was making skinny trees bend over and look like they were about to snap.

But when the people in the crowd looked a little closer, they saw a little bird sitting on a branch of one of the trees, protecting her nest of eggs. The bird's eyes were closed, and it looked like she was singing.

This was the painting that won the contest because it showed what true peace is. Peace isn't when there's no war, no fighting, no problems, and no suffering. Peace is when all those things are happening around you, but you trust God so much that, like the little bird, you can go through life calmly and without fear.

When God's Holy Spirit lives in you, He gives you that kind of peace.... And others can see it too!

Got More Time?

If your idea of peace has changed after reading the devotion, draw a second picture of what peace means to you. You can either draw what you think the last painting in the story looked like or come up with your own idea.

Get Ready for a New Week!

Winners never quit and quitters never win.

Shout for Joy!

Truth
God is so good that He deserves constant worship from us.

Do you get excited when it's time to visit your grandparents? If you haven't seen them in a long time, you might run into their house yelling, "Hi, Grandma! Hi, Grandpa! I love you!" and then give them big hugs. When you see your best friend, do you feel happy inside and start chatting with her about all kinds of things that are important to the two of you?

It's strange that sometimes when people go to church—the place where we go to worship and talk to God—they don't feel that excited. What about you?

Today's Bible reading says that you should rejoice when it's time to pray or worship. Think about it: You get to spend time with the Creator of the universe, the God who loves you so much that He died on the cross to save you from your sins.

That's a great reason to shout for joy!

DARE Rejoice when you worship God!

TRIPLE-DOG DARE!

1. On your way to church on Sunday, instead of chatting about everyday things, quietly ask God to prepare your heart and mind to worship Him.
2. During prayer times at church, instead of peeking around or daydreaming, talk to God, telling Him how great He is.
3. Memorize all of Psalm 100. You can do it!

Journaling How did it go? What did you learn?

John 14:6

Only One Way

Truth
Believing in Jesus is the only way to reach God.

When you or your parents need directions to get somewhere, you might pull out a map or look up directions on the Internet. Your parents might even have a GPS system in the car that guides the driver.

Most of the time, there are different ways to get to a certain spot. Some ways might take longer than others, or some routes might go through prettier scenery. Even when you're taking the bus or subway, there might be different ways to go.

Jesus made it clear that going to heaven is not like looking up directions on a map. You don't even need a map because the way to God is very simple: It's through knowing and believing in Jesus.

Remember this truth when you hear people saying things like, "There are many ways to go to heaven, not just through Christianity" or "All religions are good and lead to God" or "As long as you do your best to be good, you'll go to heaven."

DARE
Don't follow any path except the one Jesus is on!

TRIPLE-DOG DARE!

1 Write down today's verse. Memorize it and then challenge your best friend to memorize it too.

2 Do you have a friend who's confused about God or different religions? Explain this verse to her.

3 Write this verse on ten sticky notes and leave them in random places, such as a bus stop or public bathroom.

Journaling
How did it go? What did you learn?

Look at the Heart

Truth
Thoughts and character matter more than looks do.

Most girls spend a lot of time thinking—and even worrying—about how they look. There's a lot of pressure to dress a certain way and have the "right" shoes or bag or accessories to fit in. Magazines and TV shows can make you feel like you're ugly if you don't have the shiny hair, perfect teeth, skinny legs, clear skin, or long eyelashes that you see on models and celebrities.

Unfortunately, even though we all know what it's like to feel worried about our own looks, we often judge others by their looks! You might look at a girl wearing glasses and think, *She's probably smart.* Or you might see a pretty girl with nice clothes and imagine that she's a snob. Chubby kids are often ignored or made fun of by other kids who have no idea what they're like on the inside.

This story about God choosing David as king reminds us to pay more attention to the inner beauty than the outward appearance of others … and ourselves, too.

DARE Don't judge by outward appearance.

TRIPLE-DOG DARE!

1. How much time do you spend flipping through fashion magazines or playing with your hair? Challenge yourself to spend *more* time than that on your spiritual growth.
2. If you've been judging people you don't know because of how they look, make the effort to get to know them.
3. Write "The Lord looks at the heart" on a sticky note and place it on your mirror.

Journaling How did it go? What did you learn?

proverbs 17:17

BFF ... Really?

Truth *A true friend loves always ... no matter what.*

Do you ever wonder if people really know what the word *friend* means? You may know some girls who seem to make new friends and drop them as often as they change their shoes or the weather changes. As long as everyone agrees with everyone else, they're friends, but if someone says or does something they don't like, they're not friends anymore. "Best friends forever" do this to each other too!

According to the Bible, though, a real friend doesn't take off running at the first sign of trouble. True friends stick together even in bad times because they love each other and want what's good for their friends ... not just for themselves.

Having real friends you can count on is important as you're growing up, so don't be too quick to call someone a "friend." A true friendship will prove itself during hard times.

DARE Love your friends the way Jesus loves you!

TRIPLE-DOG DARE!

1 Make a list of people who love you even when you don't deserve it. In the next few days, thank them all for their friendship.

2 Are you having trouble getting along with a friend? Ask God to help you continue to love her.

3 Ask your parents to tell you about a time someone was a true friend to them.

Journaling How did it go? What did you learn?

Totally Satisfied

Truth When you trust in God, you'll never feel like you're missing something.

Fill a clear drinking glass with grapes, marbles, or anything about that size. Is the glass full? Not really. You can see a lot of gaps between the objects, right?

Empty the glass and then fill it again with something smaller, such as small beads or blueberries. Is it completely full now?

What if you filled it with sand? It would *look* full, but you would still have invisible gaps between the grains of sand. In fact, you would even be able to pour some water into the glass, which would fill in those gaps.

If you poured *only* water into the glass, then it would be completely filled, with no gaps.

Trying to find happiness in "things"—money, clothes, or fun activities—doesn't work. It always leaves gaps in your heart. But inviting Jesus into your life is a lot like filling your glass with water. Psalm 23:1 says that when God is your Shepherd, you "shall not be in want." That means you will be totally satisfied!

DARE Follow Jesus for true happiness.

TRIPLE-DOG DARE!

1 Make two lists: ten things you *need* and ten things you *want*. Do you have everything you need? Take time to thank God for those blessings in your life. Ask Him to help you want Him more than the things on your second list.

2 Make yourself a pretty bookmark with the words of Psalm 23:1.

3 Explain today's devotional to a friend using the drinking glass example.

Journaling How did it go? What did you learn?

Read Galatians 5:22 and Ecclesiastes 7:8.

Interesting fact: More than forty verses in the Bible use the words *patient, patience,* or *patiently.* God obviously wants us to have patience! So it's not surprising that one of the qualities listed in the fruit of the Spirit is patience.

There are two ways to think about patience. They're similar but not exactly the same. Patience can mean …

1. not easily getting angry or upset when someone does something that bothers us

2. being able to wait for something that is taking a long time

What are some things that are hard to wait for because you want them right away? We've given a couple of examples …

- Your favorite cake baking in the oven
- Glue to dry on a craft project you worked on
- Presents under the Christmas tree
- _____
- _____
- _____
- _____
- _____

Sometimes we don't have a choice, and we *have* to wait (for example, if you're looking forward to a trip), but we still get nervous and antsy and end up annoying the people around us.

Sometimes we do have a choice, but if we don't wait, we can end up ruining what we weren't willing to wait for. If you take a cake out of the oven before it's done, you won't be able to eat it! If you don't wait for the glue to dry on your project, everything will fall apart. And if you open your Christmas presents before you're supposed to, you'll ruin all the fun for later.

We also said that patience is when you remain calm when someone or a situation upsets you. Having patience with people doesn't mean that you think what they're doing is okay; it just means that you're willing to give them a chance to make things right on their own.

Patience takes hard work sometimes, but when God's Spirit lives in you and you start to grow spiritual "fruit," it does get easier.

Got More Time?

To practice patience, take a walk with an elderly person or a small child who can't walk very fast. Resist the temptation to go faster. Instead, think about how happy you're making the other person feel.

Journaling

Get Ready for a New week!

Courage isn't about not being afraid. It's about being afraid but doing the right thing anyway.

"I Remember You ..."

Truth *Your Christian leaders and friends need your prayers.*

How often do you pray for your pastor? Your Sunday school teacher or youth-group leader? How about that lady at church who never forgets your birthday or the missionary whose picture is up on the bulletin board?

When the apostle Paul wrote a letter to his friend Philemon, he told him that he not only prayed for him often but that he thanked God for him each time. Paul knew that Philemon served God faithfully and shared his faith with many people, and he appreciated that. It encouraged Paul to continue serving God too.

If you've ever had anyone tell you they're proud of you, or that they're praying for you, or that you're doing a great job, you know how good it feels to know that someone is thinking of you. You can also make others feel cared for and encouraged by praying for them and telling them how thankful you are for their dedication to God.

DARE Encourage someone today!

TRIPLE-DOG DARE!

1 Write the words of Philemon 1:4–7 on a blank card (don't forget to include the verse reference!), sign your name, and give the card to your pastor on Sunday. If you have time, make a few more cards for other Christians you appreciate.

2 Pray for the people you gave the cards to, asking God to give them strength to continue in their work.

3 Say positive things about these people "behind their backs" to remind others to appreciate them.

Journaling How did it go? What did you learn?

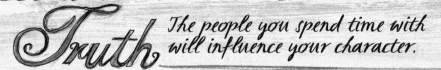
Walk with the Wise

Truth The people you spend time with will influence your character.

There's an old Turkish saying that if you hang around with a donkey for too long, you're either going to start acting like a donkey … or smelling like one!

You don't always have a choice about the people you spend your time with. Your family, your classmates, and your neighbors are there whether you like it or not. But you *do* have a choice about the friends you hang out with on your own time.

It's important to choose your friends carefully. If your friends spend hours talking about silly things or only doing fun activities that don't help them learn or grow or serve others, they won't have a positive influence on you. But if you spend time with people who are wise, who make time for others and for God, and who set a good example for you, that will help you to grow and mature into the kind of girl God designed you to be.

DARE Choose wise friends.

TRIPLE-DOG DARE!

1. Make a list of people in your life who seem wise, such as your grandparents or a girl in your youth group who really loves God. Try to spend more time with them.

2. Ask your parents to tell you about wise people they learned from when they were younger.

3. Pray that God will help you be wise so that you can be a good influence on your friends.

Journaling How did it go? What did you learn?

God's Peace

Truth   *God's peace can take away your fear.*

When most people hear the word *peace,* they think about what it would be like if the world, or even their own country, didn't have any war or fighting. Many people even pray for world peace, asking God to do something about the wars going on in many different countries. They seem to think that if all the fighting stopped, everyone would feel better.

Jesus told His disciples not to expect this kind of peace, even though many people thought that Jesus had come to earth for that reason: to bring world peace. Instead, He said that He came to bring us *His* peace—something even greater than no war.

When you trust Jesus with your life, His Holy Spirit creates a special peace in your heart that helps you be calm instead of afraid when problems come your way. God's peace is something that starts inside your heart and spreads out around you.

DARE   Turn to Jesus for true peace.

TRIPLE-DOG DARE!

1 Whenever you hear about a war, pray that the people involved will find *God's* peace inside.

2 Think of someone you know who is going through a difficult time. Send him or her a cheery card with the words of this verse.

3 Memorize today's verse with your best friend.

Journaling   How did it go? What did you learn?

How's Your Memory?

Truth — Just reading the Bible isn't enough.

Our brains are amazing—even more amazing than today's top computers! A healthy brain can hold huge amounts of information, figure out problems really quickly, and remember tiny details instantly. It's a good thing too, because can you imagine how confusing it would be if you couldn't remember anything?

You wouldn't be able to learn a language, read a book, make a sandwich, or even remember your own name. In fact, you would forget what you looked like the second you turned away from the mirror!

These verses warn that if you read your Bible without paying attention to the message and doing what you learned (just as you're dared to do every day in this book), it's just as bad as forgetting what you look like after seeing your face in a mirror.

But when you study God's Word and then obey it, God will bless you!

DARE — Remember and obey what God teaches you through His Word.

TRIPLE-DOG DARE!

1. When you read something in the Bible that you don't understand, instead of skipping over it, ask your parents, pastor, or Sunday school teacher to help you with it.
2. If you need courage to do what you learned from your Bible reading, ask a friend to work on it with you.
3. Keep a notebook or blank paper with your Bible to write down things you learn at church or in Sunday school. Review your notes when you get home.

Journaling — How did it go? What did you learn?

Ooh, Pick Me!

Truth   *God looks for Christians who want to serve Him.*

When the teacher asks who wants to read out loud from the textbook, do you quickly put your hand up or do you sink down in your chair a little, hoping she won't notice you? What if she asks for a volunteer to stay in class during recess to help her make posters for an upcoming fund-raiser?

What if she asked for a volunteer without telling the class what the job was? You might be nervous about putting your hand up, right?

In today's reading, Isaiah quickly volunteered when God looked around for someone to send on a mission … even before he knew what he had to do.

God may not ask you to be a missionary, but He may want you to tell a friend about Jesus, or to help wash dishes at church, or to walk your sick neighbor's dog. Are you ready to do whatever He wants?

DARE   Have a "Pick me!" attitude with God.

TRIPLE-DOG DARE!

1 When you wake up in the mornings, tell God that you want to serve Him today and ask Him to show you what you can do.

2 When your church is looking for volunteers, ask your parents if you (or even your whole family) can help out.

3 Today, tell someone who doesn't know God that He loves her. Then invite her to church to learn more about Him.

Journaling   How did it go? What did you learn?

Read Galatians 5:22.

You've probably heard people talk about practicing "random acts of kindness." This idea has become really popular, and some of the good deeds that people do in groups or on their own are pretty cool!

In case you're not familiar with RAOK (random acts of kindness), it's when you do something nice and unexpected for someone—it could even be a stranger—for no reason at all except that you wanted to make them smile or feel special. Sometimes people will add change to parking meters that are about to run out, surprise someone by giving her flowers, or secretly wash someone's car. There are hundreds of examples, and you can probably think of quite a few yourself.

Practicing RAOK can be fun and even easy because, if you really think about it, it makes *you* feel good. The good deeds might be unselfish, but most people also enjoy the satisfaction and pride they feel after doing them.

The sort of kindness the Bible talks about—part of the fruit of the Spirit—is a little different. True kindness is treating someone well even when you *don't* feel like it. It's when that person is someone you can't stand being around, when it might be uncomfortable for you, or when your kindness may not be appreciated.

In other words, it's more than just random. The kindness you show as a Christian should come from having God's Holy Spirit living in you, not just because you're feeling good and have the time.

Think of two people you would *like* to show kindness to this weekend:

1. _____
2. _____

Now think of two people you would find it difficult to show kindness to:

1. _____
2. _____

Pray for the last two people and ask God to help you show *His* kindness to them. Then write down your plan for showing them kindness this weekend, or as soon as you can:

_____
_____
_____
_____

Got More Time?

With one or two friends, come up with some ideas for showing kindness to others on a regular basis. You might even want to come up with a name for your "team," such as The Kindness Kids or The Daring Darlings.

You might find making a list like this (we've included a suggestion to get you started) helps you get organized.

Tip: Think of *who* you want to show kindness to first, then think of what you can do … not the other way around.

Who	What	When	How did the person react?
A teacher who never smiles	Bake cookies and wrap them nicely. Secretly leave them on his desk.	Before the end of next week.	He looked surprised and didn't stop smiling until the end of class!

Every week or every other week, work on this list with your friends to add more acts of kindness. You might want to record your ideas and results in a notebook!

Get Ready for a New Week!

You're not alone!

The Words of Your Mouth

Truth
Your words and thoughts should always please god.

Someone who always tries to make others like her by the things she says and does would be called a "people pleaser."

Suppose you went to your cousin's house for a sleepover, and all the girls wanted to paint their nails and experiment with makeup, but you wanted to play your new board game that your cousin had asked you to bring over. If you thought, "Oh well … Even though I really don't want to, I'd better go along with the other girls, otherwise they'll think I'm weird," that would be an example of pleasing people.

Of course, it's not always bad to be a people pleaser, as long as pleasing people isn't more important to you than pleasing God and it doesn't go against God's Word or desires.

Today's verse is a reminder to keep your mind and heart focused on God so that your thoughts and feelings—and the words of your mouth—always honor and please *Him*.

DARE
Dedicate the words of your mouth to God.

TRIPLE-DOG DARE!

1 Read all of Psalm 19. Pause after each verse to think about what you just read.

2 Write out and then memorize verse 14. Repeat it throughout the day as a prayer to God, asking Him to help you honor Him with all your thoughts and words.

3 Make a pretty design with the words of verse 14, small enough to put into a frame and place it where you'll see it every day.

Journaling
How did it go? What did you learn?

psalm 32:1-5

The Exterminator

Truth Trying to hide your sins from god leads to worse problems!

No matter how friendly your parents are when it comes to inviting visitors over for dinner, there's one kind of guest they definitely *don't* want eating at your house: termites!

Termites are little insects that love to eat wood, dead leaves, soil, and even animal dung. They can ruin farm crops and even destroy buildings as they munch on the wood.

If the owner of a house with a termite problem said, "They're just little bugs. How much damage can they do?" or, "I'm too embarrassed to admit my house has termites so I'll just pretend they're not there. Maybe they'll go away," or even, "I won't call an exterminator. It'll be too expensive and messy, and my house might smell from the chemicals," what do you think would happen to his house? It would fall apart after a while!

That's what it's like when we don't admit our sins to God: They start to eat us up inside like termites. But God can exterminate those sins … and the sooner, the better!

DARE Confess your sins to God … right away.

TRIPLE-DOG DARE!

1. Before you ask God to forgive your sins, make sure you have forgiven others who may have hurt you.

2. Take about ten minutes to talk to God about your sins. Ask Him to show you what you still need to ask forgiveness for.

3. Write out a plan of how you will avoid doing the same sins again.

Journaling How did it go? What did you learn?

"Do Not Fret"

Truth
You don't need to worry about people who do evil—God will deal with them.

Sometimes when rich and famous people break the law it seems like they become even bigger celebrities or more successful after that. Many popular artists sing songs that really dishonor God. Maybe the kids at school who cheat the most get the highest grades and because of that, better treatment from the teacher.

Isn't it unfair? Do you ever wonder why God doesn't punish these people? Some Christians seem to feel that if God isn't going to do anything, they should!

Unfortunately, because we don't have God's wisdom, we can make situations worse when we try to deal with evil ourselves. God wants us to trust Him in all situations, especially the confusing and upsetting ones.

Of course, there may be times when you need to speak up to help someone in trouble, but your first reaction should always be to pray and then trust God to do what He wants to do and to show you what He wants *you* to do.

DARE
Have patience when bad people seem to succeed in what they do.

TRIPLE-DOG DARE!

1. When someone at school does something really bad, pray for him or her, remembering that God can change hearts.

2. If your friends ever sound jealous of successful people who make bad decisions, share what you learned today.

3. Are you scared of people who do evil? Ask God to give you peace and to help you trust Him.

Journaling
How did it go? What did you learn?

Proverbs 18:13

Listen ... Then Answer

Truth *Talking without thinking can make us look very foolish.*

If you asked your parents to list five things that make them feel angry or disappointed in you, what do you think they would say?

How about talking back? Is that something you can't seem to stop? Many kids who say they love their parents get into a lot of trouble because of their bad habit of reacting disrespectfully. Usually it's because they just didn't have the patience to really listen first. For example, your dad may say, "You didn't take out the trash yesterday." If you quickly answer, "Why does it always have to be me? It's not fair! I was doing my homework," you might not realize that he was about to say, "… but it's okay because I saw that you were working hard so I did it."

How you react toward people will make a big difference in your relationships. If you're too quick to answer, you may end up looking foolish … and losing people's trust.

DARE Listen before you answer.

TRIPLE-DOG DARE!

1 If you talked back to your parents this week, admit it to them and ask for forgiveness.

2 When you feel tempted to react quickly when someone says something, first repeat what he or she said (quietly, in your head) to understand it better and to answer more carefully.

3 Write this verse on a sticky note and put it up in your locker at school.

Journaling How did it go? What did you learn?

Your Heart's Desires

Truth When your relationship with God makes you happy, other things don't seem as attractive.

Stephanie liked a lot of the same things most girls like: games, swimming, camping with her family, cartoons, ice cream, cute dresses, and puppies.

One day, Stephanie's family met a very generous lady who owned a ranch. She invited Stephanie's family to visit and said that Stephanie could have free riding lessons as often as she wanted and even pick out a horse of her own to keep!

Stephanie enjoyed riding and realized that she liked riding horses more than anything!

Now, imagine if Stephanie (who is only a pretend girl in our story) continued playing with her dolls and watching cartoons on TV and swimming at the pool. That wouldn't make sense, would it? Stephanie would probably gladly give up other activities for the one thing she liked best: horses.

When you really love God, He fills your life with so much joy that you stop craving things you used to think would make you happy. But if you keep looking for those other things, you'll miss out on the joy God can give you.

DARE Stay close to Jesus!

TRIPLE-DOG DARE!

1. List five things that make you happy. For each one, think of a way that God makes you even happier and thank Him for it.

2. Ask God to help you be joyful about your relationship with Him so that you don't look for happiness in other things.

3. Make two bookmarks with the words of verse 4. Give one to a friend!

Journaling How did it go? What did you learn?

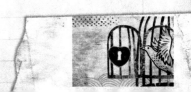

Nice ... or Good?

Read Galatians 5:22 and 2 Peter 1:5.

Olivia had a problem. Whenever she went to school, she noticed that some of the girls would look at her strangely and whisper among themselves, sometimes even pointing at her and giggling. They wouldn't sit near her unless they had to, and she didn't know why.

Let's pretend that you went to Olivia's school, and she knew that you were a Christian and that you were always nice to people. One day Olivia came to you and told you her problem and asked you for advice.

While Olivia was talking to you, you noticed that, well, she didn't smell very good. And suddenly you realized why the other kids were being mean to her. What would you do?

A. Pat her arm and say, "Don't worry about it, Olivia. Those girls really do like you. They just like to tease a lot. There's nothing wrong with you."

B. Tell her gently that you think it might have something to do with how she smells sometimes. It could just be something she eats or the perfume she uses. Offer to help her figure out what it is. (Maybe she just needs some deodorant or to wash or change more often.)

If you chose A, you probably try to be nice all the time, which is great ... sort of. Sometimes being nice makes people feel good, but it doesn't really help them.

If you chose B, you are willing to take the risk that someone might not like you for trying to do the right thing. Choice B is not as *nice* as Choice A, but it's *good*. Your honesty and kindness can help Olivia solve her problem, and it shows that you care more about her than you do about yourself.

One of the qualities—or fruits of the Spirit—that we should develop is goodness. Being good means doing the right thing. Not the easy thing, not the popular thing, and sometimes not even the *nice* thing ... but the *right* thing.

Ask God to help you develop goodness in your life.

Read Mark 11:12–19, which is a great example of Jesus being *good* but not exactly *nice*.

Make up your own story about a situation where being good wasn't the easy or popular thing to do but was the *right* thing to do.

Journaling

Get Ready for a New Week!

"Be still, and know that I am God."

—Psalm 46:10

Healthy Words

Truth *Words can destroy people ... or "repair" them.*

If you care about your health and want to have strong teeth and bones, a healthy heart, and clear skin, you know that eating junk food, drinking a lot of pop, and spending hours in the sun without protection are all bad for you. You also know that things like vegetables, fruit, nuts, cheese, fish, whole grains, and water can strengthen your body.

People sometimes forget that words can harm someone even more than junk food or dangerous activities. Hurtful words can include ...

- swear words (they dishonor God)
- dirty jokes (they pollute our minds)
- mean words (they break hearts)
- rude words (they show disrespect)
- angry words (they ruin friendships)
- dishonest words (they make people stop trusting)

The Bible says that everything you say should build others up, just like vitamins and calcium and protein and fiber build up your body.

DARE Use your words to build people up.

TRIPLE-DOG DARE!

1 Looking at the list above, confess to God any "unhealthy" words you have said lately and ask for His help to speak only "healthy" words.

2 List five people you want to build up with your words today. Give them encouraging notes or say something kind to them.

3 Challenge your closest friends to do today's dare too. You can work as a team to build people up!

Journaling How did it go? What did you learn?

Proverbs 17:9

What Not to Share

Truth Talking too much about others' mistakes can ruin friendships.

We all do it at times. You're having problems at home that make you feel angry or worried, and you tell your friends about it. Sometimes you just need to get things off your chest, right?

If your parents have been fighting or your dad lost his job or your older cousin got pregnant or your neighbor was arrested, you might feel like you really need to tell someone or you're going to burst.

The problem is that even if you tell a friend you trust not to repeat your words to others, you can't control what she will think of what you shared or how she will feel about the people you talked about. Sharing too much can create little "cracks" in relationships that grow and grow until they cause a lot of damage.

It's okay to ask someone you trust for advice about a problem, but don't blab your thoughts to just anyone without thinking.

DARE Protect your relationships by learning what not to share.

TRIPLE-DOG DARE!

1. When you hear bad news at home or you're upset about something, talk to God about it until the temptation to blab to a friend is gone.
2. If you have a friend who tells everyone her problems, share this verse with her and encourage her to be more careful too.
3. When a friend does something she feels ashamed of, let her know you won't tell others about it.

Journaling How did it go? What did you learn?

Bonus!

Truth
When your focus is on loving and obeying God, other good things come your way!

Have you ever looked for a jacket or a pair of jeans that you put in the wrong place, and then when you finally found it, you discovered five dollars in one of the pockets? How fun!

We all love to get a little more than we expected. For example, sometimes you buy shampoo, and a free sample of conditioner is attached as a bonus. Or you take a gift to a friend's birthday party and come home with a bag full of candy and small toys. Maybe you offer to shovel snow off your neighbor's walk one day because she's sick, and afterward she gives you a tin full of her delicious oatmeal cookies. Nice!

The Bible says that when you make righteousness (obeying God) and love your top priorities, God will bless you with a good life full of unexpected bonuses!

DARE Look for the right things.

TRIPLE-DOG DARE!

1 Instead of trying to become friends with the most popular kids at school, try showing friendship to the least popular ones.

2 Make a list of at least five wonderful things God has surprised you with in your life. Take time to thank Him for them.

3 Before you ask your parents for something, make sure you haven't been disobeying or disrespecting them. If you have been, make things right first.

Journaling How did it go? What did you learn?

James 4:13-16

"God Willing"

Truth Only god really knows what will happen tomorrow.

You may sometimes hear your parents or people at church say "God willing" when they talk about future plans. It's a way of showing that they understand today's lesson: That we may make our plans, but God has the final say in everything.

It's like telling your friend, "Sure, I'll come over and watch that movie with you tomotrow … if my mom says it's okay." Because you know your mom pretty well, you can probably guess ahead of time whether or not she would let you. But you might not know if she already has other plans for you, so you still have to ask her and let her make the final decision.

There's nothing wrong with making plans for your future, as long as you never forgot to pray and ask God to show you what *He* wants for you. Saying "God willing" is a good way to remember that anything you do is only because He gives you life and strength.

DARE Don't forget God when you make plans.

TRIPLE-DOG DARE!

1. Even if you don't say it out loud, try to make it a habit to remember "God willing" whenever you talk about things you plan to do.

2. List ten great experiences you've had and then thank God for allowing those things to happen.

3. Think of something you're hoping for but aren't sure if you'll get to do. Ask God to give you patience as you wait to find out if it will happen.

Journaling How did it go? What did you learn?

First Love

Truth
Serving God doesn't count for much if you don't love Him.

Have you ever watched young kids open Christmas presents? They excitedly rip open the packages and scream with happiness when they see the toy they wanted for months. They start playing with it right away and then talk about it and show it to everyone for the rest of the day. They go to bed holding it and play with it the moment they wake up.

But what happens a week or a month later? They may have forgotten the toy that, at first, was their favorite thing in the world!

That's how some Christians are with God. When they first become Christians, they are excited about knowing and serving God. They tell their friends about Jesus, read their Bibles, pray a lot, and go to church as much as possible. But after a while, they seem to lose their excitement and they spend less time with God.

It makes God sad when we lose our first love for Him, even if we continue acting like believers. He deserves to always have our first love!

DARE — Stay excited about God!

TRIPLE-DOG DARE!

1. Start each day by thanking God for your blessings and telling Him how much you love Him.

2. Ask God to forgive you if there are things in your life that you're more excited about than Him.

3. If you have a friend who hasn't been coming to church for a while, tell her what you learned today (without criticizing her).

Journaling — How did it go? What did you learn?

Read Galatians 5:22.

What do the following things have in common?

- postage stamps on an envelope
- permanent marker on your desk
- crazy glue on an art project
- freckles on a face
- insects on a spider web
- dye on an egg
- iron-on patches on clothes
- fingernails on fingers
- tattoos on skin
- annoying songs in your brain
- melted cheese on a burger
- bubble gum in your hair

If you guessed that they're all things that are stuck on—sometimes for good—you're right! You might say that they're all examples of *faithfulness* except for one problem: In each case, the things that are stuck together didn't choose to be stuck together. They just are. And sometimes it's not a *good* thing that they're stuck (such as gum in your hair)!

Real faithfulness, on the other hand, comes from choosing to follow and obey God. It's one of the things that the Holy Spirit develops in you, helping you to continue trusting and obeying God no matter how difficult it is sometimes. Faithfulness also helps us in other relationships, such as friendships and marriage. It means we stick to another person even when our feelings tempt us to ignore him or her. It means that when we make a promise, we keep it.

God gives us the perfect example of faithfulness because, even though we disobey Him, He never stops loving us, and He never breaks His promises. First John 1:9 says, "If we confess our sins, he is faithful and just and will forgive us our sins and purify us from all unrighteousness."

Write out a short prayer, asking God to help you be more faithful in relationships or areas of your life that you might be struggling with right now:

_____

_____

_____

Got More Time?

- Look up Deuteronomy 7:9 and 32:4 to read more about God's faithfulness.
- Read the story of Ruth this weekend (the book of Ruth is only four chapters long). In your journal, write all the different ways she showed faithfulness to God and in her relationships.

Journaling

Remember to love people and use things ...
not to love things and use people.

You Are Not Your Stuff

Truth — *Trying to be physically rich will make you spiritually poor.*

How do the kids at school decide who's cool and who's not? Is it by the brand of sneakers you own? How many charms are on your bracelet? What kind of jeans you wear? How expensive your MP3 player or digital camera is? What kind of car your parents drive?

There's a lot of pressure on girls to have the best "stuff." Every day you see ads and commercials about new and cool things that, according to the companies selling them, you just can't live without!

It's easy to forget that you are a special girl God created, and who you are on the inside does not change, no matter how poor or rich you are. You could place a valuable diamond in a paper bag or in an expensive jewelry box, but the value of the diamond would not change.

What *does* change you on the inside is having a relationship with God. When your happiness comes from knowing Him, you will feel richer than any amount of "stuff" or money could make you feel.

DARE Be rich in God!

TRIPLE-DOG DARE!

1. List twenty things you're thankful for that you can't buy with money and then thank God for them.

2. List ten things you'd like to buy. Choose one thing to cross off your list and find a way to help a poor family with what you already have.

3. Ask God to help you care more about growing spiritually than becoming rich or popular.

Journaling How did it go? What did you learn?

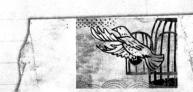

Jude 1:17-21

Don't Give Up!

Truth
We shouldn't be surprised—or discouraged—when people make fun of Jesus and His followers.

All kinds of people make predictions every day. The most common kind is probably about the weather. The newspaper or radio tells you whether it's going to rain or be sunny and how hot it will be all week. Of course, they're not always right!

Scientists and other experts try to predict what will happen in the world or in people's lives … when the world will end, what color will be in style, how many people will buy houses, which countries will have earthquakes, and so on.

Amazingly, the most correct predictions ever made can be found in the Bible! Today's verses were written over two thousand years ago, and yet they describe the world we live in so perfectly. As you read, many people reject God and Jesus and choose to give in to temptations instead. Some people might try to influence you to stop believing too, so the Bible warns not to give up on growing spiritually and not to go far from God.

DARE Never stop growing in your relationship with God.

TRIPLE-DOG DARE!

1. When other kids or even adults put down your faith in God, don't get upset. Just pray for them.

2. If you're really daring, invite them to go to church with you!

3. Think back to the past month or two. Have you grown as a Christian? If not, or if only a little, ask God to help you to keep going.

Journaling How did it go? What did you learn?

Choose Contentment!

Truth You can be content in any situation ... if you choose to be.

Have you ever heard the expression, "There's no use crying over spilled milk"? It makes sense, doesn't it? But, as another saying goes, "It's easier said than done." In other words, sometimes we know what the right or smart thing to do is, but we still have trouble doing it.

Sometimes, when something bad happens or if we lose something very special to us, we can become upset or sad or scared and lose all our happiness. We forget that getting upset doesn't actually change the situation. Of course, it's natural to feel sad if, for example, your mom loses her job, your cat dies, or your best friend moves away. God understands that.

But He always wants you to (a) be thankful for the past and (b) trust Him with the future. When you really believe that He will take care of you no matter what, you can find peace and happiness even in difficult situations.

You can't always change your situation, but you can always change your attitude!

DARE Be content—no matter what!

TRIPLE-DOG DARE!

1 List ten things you're tempted to complain about. For each one, think about how much worse it could be and thank God that it isn't!

2 See how long you can go without buying new "stuff" that you don't need while still being happy with what you have. To help you remember this dare, write today's verse on a small card and tuck it into your wallet.

3 Instead of comparing yourself to people who have more than you, think of those who have less.

Journaling How did it go? What did you learn?

Forgive Everything

Truth *God always forgives you, so He wants you to forgive others also.*

Imagine your mom bought you a package of your favorite cookies—for no reason at all except that she loves you. Now, suppose your little sister asked you if she could have just one of those cookies and you said no.

Would that be fair? You might think, *Yes, that's fair.... Those are my cookies.* Or you might realize that since the cookies were a gift to you from someone else—not something you worked for or bought with your own money—it wasn't really "fair" that you got the cookies either. Your mom gave them to you because she loves you, not because you deserved them.

That's how it is with forgiveness. When you ask Jesus to be your Savior, He forgives all your sins—not because you deserve it (we all deserve to be punished for our sins), but because He loves you. So, it wouldn't be right for you not to forgive someone who hurts you, would it?

DARE Forgive the way you've been forgiven!

TRIPLE-DOG DARE!

1. Try to count all the sins that God has forgiven you for (even the "little" ones). Ask God to help you remember how much you've been forgiven when someone hurts you.

2. Are you avoiding or ignoring someone because you're angry? Make peace with him or her today.

3. When someone apologizes to you, resist the temptation to make her feel bad before you forgive.

Journaling How did it go? What did you learn?

Cut It Off!

Truth — *Sometimes you have to take drastic action against temptation!*

Did today's verses seem a little extreme to you? Jesus used strong language to make a point. He said, "*if* your hand causes you to sin," so He didn't actually mean to cut off your hand. He knew that your hand doesn't make you steal, hit, or write mean things. Those temptations come from inside.

Jesus told His disciples—and you and me—to get rid of anything in our lives that tempts us to sin.

If you read magazines that make you feel unhappy with how you look, fantasize about an actor, feel jealous of other girls, or forget to read your Bible, you might need to stop reading them.

If a friend encourages you to disobey your parents, listen to music that doesn't honor God, cheat, or gossip about others, you might need to look for a new friend.

Giving up something you like might seem hard, but it's better than giving up heaven!

DARE   Don't let anything come between you and God.

TRIPLE-DOG DARE!

1. Make a list of your friends, hobbies, or activities that don't help you get closer to God. Ask God to show you which ones you might need to "cut off" or replace. Then ask Him to help you do it.

2. Share these verses with a Christian friend who has told you she's struggling with a sin.

3. Ask your parents to tell you about a time they had to "cut off" something that tempted them to sin.

Journaling — How did it go? What did you learn?

Read Galatians 5:22-23.

Have you ever heard someone say, "She was like a bull in a china store"? Stop for a second to imagine it and you might start giggling! Can you picture an elegant store full of crystal glasses and bowls and fine china dishes … and a huge, clumsy bull trying to walk around in there? It probably would take only a minute or two before everything was smashed into little pieces all over the place.

Unfortunately, sometimes we're just like that awkward bull in our relationships. When someone is going through a hard time and her feelings are delicate or sensitive, instead of being gentle and understanding, we may crash into her life with advice and criticism and useless comments that only confuse or hurt her more instead of helping.

But there's another way! When God's Holy Spirit produces "fruit" in us, gentleness is one of the qualities that develops. And we're not talking about the kind of gentleness that makes you pet your kitten ever so softly. That's easy! We're talking about the willingness to just be still and quiet, thinking of the needs of the other person, even when it's hard.

What are some ways you can show gentleness? We've made a few suggestions, but see how many you can think of on your own. Ask a friend for ideas too.

- Listening
- Praying with someone
- Hugging a friend
- Not talking back when you're in a bad mood
- Letting someone else go first
- _____
- _____
- _____
- _____
- _____

Bananas are very delicate fruits. They bruise and spoil easily so they need to be handled carefully and not kept too long before eating them.

People are sensitive too. If you're not gentle with them, they can get bruised. If someone has been mistreated a lot, he or she can become bitter and angry inside ... even toward God.

Try to have at least one banana this weekend, and as you eat it, pray and ask God to help you develop the fruit of gentleness in your life so that you can treat people with the care and love that they need.

journaling

Happiness isn't about everything being perfect in your life. It's about looking past the imperfections and still being thankful.

God Made This Day

Truth *Every day is a special occasion!*

Do you ever have days when it seems like *nothing* is going right and *everything* is going wrong and *nobody* understands you and *everybody* is against you?

Do you thank God for those days the same way you thank Him for the days when everything seems perfect and wonderful and happy?

Saying thanks about an awful day might seem strange. After all, what's so great about spilling grape jelly on your favorite white skirt, having a fight with your big sister first thing in the morning, having to wash dishes, or failing your math test?

The amazing thing about being thankful even when it's hard is that it not only makes God happy—it makes *you* happy too. When you realize how blessed you are to have clothes to wear, to have a big sister, to have food you need dishes for, and to be able to go to school, you can find a lot to thank God for!

DARE Thank God for the gift of each day.

TRIPLE-DOG DARE!

1 Find a small box to wrap up like a present and add a label with today's verse. Put it on your nightstand as a daily reminder to be thankful.

2 Sing the song "This Is the Day" to yourself (or to a friend!) throughout the day. (Look up the song online with your parents or ask about it at church if you don't know it.)

3 When you or your best friend start to complain, remind each other of this verse.

Journaling How did it go? What did you learn?

A Great Recipe

Truth — god can take all your problems and make something beautiful out of them.

Do you like milk? If so, you could probably easily drink a cupful, right?

What about sugar? Would you eat a cupful of sugar? Would you eat a whole stick of butter? How about a cupful of flour? A full teaspoon of cinnamon? A teaspoon of baking soda? A raw egg?

Okay, now it's getting yucky!

Except for the milk, you wouldn't really enjoy eating those ingredients individually. But when you put them all together, with other ingredients, you can make a delicious cake!

Sometimes you'll go through difficulties that make you feel angry, confused, sad, or scared. You might wonder why God lets bad things happen to you or to people you love.

Today's verse promises that God takes those yucky "ingredients" and turns them into beautiful experiences. You may have to wait until they go through the hot "oven" of life before you see what He's done, but you will love the results!

DARE
Trust God with the "ingredients" of your life.

TRIPLE-DOG DARE!

1. At the end of the day, list all the things bothering you. Ask God to help you believe that He will take care of you because He loves you.

2. Whenever you find yourself focusing on a problem, think about something that you're thankful for instead.

3. Share this verse (and the example of the cake) with a friend who is confused about her life right now.

Journaling
How did it go? What did you learn?

Call Jesus!

Truth
Knowing God's "number" isn't enough.... You have to call Him!

Imagine you're at school or at a friend's house and you need to ask your mom to come and pick you up. Do you stare at a telephone and think about how much you want to talk to your mom? Do you say your phone number or her cell-phone number over and over in your head or out loud and hope that the phone will dial itself? Do you look up your dentist's number and call him? Do you pick up the phone and press random numbers?

Those are all silly ideas. If you want to reach your mom, you just have to dial her number!

Many people read the Bible and know in their heads who Jesus is, but they don't "call on Him" and ask Him to save them from their sins and give them eternal life.

These verses promise that when you believe that Jesus died to take the punishment for your sins and you ask Him to forgive your sins, He will save you!

You know how to reach Jesus; have you "called" Him yet?

DARE   Get connected with Jesus.

TRIPLE-DOG DARE!

1. If you've never asked Jesus to forgive your sins and promised to follow Him, do it today!

2. Do you have a friend who isn't sure if she's going to heaven? Share these verses with her.

3. In your phone book, write "Jesus" under the letter *J* and then the words of verse 13. Whenever you see it, take a moment to thank God for saving you.

Journaling   How did it go? What did you learn?

Ecclesiastes 4:9-12

The Braid

Truth
When you include God in your relationships, He makes them stronger.

Whether your hair is thick and curly or thin and straight, you've probably had it in a braid or braids at least once. If not, you've most likely seen braids in other girls' hair. Maybe you've braided string to wear as a bracelet or have a belt made of braided leather or rope.

What is the most important thing about making a braid? It's having three pieces, right? If you twist together only two strings or two strands of hair, they'll quickly come apart. The cool thing about braids is that they're made with three pieces, but it looks like there are just two. It's like the third strand is invisible.

Relationships are like braids. When you have a strong relationship with Jesus, He becomes part of your other relationships and friendships, and they become strong like a braid that doesn't easily unravel. He may be invisible, but you can't be without Him!

DARE Make Jesus the center of your relationships.

TRIPLE-DOG DARE!

1. If your hair is long enough, ask your mom or a friend to braid it and tell her what you learned in today's devotional.

2. Pray about your future husband and promise God that you'll make Him the center of your marriage.

3. Braid matching bracelets out of colorful string for you and your closest friends. Tape an extra one to this page. As you give the bracelets to them, tell your friends about today's verses and that you're praying that God will make your friendships strong. (Don't forget to pray!)

Journaling How did it go? What did you learn?

No Favorites

Truth
It doesn't please God when we treat some people better than others.

You may not realize it, but your eyes make a lot of your decisions. For example, if your mom put a plate of cookies on the table, would you go for the small, broken one or the big, perfectly round one? If you had to pick out a puppy, would you choose the cute one with the bright eyes and waggly tail or the quiet one with crooked ears and ugly spots on its nose?

Sometimes we also choose whom we're nice to because of what our eyes see. On the first day of school, most kids will look around to see who's pretty, who has cool sneakers, who runs fast, who brings the best snacks to school, or who sings well, and try to be friends with them. Not too many will look for the kids who don't dress nicely, are chubby, have difficulty speaking, or live in a poor part of town.

But the Bible gives a serious warning against "favoritism"—God wants you to treat everyone equally.

DARE Don't play favorites with people.

TRIPLE-DOG DARE!

1 Show kindness and friendship to someone at your school or church whom others seem to ignore.

2 If you've been unkind to someone because she's not popular, ask for forgiveness and try to be a better friend.

3 In your journal, write how you think it would feel to be ignored by everyone. Then ask God to help you treat others equally.

Journaling How did it go? What did you learn?

Know When to Stop!

Read Galatians 5:23-22 and Proverbs 25:16.

I read a story about a boy who liked pepperoni so much that he wouldn't just eat it off pizza, but he'd eat it right out of the package! In fact, he'd get up early in the morning, find the pepperoni, and start eating it. But one day he ate so much pepperoni that it made him really sick.

At his fifteenth birthday party, there was pepperoni pizza and plain cheese pizza. Guess which one he ate. Yup … the plain cheese. He'd had enough of pepperoni!

Do you ever find it hard to stop doing something that you really enjoy or something that has become a habit? The last fruit of the Spirit listed in these verses is self-control. That means that when you love Jesus, He helps you to have discipline in your life. He gives you the strength to say no to temptations and to manage your feelings, your time, and your habits.

What are some ways girls might struggle with self-control? We've given a few examples to get you started.

- Biting nails
- Lying
- Getting angry quickly
- Going along with whatever friends do, even if it's wrong
- _____
- _____
- _____
- _____

Circle anything on the list that you have difficulty with and ask God to help you have more self-control.

If good things (such as honey or pepperoni) can be bad for you when you don't have self-control, imagine how much worse it is when you can't control the temptation to do bad things.

Got More Time?

In the 1960s, a group of four-year-olds were given one marshmallow each. They were promised that they could have a second one, but only if they waited twenty minutes before eating the first one.

Some of the children waited.... But some couldn't wait and ate their first marshmallow before the twenty minutes had passed. Later, when these children were teenagers, researchers discovered that the ones who were able to wait—the ones who had *self-control*—were doing better in school and were trusted more.

Try the same experiment with a group of your friends. You can use a cookie or piece of candy instead of a marshmallow. See how many of them are able to wait and how many aren't. Afterward, tell them what you learned about self-control this weekend!

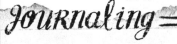

Journaling

Be kind and be truthful, and
your life will be fruitful!

Give Jesus Your Backpack

Truth You don't have to carry all of life's problems on your own.

Does it seem like every fall, when you get ready to go back to school, you have more books and school supplies to carry? It's amazing to see young children with backpacks that seem almost as big as they are!

As heavy as your backpack might be, some problems or worries in life might seem even heavier and harder to carry around in your mind and heart. Will you get along with the other students in your class? Will they make fun of your new braces? Will you do better in math this year? Will your dad find a new job? Will your little sister get better soon?

Life can put a lot of burdens on you, but there's good news: Jesus will carry your load if you ask Him! You don't need to struggle alone because God is big enough to handle all your burdens.

DARE Let Jesus carry your "backpack" of worries.

TRIPLE-DOG DARE!

❶ Write down all the things you're worried about and put the list at the bottom of your backpack or purse. Ask God to help you trust Him with those problems. Whenever you feel like you've stopped worrying about something, cross it off the list.

❷ Share this verse with a friend who is struggling with worries.

❸ Help carry your parents' "burdens" today by offering to help out around the house.

Journaling How did it go? What did you learn?

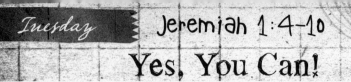

Tuesday — Jeremiah 1:4-10
Yes, You Can!

Truth
When God asks you to do something, He also helps you do it.

"I can't do it!" Have you ever said that? Maybe you were working on a math problem or a difficult piano piece, or maybe you were learning to ice-skate or fly a remote-control plane.

Of course, we all have certain things we may never be good at no matter how much we practice, such as singing or swimming or drawing, because everyone has different talents. But sometimes you may be tempted to say, "I can't do it!" before you even try. You might feel nervous or scared and think you'll never succeed.

You may feel tempted to react that way when you know you should invite a friend to church or when you need to help someone you don't know very well. Like Jeremiah, you may wish God would ask someone else to do it.

But God promises to be with you and help you when you have the courage to obey Him. You can do it!

DARE Say yes to God!

TRIPLE-DOG DARE!

1. Write down all the things you think you can't do and circle the ones that, deep down inside, you just don't *want* to do. Ask God to give you the courage to do the things He wants you to do.

2. Ask your parents to tell you about a time God helped them do something they thought they couldn't do.

3. Make a bookmark with the words of Jeremiah 1:7–8. Keep it in your Bible or give it to a friend.

Journaling How did it go? What did you learn?

Let Your Light Shine

Truth
*When your light shines,
others can see God.*

Have you ever seen those birthday-cake candles that don't blow out? You can blow on them as much as you want, but you can't put out the flames. This can create lots of laughs at a birthday party when the birthday girl keeps trying to blow out the candles on her cake!

Do you know how "trick" candles work? The wicks of these candles have a thin coating of magnesium (a metal) that catches fire very quickly. When you blow out a trick candle, the burning magnesium creates little sparks, and these ignite that thin ribbon of smoke (which contains candle wax) that you always see after blowing out a candle. And that lights up the candle again!

As a Christian, you have the "light" of Jesus inside you, which helps you see where you're going in this dark world. That light can also help others if you let it shine, and no one else can blow it out—not even the Devil!

DARE Let others see Jesus' light inside you.

TRIPLE-DOG DARE!

1 Ask your parents if you can buy some trick candles. Then tell your family (or friends) how they work and about today's devotional.

2 If you haven't been a very good example of a Christian to your friends lately, ask God to help you shine your light brighter by getting closer to Him.

3 Memorize today's verses. It's a long passage, but you can do it!

Journaling How did it go? What did you learn?

The Real Thing

Truth *When you serve others, don't fake the kindness.*

We live in a world full of artificial, fake, and imitation things. People wear false eyelashes, false teeth, fake nails, and wigs. They use artificial sweetener in drinks or when they bake, wear imitation leather shoes, and decorate with fake flowers.

Artificial things aren't necessarily bad. For example, fake flowers last longer than real ones. But they don't smell or feel as nice, and they usually don't look very realistic.

Today's verses remind us that whatever we do, we should do it with the love of Jesus in our hearts; otherwise it's not *really* serving. If you do something just because you were asked to, and it feels like a chore or a job—if you're not doing it with the joy of knowing you're helping someone—it's not the real thing.

If you remind yourself that everything you do is for God, your attitude will change drastically!

DARE Do whatever you do to please God, not others or yourself.

TRIPLE-DOG DARE!

1 Before you do your chores at home, take a moment to pray and dedicate the job to God. Imagine you're serving Him while you work, and see how much more you enjoy it.

2 Don't wait until your parents are home to do your chores. Do extra work when they're not home ... even if they never figure it out and thank you for it!

3 If you help out at church or school, pray for the people in charge.

Journaling How did it go? What did you learn?

Faith + Deeds

Truth
Believing in God but not doing anything about it just doesn't add up.

What if you went to the best dentist in the country and he told you all about his education and what a great dentist he is and showed you all his shiny, modern tools … but he never actually examined your teeth? Would you go back to that dentist?

Or can you imagine a well-trained police dog that had the ability to sniff out drugs or track a human being, but when its help was needed it just flopped onto the ground and chewed on a dog toy? Do you think the police would use that dog again?

These verses in James warn that if you call yourself a Christian and trust in God but don't live in a way that shows what you believe, it's as if your faith is dead. It's as useless as a dentist who doesn't examine teeth or a dog that doesn't do what it's trained to do.

DARE Make your actions back up your words!

TRIPLE-DOG DARE!

❶ When your church has a dinner, help wash dishes afterward instead of just hanging around with your friends.

❷ When your mom asks if you have anything to be washed, don't just give her your dirty clothes; offer to do the laundry for her.

❸ When a friend is sick, don't just send a "get well" card. Find out if you can help in some way.

Journaling How did it go? What did you learn?

Read Exodus 20:3.

In the spaces below, list your five favorite …

Friends		Singers	
1. _____		1. _____	
2. _____		2. _____	
3. _____		3. _____	
4. _____		4. _____	
5. _____		5. _____	

Actors/Actresses		Family members	
1. _____		1. _____	
2. _____		2. _____	
3. _____		3. _____	
4. _____		4. _____	
5. _____		5. _____	

People at church		People at school	
1. _____		1. _____	
2. _____		2. _____	
3. _____		3. _____	
4. _____		4. _____	
5. _____		5. _____	

What would you say if someone asked you, "Who's your favorite god?" You might think that was a strange question! Of course, you know that there's only one God, and you probably can't imagine worshipping any other god, right?

When God gave the Ten Commandments to Moses (we'll be looking at them for the next ten weekends), He started with a short and simple one: "You shall have no other gods before me." God knew that people often put other people and even things before Him in their hearts … even if He's the God they sing to at church or pray to every day.

Look at the six lists you made above. Circle any people you think about more often than you think of God. Ask God to forgive you for the times you've put other "gods" before Him. Then ask Him to help you make Him your one and only Number One.

Got More Time?

Make a small notebook using any kind of paper you like. (Hint: Cut five sheets of photocopy paper in half, put the ten pieces together, fold them in half, and then staple twice on the fold.) Design a cover that says, "Only One Number One."

Keep the notebook and a pen with you all weekend, and whenever you think of a reason God is awesome, write it in your notebook. Or draw pictures that show what you're thankful for or something great God has done.

At the end of the weekend, you'll have a great reminder of why God deserves 100 percent of your worship.

Journaling

Get Ready for a New week!

Feeling down? Take time to count your blessings.

Wise or Foolish?

Truth — *Knowing God's Word but not obeying it is foolishness.*

Who is the smartest person you know? Your dad? Your science teacher? Your next-door neighbor who works as a lawyer? Your librarian? What makes these people smart? Is it their education? Their years of experience? Their ability to do the things they have learned?

There's a difference between being *educated* or having *knowledge* … and being *wise*. A builder may know how to build the biggest and strongest houses, but if he builds them on sandy or muddy land, he's not very wise, is he? All his education would go to waste if he built a house that came crashing down during a storm.

Reading the Bible—even memorizing lots of verses—without doing what it teaches is just as foolish as building a house on a weak foundation.

DARE — Live out what you learn from the Bible.

TRIPLE-DOG DARE!

1. Have any of the dares in the last couple of weeks been difficult? Ask God to help you and try them again. If you're still stuck, ask your mom or dad for advice.

2. Get a small, inexpensive toy house that you can put on your shelf. Whenever you see it, remind yourself to be like the wise builder and practice what you learn.

3. If you have a good friend in your Sunday school class or youth group, make a point of giving each other ideas on how to live out what you learned after each meeting.

Journaling — How did it go? What did you learn?

Just Like Family

Truth Other Christians are part of your spiritual family. Treat them that way!

You've probably heard people at church talk about each other as "brothers" and "sisters" even though they're not actually related. That's because we're all children of God, our heavenly Father, and that makes us a big "family"!

Today's reading gives instructions on how to treat the members of your spiritual family. Older men and women—especially people like the pastor, your teacher, or the youth leader—deserve your respect and honor. That doesn't just mean being polite to them but also listening to their advice, helping them, and showing them love.

That part might be easy. What you might find more difficult is treating the younger people as family. A lot of girls and boys tease and flirt with each other at church, which can take their minds off the real reason they're there. But if you thought of the boys at church as your brothers, you would treat them very differently, wouldn't you?

Church should be a place of love and respect—just like your home should be.

DARE Love your Christian family!

TRIPLE-DOG DARE!

1 Surprise an older lady at church whom you look up to with a flower one Sunday and thank her for her good example.

2 On your way to church, silently pray for your pastor—that God will give him strength and wisdom as he leads the service and teaches.

3 Whenever a new child comes to your church, introduce yourself and help him or her feel welcome.

Journaling How did it go? What did you learn?

Take Care of Your Family

Truth
Caring for your family is serious business to God.

You're probably not yet thinking about the fact that one day your parents will get old and need your help. Right now, they are taking care of you and providing your shelter, food, clothing, and education. That's part of the job of being a parent.

But just because you're still young doesn't mean that God doesn't expect you to take care of your family. In fact, today's verse gives a very strong warning that not looking out for your family is as bad as not believing in God!

You don't have to get a job to support your parents right now, although you may have to provide for them in the future, but you do have to think about your family members and their needs … not just your own. Even when you're young, you can do a lot for your parents, your siblings, your grandparents, your cousins, and other relatives.

You can offer your time, kind words and actions, prayers, and much more!

DARE Take care of your family!

TRIPLE-DOG DARE!

1 Before you ask your parents for something you don't really need, think about how that money might go toward something more important in the future.

2 Find special ways to thank your parents for providing for your needs.

3 If your grandparents or other relatives live nearby, visit as often as you can and offer to help them with chores.

Journaling How did it go? What did you learn?

Turn the Other Cheek

Truth god didn't design you to pay back evil with evil.

Have you ever been hit or kicked by a two-year-old who didn't get what he wanted or didn't realize how much it could hurt? Did you hit back? Of course not! You probably had patience and just moved away a little because you understood that he didn't really know any better. Also, hitting back would probably just make him continue hitting.

God wants you to show the same kind of patience to others—whether they're your age or older—and to control the temptation to hurt someone the way he or she hurt you. That goes for physical hitting as well as saying mean words or doing anything that can hurt someone's feelings.

This doesn't mean that you shouldn't get help if you're in danger, but if someone is being annoying or unfair, showing forgiveness will solve the problem much quicker than payback.

DARE Be patient and forgiving.

TRIPLE-DOG DARE!

1. When your little sister (or a friend) purposely annoys you, smile and say something like, "I love you anyway!"

2. List all the ways you have hurt God that He was patient with instead of punishing you.

3. List any situations you feel angry or hurt about. Cross out each one as you pray about it, asking God to help you forgive the people involved.

Journaling How did it go? What did you learn?

First Things First

Truth   When you make God your top priority, He takes care of the rest.

Scavenger hunts are fun! You're given a list of things to look for, and then you have to race around trying to find everything as quickly as you can.

Let's imagine a scavenger hunt where the first item on the list is a key that opens the door to a special house that contains everything you could possibly imagine.

Would you search for all the other items on your list or would you look for that key first? The smart thing would be to find the key because that would lead you to all the other things on your list!

In life, we sometimes think we'll be happy if we buy more stuff, have more fun, go on more road trips, have more friends, or look more beautiful. But the Bible says that when we focus on being right with God, that's how we find true joy.... And we're able to trust Him with all the rest.

DARE   Make God #1 in your life!

TRIPLE-DOG DARE!

1 Start each day by worshipping God: Think (and tell Him) about His greatness and how much He deserves your honor. Keep your mind focused on Him.

2 Memorize this verse and tell a friend about it.

3 Replace some of the time you normally spend in front of the mirror with time spent reading your Bible.

Journaling How did it go? What did you learn?

Read Exodus 20:4-6.

1. Cross out all colors in columns A and D.
2. Cross out all words beginning with *B*.
3. Cross out all animals in rows 4, 6, and 7.
4. Cross out all words that rhyme with *cat*.
5. Cross out all clothing in column C.
6. Cross out all foods in rows 2, 3, and 8.
7. Write the remaining words (reading from left to right) here:

(The answer is at the end of the book.)

	A	B	C	D
1	RED	YOU	SHIRT	BROCCOLI
2	MEAT	SAT	SHALL	YELLOW
3	NOT	VEGETABLE	BIRD	PEACH
4	DOG	MAKE	PAT	ELEPHANT
5	GREEN	BASKET	DRESS	FOR
6	FLAT	YOURSELF	TURTLE	PURPLE
7	AN	ZEBRA	SOCK	MAT
8	CARROT	BELT	IDOL	CHERRY

The second commandment that God gave us goes with the first one, which we looked at last weekend. If we have no other gods before God, then we shouldn't have any idols, either. But God knew that even when we love Him most, we'll still be tempted to have idols—other things and people we worship. Just because we don't put them above God, it doesn't mean it's right to worship them!

What are some "idols" people worship today? For example: money, celebrities (Hello! We have shows with names like *American Idol),* being popular, having nice clothes … What else can you think of?

_____

_____

_____

Go through your bedroom and look for things that might take your attention away from God and tempt you to "worship" them. Do you have posters of actors or singers that you daydream about or wish you could spend time with? Do you have stacks of fashion magazines that make you think about clothes and makeup all the time? Do you have books and DVDs that you wouldn't show God?

Pray for wisdom to know what to do with those things if they have become "idols." Ask your mom or another Christian woman for advice too.

Journaling

*Most of the things you worry about
will probably never happen!*

Keep It a Secret

Truth god won't bless you for good works if you do them to get admiration from others.

When Hannah was nineteen, she worked in a warehouse putting price tags on scarves. After a while, she moved to a better section and made more money. Hannah was happy, but she kept thinking about Emma, another worker who had just moved from a poor country with her family and who needed money more than Hannah did.

Hannah asked her boss if her pay increase could be given to Emma instead. Her boss was shocked, but he agreed to do it, promising not to tell anyone. Of course, Emma was happy to find out she was going to get more money, but she never knew why. Hannah smiled inside, feeling good about what she had done.

When you do something nice for someone, it's natural to want to hear "Thanks!" or to hear people talk about what a good person you are. But God says that when you keep your kind deeds secret, He will bless you in a way that's much more special than hearing someone say, "Thank you."

DARE Do your good deeds in secret.

TRIPLE-DOG DARE!

1 On sticky notes, write happy messages such as "You are beautiful!" and secretly leave them in random places (such as bathroom mirrors at school).

2 Sneak your friend's favorite candy into her bag when she's not looking.

3 Put some of your own spending money into the offering plate at church this Sunday.

Journaling How did it go? What did you learn?

1 Corinthians 6:18
A Dangerous Sin

Truth *Sexual sin is no joke.*

You might feel a bit awkward about today's devotional and think, *Why are we talking about ... you know?* The thing is, even if you're still in elementary or middle school, you probably already know more about sex than your mom and grandma knew at your age. That's just the kind of world we live in today.

A lot of movies, TV shows, magazines, and advertisements send confusing messages about love and sex, and you may wonder what's wrong or right. Even some of your relatives or friends may be involved in relationships that don't honor God's design for marriage.

The danger with sexual sin is that it can damage your body, your mind, and your heart. That's why the Devil makes it such a big temptation for many people.

It's never too early to promise God—and yourself—that you will keep yourself pure. If you have questions about sex, talk to your mom or another woman you trust. Don't trust the Internet, magazines, or library books to teach you what's right.

DARE Run away from sexual temptations!

TRIPLE-DOG DARE!

1 Save kissing until you're older. Kissing leads to other things, and once you start, it's hard to stop.

2 Avoid dressing "sexy." It will send the wrong message about you to others.

3 Avoid books, movies, TV shows, or magazines that fill your mind with inappropriate relationships.

Journaling How did it go? What did you learn?

Don't Get Bored

Truth
If you don't give up on doing good, God will bless you.

Some people have really boring jobs! They may have to stuff letters into envelopes all day or sit in a factory watching spatulas go by on a conveyer belt as they try to spot the ones that aren't perfect. When you have to do something over and over again, it can drive you a little crazy! Some of your classes might seem boring if you're just doing a lot of reading or memorizing.

The Bible warns us not to get tired of doing good deeds, no matter how difficult it becomes or how little thanks we get. God wants you to cheerfully do good for others—not just once in a while, but every chance you get. He wants you to look for ways to be a blessing to others and to share His love with them.

God also promises to bless you in amazing ways when you do this. You'll feel great knowing that you helped someone and that you honored God, and you'll be rewarded later if you've done your good deeds with joy and love.

Don't give up…. It's all worth it!

DARE Do as much good as you can.

TRIPLE-DOG DARE!

1 Try to get to church early, and instead of sitting down right away, ask an adult if there's some way you can help out.

2 Give up some of your "play" time to do extra chores for your parents.

3 Bake some cookies and surprise a family at church with them on Sunday!

Journaling How did it go? What did you learn?

You Get What You Plant

Truth You can't be selfish and still receive God's gifts.

Everyone knows that if you plant strawberries, you grow strawberries—not watermelons! If you plant an apple tree, you won't see pumpkins on the branches.

This logic works in other areas of life too. If you spend all your time watching TV, you'll turn into a couch potato. If you work hard on your violin homework, you'll improve between lessons. If you are kind and loving to others, you will enjoy better relationships.

You get what you "plant" in your spiritual life, too. If you make your relationship with God your first priority in everything you do, He will bless you ... not only here on earth but also forever in heaven. But if you do only the things that make *you* feel good and that you know are wrong, your life and soul will be in danger.

How you live is a serious matter to God, so make sure you take it seriously too.

DARE Put your efforts into good things.

TRIPLE-DOG DARE!

1. Ask God to show you any selfishness in your life that you might need to change. After you pray, take some quiet time to think about what He says.

2. Make a list of five things you could do to please God. Try to do one each day for the next five days.

3. Before you agree to do something with friends, ask yourself if you'd want God to join you. Make your decision based on the answer.

Journaling How did it go? What did you learn?

Don't Forget!

Truth It's important to remember all the great things God teaches and shows you.

"Selective memory" is when you remember things you want to remember and forget the things you don't really care about. For example, if your dad promised you (in May) a puppy for Christmas, there's no way you would forget that in December! But when your mom asks you in the morning to take out the trash after school, well … You might forget that.

It's normal for adults to forget some things as they get older, but have you ever noticed that your great-grandparents can remember stories from when they were little? Special things have a way of staying in our minds. That's because we think about them over and over again.

We can do that with God. When we love God and feel excited about serving Him and learning about Him through His Word, those special thoughts stay with us for a long time. But if we don't care, we will forget them quickly.

DARE   Keep your thoughts on God!

TRIPLE-DOG DARE!

1 If you don't already have one, start a journal where you write down all the great things God teaches you and all the things you're thankful for.

2 Ask an older Christian to tell you about something special God has done in her life.

3 Offer to read a Bible story to your little sister (or a child at church).

Journaling How did it go? What did you learn?

Read Exodus 20:7.

When Tamara, who lives in Montreal, Canada, was eleven years old, she was part of a performance theater class with older teens. She probably never expected to face the challenge of obeying God's third commandment: *"You shall not misuse the name of the* LORD *your God, for the* LORD *will not hold anyone guiltless who misuses his name"* (Ex. 20:7).

One day, she was given a difficult script for a very interesting play that she really wanted to participate in. However, she noticed that close to the end of the play, her character had to say God's name in a bad way. "I knew I wouldn't be comfortable with that," she said, "because the Bible says we're not supposed to do that."

Tamara talked to her parents about it, and they told her she could either skip that part of the play or talk to her drama teacher. "I decided to talk to her, and she was okay with me changing what it says," explained Tamara. "I told her that I don't like saying words like that because I know it's wrong in my religion so I'd like to change what it says, and she agreed. She respected what I said."

Although she was nervous about talking to her teacher because it was her first speech in the play and there wasn't anyone to cover for her, Tamara took a stand. "I was worried that my teacher would insist that I had to do what the script says or else I'd have to be in a different skit, but I liked that skit—it was just the ending. I felt happy that I didn't have to worry about it after all. I did the play and it went well."

Tamara prayed for God to show her the right thing to do—whether she should actually defend what she believed or just pretend not to care.

What about you? How do you react when people around you are saying God's name in a disrespectful way?

Got More Time?

Think about this: Do you ever say, "Oh my God!" without thinking about it? Do your friends? What about writing "OMG" when chatting online or sending text messages? Ask God to help you stop using His name thoughtlessly.... And encourage your friends to stop doing it too.

Jot down some ideas for more appropriate expressions of surprise. We've suggested a few to get you started, but see if you can come up with some fun ones. Get your friends involved!

Whoa!

No way!

Sweet!

_____

_____

_____

_____

Journaling

"*Life is like riding a bicycle. To keep your balance, you have to keep moving.*"

–Albert Einstein

Higher Thoughts

Truth　*Even your greatest ideas don't come close to God's amazing thoughts.*

If you've ever asked a five-year-old to explain something difficult, such as how airplanes fly or how to make a pizza, you might have giggled at his or her response. Maybe some of it made sense, but the rest was probably kind of silly. When children know a little bit about something, they think they know *everything!* And we just smile because we know they're too little to understand.

As humans grow up, that attitude of thinking we know a lot doesn't change very much. There may be times when you'll say to yourself, *My parents have no clue!* You may think you're as smart as they are. It's not until we get older that we look back and realize how little we knew before.

You might be tempted to think you know what's best for you, but remember that God may have other plans—and He really does know everything!

DARE　Don't forget to ask God what He thinks about your situation.

TRIPLE-DOG DARE!

1. Before you make your next big decision, pray about it and ask God to help you choose with His wisdom instead of your feelings.
2. Write these verses on stationery as if it's a letter to you from God. Put the letter up on your bulletin board or somewhere else so you'll see it often.
3. If you've acted like a know-it-all lately, ask God to forgive you.

Journaling　How did it go? What did you learn?

Simpler Than You Think

Truth god's expectations are simpler than you think.

When some people hear words like *Christian* or *church,* they either feel nervous or become a little bit angry. They may tell you about all the bad things they've heard that religious people do.

What many people don't realize is that true Christianity is not a religion the same way that Buddhism, Mormonism, or Islam are. Most religions are all about following strict rules, doing good deeds, participating in special ceremonies, or repeating certain prayers. Christianity may have a little of that, but what makes Christianity different is that it's mainly about having a personal relationship with God.

This verse in Micah tells us that God wants us to act justly (that means being fair and standing up for what's right), to love mercy (kindness and forgiveness), and to walk humbly with God.

When you make every effort to be close to God and to obey Him, He will help you with all the other parts of being a Christian.

DARE Walk with God.

TRIPLE-DOG DARE!

1 Before you go to church next Sunday, make sure your heart is ready to worship God and that you're not just going because you have to.

2 If you have trouble making time for prayer, take daily walks around your house (or in your backyard) and use that time to focus on God.

3 Write down and memorize today's verse.

Journaling How did it go? What did you learn?

What God Really Wants

Truth

A good heart is more important to God than good actions.

In the Old Testament, when people sinned, they had to go to the temple and offer a sacrifice, such as a pure white lamb or doves. They had many different rules to follow and ceremonies to participate in. The people had to pay for doing wrong, but that didn't always stop them from repeating their sins.

Have you ever disobeyed your parents and thought, *I'll just say I'm sorry afterward?* Your parents may accept your apology. But think about it: Were you really sorry if you did something on purpose that you knew they wouldn't like?

In this verse, God is saying that He wants you to do things right the first time: to honor Him and love others and obey all His commands. He's promised to forgive all your sins when you confess them … but wouldn't it be better not to sin in the first place?

DARE
Make a habit of doing right … not of apologizing after doing wrong.

TRIPLE-DOG DARE!

1. Think of a sin that you seem to do over and over again. Ask God to help you love Him so much that you start hating that sin and are able to stop.

2. Make your mom smile by doing a chore that she doesn't expect you to do.

3. Tell a friend what you learned in today's devotion.

Journaling
How did it go? What did you learn?

Galatians 3:28

We're All Equal

Truth *In god's eyes, we're all equal to each other.*

Today we're going to do a bit of simple arithmetic. Write the answers to these equations:

$1 + 2 + 3 + 4 =$ $20 \div 2 =$

$2 \times 5 =$ $8 + 1 - 4 + 5 =$

Okay, so that was easy, but there's a point to the little exercise. There are a lot of *different* ways to get *equal* answers of ten, right? Each of those equations has the same answer, but they all look different.

There are nearly seven billion people on this earth, and you won't find two exactly the same. Even identical twins have differences between them! It's amazing how God has made each person so unique, but sadly, we sometimes judge people because of the ways they're different from us. It could be their skin color, how much money they have, how smart they are, what part of town they live in, or how they dress.

The Bible reminds us that we're all created equally by God, and none of us is more important to Him than another.

DARE Treat everyone equally.

TRIPLE-DOG DARE!

1. Look up the definition of *prejudice,* and ask God to help you get rid of any prejudice you have in your heart.
2. At church, show kindness to someone who is older than you and from a different cultural background.
3. Take #2 a step further by asking her to tell you about her childhood and how she became a Christian.

Journaling How did it go? What did you learn?

1 Timothy 4:8

Training for Life

Truth *Practicing living for god brings joy!*

Did you know that basketball players have to go through physical training all year long, not just when they're playing?

To be strong players from the first day they join their team, they have to do all kinds of exercises and practice different techniques every day: dribbling, passing, jumping rope (to be quick on their feet), running up and down steps, and, of course, shooting.

Every sport has its own kind of training to make players strong and good at what they do. It can be really tough, but the players who train hard enjoy success later because of their hard work.

The training you do by studying your Bible, saying no to temptation, putting others before yourself, and obeying your parents will result not only in everlasting life with God in heaven but also in a more joyful life here on earth too!

DARE Train hard in your life with God!

TRIPLE-DOG DARE!

1 Resist the temptation to skip your devotions "just for one day." It will make it too easy to skip them the next day too. When it's hard, give it the best effort you can.

2 Ask a friend (or your mom) to "coach" you by asking you once a week how your devotions are going.

3 Memorize this verse and recite it to yourself on your way to gym class each day.

Journaling How did it go? What did you learn?

Read Exodus 20:8–11.

It's interesting that the longest commandment in this set of ten is the one that talks about resting. It should be the easiest one to follow, right? So why did God make a big deal about it?

Maybe it's because God knows how much His children struggle with getting their priorities set up in the right order! How many times has your mom said something like:

"Do your homework first and then you can watch TV."

"Clean up your room before you go outside to play."

"If you want that new bike, you have to get your grades up first."

"You can't go to Katie's birthday party because it's on a Sunday morning, and we will be at church."

You probably have to finish up your vegetables before you can have dessert too, right?

You may be tempted to grumble when your parents ask you to do things you don't enjoy, especially if you're excited to do something else that's more fun. But you probably also secretly think, *They were right!* when you finish your chore and then have free time.

God, our heavenly Father, also knows what's best for us. He knows that we will enjoy life more if we do all our work during the week, instead of leaving it for later, saving ourselves one day to rest. But that special day isn't just for us to sleep in and do nothing! The Sabbath, or the seventh day, is a day to focus on God, which is why most of us go to church on Sundays.

God wants us to save one day—with no homework or chores to catch up on—that we can dedicate to worshipping Him and spending time with Him. Not just one hour in church, but the whole day.

Got More Time?

In the schedule below, try to describe what a normal Sunday is like for you. Include things like showering, breakfast, church, and anything else you might do.

Time	Activity
8:00 a.m.	
9:00 a.m.	
10:00 a.m.	
11:00 a.m.	
Noon	
1:00 p.m.	
2:00 p.m.	
3:00 p.m.	
4:00 p.m.	
5:00 p.m.	
6:00 p.m.	
7:00 p.m.	
8:00 p.m.	

How much of your time is spent with God? This weekend, think about how you can make your Sundays more holy and focused on God. With a different color pen or pencil, add your ideas to the schedule above. Get your family involved too! Ask your parents and siblings for ideas on how you can all dedicate your Sundays to God together.

Get Ready for a New week!

It's more important to want what you
have than to have what you want.

Danger! Don't Touch!

Truth — *Witchcraft is seriously dangerous stuff!*

In cartoons, witches are ugly old ladies with crooked noses, warts, and green skin. They wear long black dresses and pointy black hats, fly on brooms, and boil gross ingredients in a big black pot.

The Devil is usually shown as a fat red guy with horns, goat legs, a tail, and a pitchfork.

The problem with these images is that they make the Devil, witches, and other evil things seem funny and not really dangerous. But God gave many warnings to His children to stay away from evil practices.

It might seem impossible that a Christian would get involved with anything evil, but movies and books about witchcraft, vampires, and ghosts have become very popular. Ouija boards, horoscopes, and other seemingly innocent things can also introduce us to the occult.

Don't worry: God can protect your heart and mind from all these influences, but you have to be wise and careful too.

DARE — Stay far away from evil!

TRIPLE-DOG DARE!

1. Look up the definition of *astrology*. Since horoscopes are a type of astrology, resist the urge to read them.

2. If your teacher asks you to read a book about witches or other supernatural things, talk it over with your parents first. Don't be shy about asking if you can read something else, and explain why.

3. Pray for any friends or classmates who seem fascinated by astrology or the occult (look up that word, too, if you don't know it).

Journaling — How did it go? What did you learn?

1 Thessalonians 5:14-15

Help the Weak

Truth *Your life should bless others.*

Some people think being a Christian is like taking a trip on an airplane. You buy the ticket, pack your bags, sit back, and let the pilot take you to your destination. You may have a few rules to follow, such as not carrying dangerous items with you, wearing your seat belt, and not using your cell phone while in the air. But you don't actually have to *do* anything.

When you become a Christian, you can't just say, "Okay, I got my ticket to heaven. Now I'll just relax and wait until I get there."

Following Jesus is more like a hike—you have to get involved, and sometimes it's hard. You will also meet people along the way who feel discouraged, who are injured, or who feel like giving up. With God's help, you can share His love with others and make their journeys a little easier.

DARE Look for people you can help.

TRIPLE-DOG DARE!

1 If you have a younger sibling, help him or her memorize a Bible verse every week.

2 Think of someone who really annoys you. Ask God to give you patience and to help you treat that person with kindness instead of anger.

3 Send a cheery note to one of your grandparents or other relatives this week. Or if they live near you, ask your parents if you can go hang out with them one day soon.

Journaling How did it go? What did you learn?

Satisfied

Truth

If you're happy with a little, you'll always be satisfied.

There's nothing wrong with money. We obviously need it for the basic necessities of life, such as food and shelter. But money can become a problem when we let it take over our lives and when all we think about is having more of it and spending it on things we want to have, see, or experience.

You probably don't have to wonder whether you will have food for supper or how long your house will stay standing. You may have enough clothes to wear something different every day of the week, a full fridge, a comfortable bed, and even some money to spend on fun stuff.

Becoming greedy for more than what you need to survive puts you on a slippery downhill path into temptations and sin. It can even lead you away from God. Be careful!

DARE   Be satisfied with what you have.

TRIPLE-DOG DARE!

1 Make a wish list of all the things you'd love to have or do. Cross out anything that's a real *need*. Ask God to help you be happy even if you never get the rest of the things on your list.

2 For your next birthday, instead of asking for gifts, collect money for your favorite charity.

3 Write a thank-you card to God listing as many things you're grateful for as you can fit on the paper. Keep it in your Bible.

Journaling   How did it go? What did you learn?

Godless Chatter

Truth Talking about inappropriate things can become a dangerous habit.

Have you ever stood in line to check out at the grocery store and noticed those big, flashy celebrity gossip magazines (tabloids)? Many people enjoy reading about the lives of actors and singers, finding out who's dating whom, who got caught using drugs or shoplifting, and who the worst-dressed celebrity is.

First of all, a lot of the things written in these magazines is just gossip and not always true (or appropriate!).

It's easy to participate in gossip and offensive jokes and to waste our words on foolish conversations, isn't it? Even at church you might find yourself chatting with friends about things like fashion, movies, and boys when you really should be concentrating on God.

This can become a bad habit that leads us away from the pure thoughts God wants us to have. With His help, you can keep your conversations God-honoring.

DARE Stop the godless chatter!

TRIPLE-DOG DARE!

1 After church, make a point of talking with your friends about what you learned that day instead of chatting about your usual subjects.

2 If you have magazines that take your attention away from God and tempt you to think about godless things, toss them.

3 When a friend starts to share gossip with you, ask her to stop, and share today's verse with her.

Journaling How did it go? What did you learn?

Like Oil and Water

Truth *Your deepest friendships should start with god.*

Try this: Fill a glass with water and then take a bit of cooking oil (just a couple of drops) and add it to the glass. You'll notice the blob of oil just floats on top of the water. Now stir the water really well. When it stops swirling, take another look. The oil might have divided into smaller blobs, but it's still floating, right?

Oil and water don't mix because, simply put, it takes more energy for them to combine than to stay separate.

In a similar way, Christians live in the same world as non-Christians. You will have classmates, relatives, and even friends who don't believe in Jesus. That's fine, but the Bible warns that, to honor God, your closest friends (that includes the person you date and marry when you're older) should be Christians.

Trying to bond with a non-Christian is like trying to mix oil and water. It just doesn't work!

DARE Keep a safe distance from the world.

TRIPLE-DOG DARE!

1. Promise God today that you will not date or marry someone who doesn't love Him the way you do.

2. If you don't have any friends at school who follow God, try to develop a friendship with someone at church or at a Christian camp.

3. Explain this verse to another Christian friend by showing the oil and water experiment.

Journaling How did it go? What did you learn?

Read Exodus 20:12.

Time for a pop quiz!

Can you match up these Bible children with their parents? Draw a line from the child (middle column) to his father (left column) and then to his mother (right column).

Note: The list of kids is longer because some of them are brothers. A couple of the children also appear in the list of parents. Don't get confused! (The answers are at the end of the book.)

FATHER	CHILD	MOTHER
Jacob	1. Jacob	Sarah
Boaz	2. Solomon	Eve
Adam	3. Isaac	Rachel
Abraham	4. Joseph	Ruth
Zechariah	5. Obed	Elizabeth
David	6. Cain	Bathsheba
Isaac	7. John the Baptist	Rebekah
	8. Benjamin	
	9. Abel	
	10. Esau	

The fifth commandment must have been pretty important to God because it's the only one that He promised to reward us for following!

It's normal for girls to struggle sometimes to obey and respect their parents. You're at an age where you've started taking care of yourself and can do a lot of things without their help. You don't want to be treated like a baby anymore. You feel like you can make your own decisions or should be able to do what you want. Maybe you don't agree with your parents' decisions or rules sometimes. And you'll only feel more and more like this as you enter your teen years!

So how do you obey this commandment to honor your parents without getting frustrated?

Here's a tip: Start by being grateful. When you recognize and feel thankful for all the things your parents do for you—and how little they ask for in return—that makes it easier to respect and obey them.

Imagine for a moment what your life would be like if your parents (or parent, if you live with only one) suddenly disappeared. Write down some ways your life would change:

_____

_____

_____

_____

_____

_____

_____

This weekend, take time to thank God for your parents and ask Him to help you give them the honor and respect they deserve. Then find some special ways to show them how much they mean to you.

Journaling

Having problems with a friend?
TALK! (Try <u>A</u> <u>Little</u> <u>Kindness.</u>)

2 Corinthians 12:7-10

Living with Thorns

Truth — *god's love and strength can get you through even the hardest times.*

We're not really sure what the apostle Paul was struggling with when he wrote about having a thorn in his flesh—it could have been a physical disease, a temptation, or attacks from an enemy. Whatever it was, it troubled him a lot. He prayed about this problem three times, begging God to take it away from him.

Paul had risked his life and ended up in prison because of his courage to preach about Jesus. You'd think God would reward him by answering his prayers, right?

But God had other plans for Paul. He promised him that His grace—in other words, His love and strength—was big enough to help Paul cope with his struggles. And Paul accepted God's answer because he understood that his life could show people how great *God* is instead of how great *he* was.

You, too, can have the strength to go through difficulties when you trust God.

DARE   Use your problems to get closer to God.

TRIPLE-DOG DARE!

1. Ask your mom or dad to tell you about a time God helped one of them get through a big problem.

2. Write a letter to God about something you're struggling with. Ask Him to help you trust Him even if the problem doesn't go away.

3. Memorize verse 9 and repeat it to yourself throughout the next day.

Journaling — How did it go? What did you learn?

2 Timothy 1:7

God Power

Truth With god, you can have real power.

A British all-girls group in the 1990s made the phrase "girl power" popular for a while. The idea was that girls can do anything and be independent and strong and successful. "Girl power" was supposed to boost the self-esteem of young girls and women.

It's not clear whether this ever had a positive influence, but girls everywhere struggle with feelings of not being good enough. You probably have your own concerns. Maybe you're shy or don't like how you look. Maybe you have trouble with schoolwork. Maybe you're afraid to tell your friends about God. Maybe you find it hard to love your little brother. Or maybe you feel guilty for not reading your Bible often.

The Bible says that you don't need to let your fears bully you around. When you put your trust in Jesus, He gives you access to an amazing gift: God power! If you ask Him, He will give you courage and the ability to live a good life.

DARE Don't be timid!

TRIPLE-DOG DARE!

1 Think of an area where you need more self-discipline, such as cleaning your room or doing your homework before watching TV. Ask your parents to help you create a plan to do better.

2 Share this verse with a Christian friend who needs encouragement today.

3 Whenever you see someone you don't like, think of one great quality she has. Feel really daring? Tell her about it!

Journaling How did it go? What did you learn?

Itching Ears

 ***Truth*** *It's easy to believe only what makes us feel good about ourselves.*

Jane had two friends: Emily and Kim. Whenever Emily saw Jane she said things like, "You're so beautiful! You're the best! Don't worry about that little lie…. God doesn't mind. He knows you're just human. You're cool just the way you are!"

But Kim said things like, "I prayed for you last night. Did you tell your mom about what you did yesterday? Are you coming to youth group tonight? Did you memorize that great Bible verse from today's devotions?"

Whom do you think Jane enjoyed hanging out with more? Emily!

Who do you think loved Jane more? Kim!

Many people don't like thinking about their sins or making the effort to please God, so they ignore the challenging things the Bible teaches and look for messages that make them feel good. This is dangerous because, as in Jane's story, it leads to believing in lies.

DARE Keep your ears tuned to the truth … not to nice-sounding lies.

TRIPLE-DOG DARE!

1 In your journal, write about the toughest parts of following Jesus. Then ask God to help you be stronger in those areas.

2 When someone tells you a sin is okay, tell her what these verses taught you today.

3 Think of someone who recently told you something true about yourself that hurt your feelings. Thank her for caring enough to be honest!

Journaling How did it go? What did you learn?

Chase Righteousness

Truth When you run after good things, temptation can't catch you.

If you've ever watched a greyhound race, you may have noticed all the dogs chasing a lure (the same thing as bait in fishing) that is basically a fake rabbit. The dogs run as fast as they can, hoping to catch that rabbit. Of course, none of them ever do, since the point of the race is only to see which greyhound will cross the finish line first.

Many temptations will try to lure you away from God's plan for your life: the desire to be beautiful or popular, attention from boys, and activities that make sin seem okay. The Devil wants you to think that these things will make you happy, but it's like the fake rabbit in the greyhound race: You will get nothing at the end.

God's promises are not like that. When what you wish for is being right with God, loving Him and others, and having a pure heart … You always get your wish!

DARE Run away from temptation!

TRIPLE-DOG DARE!

1. Spend extra time with your Bible today: Read all of 2 Timothy 2.
2. List ten things that you are tempted to do or have. For each one, write how getting your wish would affect your relationship with God.
3. If there's someone you need to apologize to, try to do it before going to bed today.

Journaling How did it go? What did you learn?

Stop Quarreling!

Truth
Arguing is a big waste of time.

Susie and her brother Steve were excited about taking their new puppy for a walk. Steve attached the blue leash and Susie said, "You're supposed to use the red one!" Steve told his sister it didn't make a difference, but she insisted that they had to use the red one because the dog liked it better. Susie and Steve yelled at each other and argued for about ten minutes.

Suddenly their mom walked into the room ... and noticed that the poor puppy had had an accident on the carpet while he waited for his walk. Oops. Now Susie and Steve were in big trouble!

Sometimes Christians get into arguments about things like music, money, proper behavior, how to study the Bible, and many small details about what we should believe. The subjects may be important, but if the arguments keep us from loving each other and serving God, that goes against His plan for us.

DARE   Say no to the temptation to argue.

TRIPLE-DOG DARE!

1 Make this a habit: Before disagreeing with someone, ask yourself if you're trying to help or just trying to prove you're right. In the second case, be humble and let it go.

2 If you argued with your parents lately, ask for their forgiveness and promise to do better.

3 Do a random act of kindness for someone who always seems to argue with people.

Journaling   How did it go? What did you learn?

Read Exodus 20:13.

Did you roll your eyes even just a little when you read the commandment not to murder? Maybe your first thought was something like, *Duh. I've never killed anyone and I never will.* You're probably right, but it's still an important verse to think about because it goes a little deeper than you might think.

Take a look at 1 John 3:15. It says, "Anyone who hates his brother is a murderer, and you know that no murderer has eternal life in him."

Jesus also said, "You have heard that it was said to the people long ago, 'Do not murder, and anyone who murders will be subject to judgment.' But I tell you that anyone who is angry with his brother will be subject to judgment" (Matthew 5:21–22).

Hmm … that brings it a little closer to home, doesn't it? The Bible tells us that murder isn't just killing someone with a knife or a gun. To God, it's just as serious and wrong to hate someone as it is to kill him or her. Does that surprise you? Does it seem strange to compare murder with hateful thoughts?

You see, God knows that murder always starts with hate. The only difference between a murderer and someone who hates is that the murderer acted out on his feelings. The consequences are much, much worse, but the heart isn't very different.

You may never hurt or kill anyone physically, but if there is hate and anger and bitterness in your heart, you will probably hurt him or her emotionally.… And you'll still be breaking the sixth commandment.

Write down some ways you've been hateful toward others lately:

_____

_____

_____

_____

Ask God to forgive you and to help you love others, no matter how difficult it is. Remember that Jesus could have killed those who made Him suffer and crucified Him.… But He forgave them instead.

Got More Time?

This weekend, whenever you catch yourself thinking or saying mean things, write about it in your journal. This will help you realize how easy it is to hate and will hopefully make you pause before hurting people you don't like.

At the end of the weekend, see if you've noticed a change in your attitude. Keep doing this during the coming week if you feel like you need to work on it some more.

Journaling

You are pretty when you smile.

Less Talking, More Listening

Truth

When you worship God, His words should matter more than your own.

How would you feel if you and your best friend had a fight, and the next day she came over and, after quickly saying, "Sorry about yesterday," checked out your fridge, took some leftover pie, flopped down on the couch, and started watching TV? What if you tried to talk with her and she just nodded and said "Uh huh" once in a while?

Most of us expect others—especially our friends and family members—to treat us with respect, to listen to us, to apologize when they've hurt us, and to thank us when we've done something nice for them.

The strange thing is that we often forget that God deserves even more respect than we do. Today's verses remind us to be humble and respectful when we worship God. We should pay attention in church and think before we pray. It's better to say only a few words that come from your heart than to use a lot of words that mean nothing.

DARE   Don't use more words than you need to.

TRIPLE-DOG DARE!

1 Before you pray today, sit quietly for a few minutes and just think about how great God is.

2 Take a notebook to church each Sunday and write down things you'd like to remember. This will help you pay attention.

3 If your friends whisper or pass notes in church, don't join in. Later, tell them why you didn't.

Journaling   How did it go? What did you learn?

Keep Your Promises

Truth — *God does not want to hear empty promises.*

A lot of people make promises without thinking about them carefully first. These examples may sound familiar to you:

"Dad, please let me have a puppy! If you let me, I promise to wash the dishes every day."

"If you vote for me as class president, I'll make sure we get less homework to do!"

"If you do my math homework for me, I'll let you ride my bike for a week."

We usually make these kinds of promises either to get something we want from another person or to make someone have a good opinion of us. But we're not always serious about doing what we've promised to do, or we hope the other person will forget about it. That doesn't make us very trustworthy, does it?

We sometimes make thoughtless promises to God, too: "I promise to pray ten times a day. I promise to pray for an hour every day. I promise never to lie again."

These are great promises, but they mean nothing to God if we don't keep them.

DARE — Keep your promises!

TRIPLE-DOG DARE!

1. Make a list of promises you haven't kept yet (for example, a chore at home) and complete them one by one (even if they're old promises!).

2. When you make promises, write them down in your journal so you won't forget.

3. Whenever someone keeps a promise they made to you, tell them how much you appreciate it.

Journaling — How did it go? What did you learn?

If ... Then

Truth
god will help and forgive us when we humble ourselves.

In philosophy (the study of knowledge), there is a subject called "causality"—or, more simply, cause and effect. That means that whenever something happens, there must have been an *action* that caused the *result*. For example, if you leave the milk out of the fridge on a hot summer day and it gets stinky by nighttime, the *cause* is your forgetting to put the milk away, and the *effect* is the milk going bad.

Pretty simple, right? You can probably think of dozens of other examples of how if you do one thing, something else happens.

This verse talks about a more important cause and effect. It says that *if* you admit your sins to God, without making excuses, and you are ready to change your ways, *then* He will forgive you and help you with your problems.

DARE Turn from your wrong ways.

TRIPLE-DOG DARE!

1 Ask God for forgiveness *only* when you're truly sorry for what you did and ready to stop doing it.

2 Every morning, before you check your email or cell phone for messages from friends, "seek God's face" and talk to Him first.

3 Challenge a friend to see which of you can memorize this verse the fastest. (Don't cheat! Start learning it at the same time.)

Journaling How did it go? What did you learn?

Everything Is Possible!

Truth — *Nothing is impossible for god.*

Have you ever sat in an airplane and wondered, *How can this huge plane, which must weigh a bazillion pounds, fly through the air without dropping to the ground?*

Or have you thought about how wonderful it is that you can pick up a gadget that fits in your palm and talk to your grandparents or a friend who lives on the other side of the country … or world?

If you could go back five hundred years in history and describe an airplane or cell phone to the people of that time, they would say, "It's impossible!" But humans have been able to invent these amazing machines…. So it shouldn't surprise us that God can do even more "impossible" things!

At times, you may worry about problems that seem to have no solution, or you may feel like you'll never succeed in a certain situation. Don't forget that what seems impossible to you isn't impossible for God. If He wants it done, it'll be done!

DARE — Trust God even in the most "impossible" situations.

TRIPLE-DOG DARE!

1. Make a list of all the things you feel anxious about. Pray for them one by one, telling God you trust Him to take care of them.

2. Ask your parents to tell you about a time in their lives that God did something they thought was impossible.

3. Pray for someone you think could never change, believing that it's possible with God!

Journaling — How did it go? What did you learn?

Selfishness Not Allowed

Truth
God wants you to care about the needs of others.

If you're thinking about getting a pet, you should probably forget about getting a crocodile. They're super fast and heavy (and probably stinky), and they have very sharp teeth. Oh, and they're hunters.

Amazingly, little plover birds are not afraid of crocodiles. In fact, they will hop over to crocodiles' mouths and pick their teeth clean! The crocodile gets clean teeth and the bird gets free food.

Zebras and ostriches help each other too. Ostriches can't smell or hear very well, and zebras can't see very well…. So they warn each other when they sense danger.

This kind of relationship in the animal world is called *symbiosis*.

The Bible teaches us to look out for each other too, instead of being selfish and thinking only of ourselves. Of course, the crocodile and the plover bird are being a little selfish because they each get something out of the deal. But we should help others even when it means we get nothing, just because we really care about them.

DARE
Show kindness … without thinking of yourself first!

TRIPLE-DOG DARE!

1. Find a way to help someone who can't pay you back for your kindness.
2. When you have time to do whatever you want, first ask your parents if they need help with anything.
3. Write a thank-you card for someone at church who works hard and drop it in the mailbox. Don't sign your name!

Journaling
How did it go? What did you learn?

Read Exodus 20:14.

Remember last weekend when we looked at how murder is something that you can do in your heart even if you never physically kill someone? The Bible says the same thing about adultery. Adultery is when a married person has sex with someone he or she is not married to. The Bible teaches that any sex outside of a marriage is wrong.

Now, you may wonder why we're looking at this verse if you're not even old enough to be married. Well, two reasons: First, it's important to know early in life what God says so that you don't feel confused about what's right or wrong when you're older. Second, adultery is all about being unfaithful, breaking promises, and cheating.... And it's good to be reminded that those are sins that are easy to do at any age.

Many of the movies, TV shows, magazines, and songs that are popular today—and even things you hear at school or from your friends—make it seem like there are no rules when it comes to relationships and marriage. It's common for couples who aren't married to live together and for married couples to cheat on each other or leave each other for new partners.

The message from the world is, "If it feels good, as long as you're not hurting anyone, do it." That's not what God says because God is wise enough to know that some sins may not *seem* like they're hurting anyone, but all sin is dangerous … not only to ourselves but also to those around us.

Imagine how you would feel if someone told you she was your best friend … and then you found out she was hanging out with another girl whenever she told you she was too busy to spend time with you. It would hurt, right? Well, the pain that adultery causes is much worse than that.

You can plan *from now on* to honor God with all your decisions about dating, marriage, and your body.

Write out a promise to God here:

_____

_____

_____

Tip: If your parents are married, take time this weekend to pray for their marriage. Also, find ways to help them have more time to spend together. Maybe do some of their chores so they can have a date night or go for a walk. The more fun your parents have together, the stronger their marriage will be … and the happier you will be too!

Journaling

The struggles you go through can make you stronger and wiser.

Willing Spirit, Weak Body

Truth
When you're alert and prayerful, you can say no to temptation.

If you've ever gone camping and had to walk around outside at night, you probably know the importance of having a good flashlight so that you can see where you're going. You don't want to trip over a branch, fall into a hole, walk through thorns, or step on a snake!

Your life as Jesus' follower will often feel like you're walking through a dark forest. Confusing situations, temptations, and difficulties in relationships can make it easy for us to "trip" and fall into sin. That's why Jesus told His disciples to be alert and to pray. He understood that even when, in your heart, you want to obey and please Him, your body might not have the strength or discipline to say no to sin.

Remembering that you need God's help at all times will help you stay close to Him and far from sin.

DARE   Don't fall asleep spiritually!

TRIPLE-DOG DARE!

1. If you have trouble staying focused while praying, try writing out your prayers in a notebook or journal.

2. What's your biggest temptation? Pray about it every morning … *before* the temptation comes to you!

3. Make a list of things you want to pray about so that you'll have something to guide you as you pray.

Journaling   How did it go? What did you learn?

The Secret to a Good Life

Truth *Obeying your parents is good for you!*

Life as a girl can be annoying at times: You might feel like your parents constantly tell you to do this or that…. And "this or that" usually isn't fun. Or they might tell you *not* to do this or that, and those are usually fun things you want to do.

When your parents' wishes go against your own, you might forget that they love you and want the best for you. You might think that *you* know what's best for you and that if you could just do what *you* want to do, you'd be happy.

The Bible promises that obeying your parents results in blessings and even a long life. That doesn't mean that obedient children never die young, but when you obey those who care about you, you will make wiser decisions that keep you from danger and other problems and, in that sense, help you live longer than you would if you were disobedient.

DARE Trust and obey your parents!

TRIPLE-DOG DARE!

1. Have you disobeyed or disrespected your parents lately? Apologize and ask for their forgiveness as soon as possible.
2. Write a letter to your parents thanking them for their love and care and telling them what you learned from today's devotion.
3. Fight the urge to whine or ask "Why?" when your parents ask you to do something.

Journaling How did it go? What did you learn?

By Heart

Truth
God's Word should always be in your mind and heart.

When your favorite song starts playing, do you need to pull out the lyrics to sing along or do you just start singing automatically?

How about when a friend mentions the name of a movie you've watched together over and over? Do you find yourself quoting all the best lines from memory?

And have you ever received a card or letter that's so special you read it ten times, until you realized that you knew all the best parts by heart?

If you read your Bible with the same enthusiasm that you have as you listen to music, watch movies, or read letters, you would naturally begin to memorize God's Word, too! And when Bible verses get "downloaded" into your brain, they can help you in all kinds of situations, whether you need wisdom, encouragement, or a reminder of God's love.

DARE   Learn God's Word by heart!

TRIPLE-DOG DARE!

1 Write out, in your planner or on notes tucked into your pocket, the verses you want to memorize and read them whenever you have a spare moment.

2 Have a memorizing competition with your friends and see who can learn the most verses in a week.

3 Whenever you memorize a verse, rewrite it in your own words to make sure you understand what it means.

Journaling   How did it go? What did you learn?

Danger Past the Gate

Truth When you spend your time with God, you won't get mixed up with sin.

Imagine you were camping in a beautiful park with lots of space to play and a clean lake to swim in, and you could to go anywhere in the park.... But you weren't allowed past the gate because of the possibility of dangers such as wild animals, poison ivy, and deep pits.

One day you're picking wildflowers and you notice that the forest behind the camp has much bigger flowers and pretty butterflies, too. You'd have to go through the gate to get there, but you know you're not allowed. What would you do?

God has promised you a life full of His love and blessings, but He's also warned you not to sin. Sometimes you will look at things the world offers and they will seem as beautiful as that forest past the gate.... But sin always leads to disaster!

When you say no to sin and stay close to God—in the safe campground—He will bless you.

DARE Stay away from people and places that tempt you to sin.

TRIPLE-DOG DARE!

1 If your friends always talk about things that you know don't please God, start looking for new friends who do honor God.

2 Read Psalm 1 twice more before going to bed.

3 Write a prayer asking God to help you always make right decisions, even when it's hard.

Journaling How did it go? What did you learn?

Getting "Big"

Truth
We need to "grow up" in god.

Who is the biggest Christian you know? Is it the oldest lady in your church? The tallest man? The heaviest person? The one with the biggest muscles?

Of course, you can't use a measuring tape or a scale to determine how "Christian" someone is. But the Bible does talk about growing and maturing as God's followers. How do we do that?

Think of how a baby grows up to be a child and then a teenager and then an adult. First she needs milk, but then she moves on to solid food. As she grows, she needs exercise, sunshine, and something else you might not have thought of: human touch and affection.

In the same way, you need spiritual food (the Bible), exercise (living out what you learn), sunshine (spending time talking and listening to God), and fellowship with other people who love Him.

Are you getting everything you need to grow as a Christian?

DARE Get big ... spiritually!

TRIPLE-DOG DARE!

1 Flip back to earlier pages in this book and read some of your journal entries. Would you say you've grown since then? If not, ask God to help you grow spiritually.

2 Ask your parents to tell you what helps them grow in God. (If they're not Christians, ask another mature Christian you know.)

3 In your journal, list at least five changes you'd like to see in your spiritual life by the end of the year and how you can make those changes happen.

Journaling How did it go? What did you learn?

Read Exodus 20:15.

Which of these things would you call stealing?

- O Robbing a million dollars from a bank.
- O Taking a dollar from your mom's wallet to buy candy.
- O Taking ten dollars from your mom's wallet to buy her a birthday present.
- O Borrowing a hair clip from a friend and then not giving it back because she forgot about it.
- O Cutting a flower from your neighbor's yard to give to your teacher. (He has dozens! Why would he care about one?)
- O Keeping the extra change when a cashier makes a mistake. After all, it's her fault—not yours.
- O Walking out of a store wearing a sweater you didn't pay for.
- O Copying homework from your friend.
- O Taking home one of those little pencils they have at church.
- O Having an extra cookie when your mom isn't looking.
- O Copying information from books or the Internet into your homework assignments and pretending you wrote it.
- O Taking a couple of fries from your friend's plate while she goes to the bathroom.

You should have twelve things checked off above. Surprised? Did you think some of the actions were not so bad?

The Bible tells us not to steal. It doesn't say, "Don't steal big stuff." That means taking anything that doesn't belong to us without asking first is a sin. It doesn't matter if what you steal is as big as a car … or as small as a safety pin. Stealing is stealing.

It also doesn't matter whether the person you stole from knows that she lost something. You can't tell yourself, *She doesn't even realize it's gone, so what's the big deal?* Don't forget that *God* sees everything and knows everything.

Why is stealing something small so serious to God? Think of it this way ...

The two chains above look different, but they work pretty much the same way. As long as each link in a chain is strong, the entire chain will be strong. But if you cut just one of the links, the entire chain is no good. It doesn't matter if the link is huge or tiny.... It will still mean the chain is broken.

Note: This is also a good way to think about the Ten Commandments. Even if you break just one of the commandments, it's like you've broken all of them.

Journaling

"If we did all the things we are capable of doing, we would literally astonish ourselves."

—Thomas Edison

Reckless Words

Truth
Talking without thinking can really hurt someone.

When you watch a basketball, football, or hockey game, the person you probably pay the least attention to is the referee, but he's very important to the game because he's *neutral*. That means that he isn't rooting for either team, and he can be (or should be!) perfectly fair when making decisions about things like penalties, fouls, and so on. For the audience, he's not one of the good guys, but he's also not one of the bad guys.

Other things in life are neutral too. Money can be used to help people or to buy drugs. Fire can be used to cook a burger or to destroy someone's house. A knife can be used to slice watermelon or to kill someone.

Words, by themselves, are neutral too. But, just like a knife, if they're used the wrong way, they can really hurt someone. Instead, God wants you to use your words to comfort and love others.

DARE Use your words wisely.

TRIPLE-DOG DARE!

1. When you're upset with someone, write your thoughts and feelings on paper first. Then rip up the paper while you ask God to help you keep your words soft.

2. If you have hurt someone's feelings lately, ask for forgiveness as soon as you can.

3. Write an encouraging note to a friend who is going through a hard time.

Journaling How did it go? What did you learn?

Jesus Will BRB!
(BRB = be right back)

Truth — *Jesus could come back at any time.*

What happens when a teacher says to the class, "I'll be back in a few minutes. Please work on your lessons and keep it quiet in here," and then steps outside the room? The class might behave well for about the first minute, but have you ever noticed that the longer the teacher is gone, the noisier and rowdier the students become? It's as if they think, *She's already been gone for a while. She probably won't come back soon.*

A smart student would know that the more time passes, the closer the time of her return!

Jesus is going to come back to this world one day too, but none of us knows when. So you need to be careful to live according to His way all the time, even at your young age. Don't be like the people who say, "Jesus isn't here right now, so I'll have fun and sin for a few more years and become a Christian later."

DARE — Get ready for Jesus' return!

TRIPLE-DOG DARE!

1. Post a sticky note that says, "Jesus will BRB!" on the fridge as a reminder to everyone.
2. Tell a friend what you learned in today's devotional.
3. When you feel tired of trying to be good all the time (it happens!) ask God to help you stay spiritually awake.

Journaling — How did it go? What did you learn?

When You Don't Have the Words

Truth
The Holy Spirit can help you pray when you don't know what to say.

If you've ever disobeyed your parents or hurt your friend in a way that made you sick to your stomach, you probably know what it's like when you want to apologize and all you can do is stand there and cry, not knowing what to say.

As you go through life, you will probably face different situations that leave you feeling like you should say something, but you don't know what.

Sometimes that will happen when you pray. You might be going through a difficult problem at home that worries you, and all you can do is stare at your ceiling hoping that God still cares. You might feel tired or sick and your words get all jumbled because you can't concentrate. Or you might be angry about something and don't feel ready to pray.

God understands. When your heart wants to pray but your brain or mouth can't manage it, the Holy Spirit can "translate" those feelings and thoughts for you.

DARE Pray ... even when you think you can't.

TRIPLE-DOG DARE!

1 When a friend is sad, offer a hug and just sit quietly with her for a while.

2 When you feel too confused to pray, focus your thoughts on how great God is instead of on your problem.

3 Instead of speaking your prayer, try singing a worship song that reminds you of God's love and care.

Journaling How did it go? What did you learn?

Do You Have Faith?

Truth Faith in Jesus can keep you from getting crushed.

Try this experiment …

Find an empty plastic pop bottle that still has its cap. Tighten the cap and place the bottle on its side on the floor. Now step on it as hard as you can. What happened? Not much?

Next, take the cap off the bottle and do the same thing. What happened when you stepped on the bottle this time? You should have been able to crush it easily!

You used the same bottle and did the same action, so why did something different happen? The difference was all in that little cap!

As a Christian, you will sometimes go through "storms"—difficult times that make you nervous or worried. You probably won't be able to change the situation…. But you *can* control how you react, just like you were able to control what happened to the bottle.

If you trust in Jesus, He can help you stay strong during the storms in your life.

DARE Have faith!

TRIPLE-DOG DARE!

1 Show a friend the pop bottle experiment and explain the message to her.

2 Ask your parents to tell you about a time they trusted God with a problem and He gave them the strength they needed.

3 Tell God about a "storm" in your life and ask Him to make your faith stronger.

Journaling How did it go? What did you learn?

Practice Makes Perfect

Truth — *Following Jesus takes practice.*

Leopold Auer, a famous Hungarian violinist and composer who lived from 1845 to 1930, once said, "Practice with your fingers and you need all day. Practice with your mind and you will do as much in one and a half hours."

What he was trying to say is that just repeating violin exercises for hours and hours without giving it a lot of thought could help a student improve, but if that student focused all her attention on her practice time and concentrated on every note, she would learn much faster!

If you don't feel excited about your lessons—whether it's piano, tennis, or Spanish—you'll be tempted not to give 100 percent when you practice or even to skip practicing. And you can't succeed if you don't practice.

The lessons you learn about God through your devotions, at church, and from your parents are not enough to make you a strong Christian. You have to practice what you learn.

DARE — Put your mind and heart into living out what the Bible teaches.

TRIPLE-DOG DARE!

1. If you've skipped any devotionals or dares in the past week or two, go back and do them this week.

2. When you learn something new in Sunday school, ask your teacher for an example of how you can "practice" what you learned.

3. Write this verse somewhere you'll see it whenever it's time to practice your lessons.

Journaling — How did it go? What did you learn?

Read Exodus 20:16.

Without using words like *true*, *truth*, *lie*, *honest*, *dishonest*, or *false*, write down how you would explain the difference between truth and dishonesty to someone:

_____

_____

_____

Take this quiz to see how your definition of honesty matches up with the Bible's.

1. You and two other girls compete in a race, and you lose badly, finishing far behind the others. When other students later ask you how the race went, you …

   a. laugh and say, "Well, I came in third! That's pretty good, isn't it?"
   b. mumble, "I lost. Big deal. It was just a stupid race, anyway."
   c. say, "It was a pretty tight race. It was hard to tell who won."

2. Your little sister puts on an outfit that's a little mismatched and then asks you how she looks. You …

   a. smile at her and say, "You know what? I think your *striped* top would look really good with those pants. Why don't we try that instead?"
   b. shrug and say, "You're five. Who cares what you wear?"
   c. pretend to get excited and say, "Oh, you look so cute!"

3. You borrowed your mom's pretty purple scarf but lost it on the way home from school. You …

   a. tell her as soon as you get home, apologizing and offering to buy her a new one as soon as you save up your allowance money.
   b. don't say anything and hope she'll forget about it.
   c. tell her that someone on the street stole it from you but you didn't see who.

4. One of your friends accidentally breaks a school window while swinging her heavy backpack around. When a teacher later asks you if you know what happened, you …

   a. tell her exactly what happened and explain that it was an accident.
   b. tell her you don't know.
   c. tell her the school bully did it, but you're sure he'll lie about it if she asks him.

Your Score

If you answered …

- **mostly A,** you're not only good at telling the truth, but you do it quickly and with a good attitude. You care about how the truth makes others feel, but you don't hide it just to avoid awkwardness. Keep up the good work, and the trust people have in you will grow.

- **mostly B,** you may not exactly *lie* in difficult situations, but you're not always willing to tell the whole truth, either, and that doesn't please God. You need the courage to tell the truth with confidence, even if you know there may be consequences for your honesty. Ask God to help you be more truthful.

- **mostly C,** you really struggle to tell the truth and sometimes give in to the temptation to make up your own version of what's true. This doesn't please God at all because honesty is very important to Him. Talk to God about your problem with lying and ask Him to help you change.

Got More Time?

Have you lied to anyone lately? This weekend, do your best to make things right with that person (or those people). Tell them the truth, apologize for lying, and then promise that you will be more honest in the future.

Remember: Just when a caterpillar thinks its life is over ... it becomes a butterfly!

Beautiful Humility

Truth

God honors those who are humble enough to serve others.

When you're scooping out ice cream for your family or a friend, do you ever feel tempted to give yourself a bit more than the others? When your favorite TV show is about to start and your mom is still putting away dishes in the kitchen, do you go help her first?

It's natural for humans to think of ourselves first and then others. We're happy if someone wants to serve us but not so happy if we have to serve him or her.

The Bible teaches that God wants you to have the attitude of a willing servant … And it promises that He will bless and honor you if you do! But if you go around feeling proud of yourself and expecting people to admire you, you may find yourself in a very humbling situation.

If you want people to respect you, you have to respect them first.

DARE — Live a life of serving others.

TRIPLE-DOG DARE!

1 Do a secret act of kindness for someone without expecting any thanks or recognition.

2 If a teacher or your parents correct or criticize you today, don't defend yourself. Instead, be grateful for the opportunity to learn something.

3 Let someone win an argument with you, even if you think you're right.

Journaling — How did it go? What did you learn?

Luke 14:12-14

You'll Get Paid Later

Truth You shouldn't be kind only toward those who can pay back your kindness.

Have you ever done this? You're invited to a birthday party so you go shopping for a gift, and you think, *All she gave me for my birthday was that book, so I'm not going to spend a lot on her gift!*

It's easy to show kindness to people who can pay us back with favors or who have something we'd like. For example, a girl who has a crush on a boy might try to become friends with his sister just to have a way of hanging around him. Or maybe your little sister lets you use her good markers because she hopes you'll lend her your new earrings.

Jesus taught His disciples that these types of good deeds don't mean a whole lot. Anyone can be nice to another nice person. What Jesus wants to see in you is the willingness to be kind to those who have nothing to give you in return. Your heavenly Father sees what you do, and He will reward you in a special way—maybe not now, but definitely later.

DARE Be generous with your kindness.

TRIPLE-DOG DARE!

1. Go out of your way to help someone today, even if it means giving up some of your time.

2. Make a habit of holding doors open for people, carrying things for your parents, and doing chores you're not expected to do.

3. Pray for someone at school who isn't usually nice to you, asking God to bless him or her.

Journaling How did it go? What did you learn?

Proverbs 1:8-9

Better than Jewelry!

Truth *Taking your parents' advice will give you something to be proud of.*

Girls love accessories, don't they? Bracelets, scarves, rings, belts, caps, hair bows, sunglasses … There are so many ways to add some color and fun to your outfit!

The problem is, once someone has noticed your pretty purple necklace or ring, that's it. That person may think, *Oh, how cute! She has good taste.* But then what? How much can a piece of jewelry really tell someone about who you are as a person?

The Bible says that when you listen to your parents' advice and focus on becoming a wise and good person—not just a girl who has cool accessories—people will notice, and that inner beauty will impress them much more than any jewelry you could ever wear!

DARE Spend more time working on your inner beauty than your outer beauty.

TRIPLE-DOG DARE!

1. When your parents correct you or tell you to do something you don't like, instead of arguing right away, go and pray about it. Ask God to make you humble enough to see the wisdom of your parents.

2. Write a thank-you card to your parents for all the guidance they have given you.

3. Write this verse out on pretty paper and put it in your jewelry box as a reminder (or stick it up in your closet).

Journaling How did it go? What did you learn?

proverbs 3:11-12

Don't Hate Discipline

Truth *god corrects and disciplines you because He loves you.*

Have your parents ever punished you for disobeying them and then explained, "I'm doing this because I love you"? How did you feel? Was it hard to believe that they really loved you if they were so angry and harsh with you?

Let's try looking at it another way. If you saw a troublemaker at school smoking, would you say anything to him? You might quickly think, *That's sad. He shouldn't be smoking.* But you might not be too concerned about it.

What if your best friend told you she wanted to start smoking? Would you still remain quiet … or would you get upset and try to talk some sense into her? You'd probably speak up because you care about her! If you ignored the subject, it would be as if you didn't love her.

These verses in Proverbs remind us that discipline and correction from someone who loves us—especially from God—is a gift that we should be thankful for.

DARE Thank God for His discipline.

TRIPLE-DOG DARE!

1 Today, make a point of telling your parents that you appreciate how they care enough about you to discipline you when you do wrong.

2 Have you been ignoring your prayer time and Bible reading lately? Ask God to forgive you.… And then spend some extra time doing your devotions today.

3 In your journal, write about positive changes in your life that have happened whenever you've accepted God's discipline.

Journaling How did it go? What did you learn?

Stop Complaining, Start Shining

Truth
Complaining and arguing take away a Christian's "shine."

Have you ever noticed how much people complain? You may know someone who whines and argues no matter what. Here are some complaints you may often hear—or that others may hear from you!

> *It's not fair! She always gets to do what she wants.*
> *I have too much homework.*
> *My parents don't let me do anything fun.*
> *It's too hot.*
> *I'm bored.*
> *I hate broccoli.*
> *It's too cold.*
> *I walked the dog three days in a row! It's his turn.*
> *There's nothing good on TV.*

How do you feel about people who have this kind of attitude? Do you try to stay away from them because they make you tired and frustrated?

These verses remind us that when we complain and argue, it doesn't show people around us that we have God's love and purity in our hearts. It just makes us seem greedy and selfish.

DARE — Let God's light shine through you!

TRIPLE-DOG DARE!

1 For one week, wear a rubber bracelet on your arm. Whenever you catch yourself complaining or arguing, snap the bracelet so that it stings a little. See if that helps you complain less!

2 Try this with your best friend: Whenever one of you complains, challenge each other to think of two positive things about that situation.

3 Design a sign with today's verses and put it up on the fridge as a reminder for the whole family.

Journaling — How did it go? What did you learn?

Read Exodus 20:17.

Once upon a time, two young women owned very successful businesses right across the street from each other. Although one sold flowers and the other sold books, they were very competitive. Every day they would watch each other's store to see how business was doing across the street. Whenever a customer entered one of the shops, the owner of that shop would silently cheer, but the other shop owner would feel upset.

One night, an angel appeared to one of the women in a dream and said, "I will give you anything you ask for, but there's a catch. Whatever you receive, your competitor will receive twice as much. You can ask to be rich, but she will have double your money. You can ask for a long and healthy life, but her life will be longer and healthier. So, what do you wish for?"

The young lady thought about it for a while. She knew that whatever she came up with, the other shop owner would have twice as much. If she asked for beauty, her competitor would be more beautiful. If she asked to be popular, her competitor would become more popular.

She finally thought of her answer. Turning to the angel, she said, "I wish to be blind in one eye."

How does that story (based on a folk tale) make you feel? Were you surprised by the ending? What was the problem between these two young women?

Romans 12:15 says, "Rejoice with those who rejoice; mourn with those who mourn." Do you think the woman who was offered a wish was following this principle? No. Instead, her jealousy was so strong that she preferred to be half-blind so that her competitor would suffer, rather than receive a blessing knowing that the other woman would also be blessed.

If you think you'd never be that jealous or mean, read Romans 12:15 again and ask yourself, "Am I happy when others are successful or happy? Or am I jealous? Am I sad when others go through hard times or fail? Or am I secretly happy that it was them and not me?"

In the left column, list people who have things or who are good at things that make you wish you were in their place (be specific). In the middle column, list the things you have or are good at that might make *others* wish they were in your place. In the right column, list people who don't have much or are going through difficult situations that you wouldn't want to be in yourself.

_____ _____ _____

_____ _____ _____

_____ _____ _____

_____ _____ _____

_____ _____ _____

This weekend, ask God to help you rejoice with the people in the first list instead of being jealous of them and to feel compassion toward (and help if you can) the people in the third list instead of feeling glad that you're not in their place. As you look at the second list, thank God for all that He's blessed you with and ask Him to help you not to be proud or boastful about the things on that list but to always give the honor to Him.

Just for Fun

Do you know why people refer to jealousy as a "green-eyed monster"? The expression comes from two different plays by William Shakespeare.

In *The Merchant of Venice,* he talked about "green-eyed jealousy," and in *Othello* he wrote, "O, beware, my lord, of jealousy; It is the green-eyed monster which doth mock the meat it feeds on." (The "green-eyed monster" could also be a cat that plays with a mouse before killing it, which is mean ... just like jealousy!)

Is it time to have a heart-to-heart chat with God?

Fellowship

Truth *going to church helps you grow in your faith ... and relationships.*

Jamie was so excited to join the science club at school! She got a bag full of gadgets, books, an official membership card, and even a cool DVD. She could go to all the meetings and events and do experiments in the lab. Best of all, she could hang out with other kids who loved science as much as she did!

But Jamie never went to any meetings. Sometimes she read a bit from the books or watched the DVD for a while. She proudly showed people her membership card and talked about how great the science club was. But ... she never went to any of the meetings!

If this was a true story, wouldn't you think Jamie was a strange little girl?

Sadly, some people are like that with church. But the Bible says that you need to spend time with other Christians to grow. Are you like Jamie, or do you get involved in church as much as you can?

DARE Make church a priority.

TRIPLE-DOG DARE!

1 Look up the word *fellowship* and write its definition in your journal. Ask your parents what the word means to them and then add that to your journal.

2 Do you have a friend who has missed church a lot lately? Share this verse with her and encourage her to go back with you.

3 When you go to church, dig in! Sing every song, listen to the sermon, and talk to people besides your friends.

Journaling How did it go? What did you learn?

1 Corinthians 12:12–13
One Body

Truth — *Every Christian is one special part of a "body."*

Quick: How many different parts of the body can you name? In thirty seconds, you could probably think of about thirty different parts, such as head, nose, arm, knee, stomach, chin, and so on.

Take another minute and keep adding to your list. Did you think of these parts: spleen, ovary, thyroid, gall bladder, or sternum? Ever heard of those before? Do you know what they do?

What about things like DNA and skin cells and blood and saliva?

God created our incredibly fascinating human bodies with millions of tiny parts that are all important—but they are useless on their own. They have to work together with all the other body parts to keep you healthy and alive.

The "body" of people who belong to Jesus works the same way. You may feel small and unimportant at times, but you make up a very special part of this spiritual body! (Just remember that *everyone* is important, so you should treat others equally.)

DARE Respect others as your equals.

TRIPLE-DOG DARE!

1. Write down different ways Christians can be like body parts; for example, a helpful hand, a listening ear, a shoulder to cry on. Which one are you?

2. Is there someone you've been ignoring? Ask God to help you show that person love and respect.

3. Write a thank-you note to someone who has encouraged you and helped you to grow in your faith.

Journaling How did it go? What did you learn?

The Greatest Love

Truth
Jesus gave us the best example of how to love.

Do you know the games Simon Says and Follow the Leader? Both games involve following instructions, but there is one important difference between them.

In Simon Says, you have to do whatever the leader *tells* you to do, but in Follow the Leader, you have to do whatever she *does*. This may not seem to matter much … until the challenges get difficult!

If the leader shouted, "Simon says, walk along that skinny log to get to the other side of the stream," you might feel a bit nervous and think, *I can't do that!* But if you saw the leader walking on the log ahead of you, that would give you the courage to believe you could do it too.

When Jesus told His followers to love each other, He set a good example for us to follow. Jesus was willing to die for us because He loves us.… And He can put that kind of love into your heart too.

DARE Love like Jesus does!

TRIPLE-DOG DARE!

1 When your mom makes your favorite dessert, let others get theirs first, even if that means you get the smallest piece.

2 Today, instead of only *obeying* your parents, do something special that shows you really *love* them.

3 Give up some of your free time to help others as a volunteer at your church or in your community.

Journaling How did it go? What did you learn?

Proverbs 15:17

The Grass Is Greener ...

Truth *There's more to life than being rich and having what you want.*

Have you ever heard the saying, "The grass is always greener on the other side"?

People usually say that when they hear someone else complaining about something in her life and comparing herself to someone who seems to have more. It's like looking over the fence between your house and your neighbors' and wishing your grass was as green as theirs ... when it probably already is!

At times you may compare your life to another girl's life and think, *She has nicer clothes. She probably has more money. I bet her dad has a really important job. Her parents are probably smarter than mine. I wish I were her!*

We often forget that just because someone else has more "stuff," it doesn't mean she's happier. This verse reminds us that it's better to have a little and be with people who love you than to have a lot and be miserable.

DARE Be happy and grateful for what you have!

TRIPLE-DOG DARE!

1. List ten things you wish you could have. Now list ten things you have that are better than the things on your first list. Joyfully thank God for them!

2. The next time your mom cooks something you don't like, think about all the poor children who have nothing to eat.... And be thankful for what you have.

3. Whenever you feel jealous of someone else, remind yourself that she may not be as happy as you think.

Journaling How did it go? What did you learn?

Can't Have Both

Truth
If your words are sometimes good but sometimes bad, something's wrong!

Imagine you wanted to put some ketchup on your hamburger, and raspberry jam came out of the bottle! Or what if you turned the faucet to wash your hands and you got paint instead of water?

You'd be surprised … and probably a little upset, too, right?

It's perfectly normal to expect things to do what they're supposed to do. A tooth-paste tube should squirt toothpaste. A saltshaker should sprinkle salt. A blue pen should write in blue and not red.

As a Christian, you can either use your words to honor God and encourage others or you can use them to lie and hurt people. But when you truly love God and try to live like Jesus did, you can't do both. Because the Holy Spirit lives in your heart, your words should be just as loving and good as His would be.

DARE Make sure all your words honor God.

TRIPLE-DOG DARE!

1 What are some things you've said this week that you shouldn't have said? Ask God to forgive you.… And ask others to forgive you if you hurt them.

2 Every time you complain or say something rude, think of three positive things to say.

3 Do you know someone who always honors God with his or her words? Thank him or her for setting a good example for you.

Journaling How did it go? What did you learn?

(erased)

Read 1 Corinthians 6:19–20.

The temple that King Solomon built for God was so grand and beautiful that it takes four chapters in the Bible (1 Kings 5—8) to describe it! The Israelites went to the temple—or God's house—to worship Him and to bring sacrifices when they sinned.

Of course, God is spirit so He lives everywhere—not just in a temple, but in heaven, all around us, and, when we ask Him to be our Savior, in our hearts.

Today's verses compare our bodies to God's temple. You may think that God cares only about whether your heart and mind are pure, but He actually wants you to take care of yourself physically, too. Your body is a gift from Him and should be kept healthy and in good shape.

Take this quiz to see how well you take care of your "temple."

1. You exercise …
    a. every time you go up and down your stairs at home.
    b. by playing outside whenever you can.
    c. by doing sports or taking swimming lessons.

2. You eat …
    a. only when you really have to.
    b. all the time!
    c. three meals plus a couple of healthy snacks every day.

3. You sleep …
    a. only a few hours because you stay up too late reading or playing.
    b. seven to eight hours every night.
    c. nine to ten hours every night.

4. You drink water …
    a. only when you have to swallow medicine.
    b. once or twice a day.
    c. several times a day.

5. You spend your free time …
    a. napping or watching TV.
    b. chatting or playing with friends.
    c. developing your hobbies.

If you answered …

- **mostly A,** you're not taking good care of your "temple." Remember that your body is a gift from God that you need to appreciate and keep healthy. Ask Him to help you develop better habits now because it will become harder as you get older.

- **mostly B,** you're doing okay but need to pay better attention to what goes into your body and how you balance your time. Think of some improvements you can make, starting this weekend.

- **mostly C,** you're doing a great job of caring for your "temple" and have developed some healthy habits. Keep up the good work and remember to do it all to honor God, not yourself.

journaling

The word "triumph" is made up of
two parts: "try" and "umph!"

Perfect Peace

Truth When your trust in Jesus is strong, you'll always have peace.

I'm going to tell you a secret about myself. (Oops … I guess it's not a secret now that it's in a book!)

I'm terrified of deep water.

Even though my brain knows that I probably won't drown because I do know how to swim a little, my heart gets scared, and I just can't go in the deep end in the pool or lake. Not without some help, at least. If I am in a boat and wearing a life jacket, no problem! I love being in the middle of a lake. I trust that the boat will keep me out of the water so I can just relax and enjoy the view.

When you believe that God loves you and has the power to help you in every situation, you can feel peace in your heart no matter how scary life becomes around you. You just have to remember that He is bigger than your worst problem!

DARE Focus on Jesus instead of on your worries.

TRIPLE-DOG DARE!

1 Write down and memorize today's verse.

2 What are you worried about today? Tell God how great He is instead of telling yourself how big your problem is.

3 Draw a picture that shows an example of how trusting in God can give you peace.

ournaling How did it go? What did you learn?

Luke 16:10

Can You Be Trusted?

Truth god wants His children to be worthy of trust.

Let's say you had a small fish tank with three goldfish. Your parents agreed to let you keep the goldfish in your room as long as you promised to feed them every day and clean the tank once a week.

Now suppose you didn't pay much attention to the fish and, one by one, they died. Then you asked your parents for a puppy. What do you think they would say?

You couldn't blame them for saying no, right? After all, if you couldn't take care of goldfish, which are easy to look after, how could they trust you to have a puppy, which would need much more attention?

The Bible reminds us that if we want to be trusted with big things, we have to prove we can be trusted with small things. If you want to serve God, you have to start with simple things, even if they don't seem important. For example, before you can become a leader or teacher, show that you can joyfully put away chairs, design a poster, or hand out programs.

DARE Prove you can be trusted.

TRIPLE-DOG DARE!

1 Are there jobs your mom always has to remind you about? Get into the habit of doing them on your own right away.

2 Volunteer to help out however you can at church to show that you want to serve God.

3 Ask someone you look up to what he or she had to do to become a good leader.

Journaling How did it go? What did you learn?

Search with All Your Heart

Truth
It's not difficult to find God ... if you want to.

If you had a pair of shoes you didn't like and your mom asked you to wear them, how long would you look before you said you couldn't find them? You might "forget" where you put them because you didn't really want to find them.

But if you lost a pair of shoes that you really, *really* liked, you might turn your whole room upside down to find them, right?

When something—or someone—is special to us, we search for it with more enthusiasm and attention than we would for something we don't care about much.

God promised that if you really want to know Him more and you *seek* Him (for example, by reading your Bible, praying, and going to Sunday school), you will *find* Him. But if you only call yourself a Christian without really caring about getting closer to God, you won't grow in your relationship with Him and it will feel like He's missing from your life.

DARE — Search for God with your whole heart!

TRIPLE-DOG DARE!

❶ List ten things you would miss if they were taken away from you. Ask God to help you value your time with Him more than those things.

❷ Read today's devotion again, but more slowly, really thinking about it.

❸ On an index card, draw a cross inside a magnifying glass inside a heart. Write today's verse on the back and use the card as a bookmark in your Bible.

Journaling — How did it go? What did you learn?

PSalm 133:1

Beautiful Harmony

Truth It pleases God when His family agrees with each other.

In an orchestra or band, you will see (and hear!) musicians playing different instruments. Each instrument has a different sound, and sometimes each musician is playing a completely different part from all the others. However, when they all play in the same key, with the same tempo (speed), the music sounds complete ... almost as if only one instrument is playing. That's called harmony.

You could also call it unity because the musicians are playing as one "unit"— they're not all doing whatever they want or playing their own songs. The orchestra members are all following the same director and playing the same song.

God has given you special talents that may be different from those of your friends, but when Christians love each other and are *united* in loving and serving God together instead of being selfish, it's like beautiful music to God's ears!

DARE Live in unity with other people.

TRIPLE-DOG DARE!

1 Have you had an argument with a friend? Call her up and try to make peace with her.

2 With a friend, think of five (or more) examples of unity, besides an orchestra. A few hints to get you started: ingredients, words, colors ...

3 Come up with a way you and a couple of friends (or your family) can work together to serve God.

Journaling How did it go? What did you learn?

How Far Would You Go?

Truth
When you look for God, you'll always find Him!

The story of Zacchaeus sometimes gets a giggle from children as they imagine a short little man running through the legs of people in a big crowd to try to get to Jesus. We don't know how short Zacchaeus actually was, but he couldn't see over the heads of the other people, so he came up with a plan B.

Sycamore trees can have very low, thick branches, so Zacchaeus probably had no difficulty climbing up one to get a better view. He didn't care if people laughed at him…. He just wanted to see Jesus, no matter what. And he did! In fact, Jesus was so pleased with his faith that He visited him at home. And that helped Zacchaeus get serious about following God; he promised to give half of his money to the poor and generously pay back anyone he had cheated.

How far would *you* go to follow Jesus?

DARE   Follow Jesus even when it seems impossible.

TRIPLE-DOG DARE!

1 If your parents say it's okay, look up the song "Take Me Away" by BarlowGirl, which sounds like it could be about Zacchaeus. Use the words as an example for your own prayer today.

2 If you're always distracted during your devotions and prayer time, come up with a plan B so that nothing interrupts your time with God.

3 Write a short story describing how you imagine a visit by Jesus to your house would be.

Journaling   How did it go? What did you learn?

Twelve-year-old Tamara had known one of her good friends (let's call her Jenny) since preschool. Everything was great until a couple of years ago when Jenny's mom got breast cancer.

Tamara noticed that Jenny started to change. She became meaner, and a lot of kids stopped liking her. But Tamara still hung around Jenny even when others were staying away from her. And Jenny was still pretty nice to Tamara. Until one day ...

"We were lining up to go somewhere and I asked her if she was okay and I guess she didn't like what I said because she threatened to give me a black eye," says Tamara. "I got scared and started to cry. My teacher noticed what happened and asked Jenny why she said that to me. I was just trying to comfort my friend, but Jenny said that her mom had gone to go get treatment that day so she was just having a bad day."

One day, some of Tamara's friends asked her why she was being so nice to Jenny. She said, "I know she's not being nice, but that doesn't mean I can't be nice back. She's going through a hard time and I'm trying to help her."

Some of Tamara's friends understood and some didn't. They thought she was weird for being nice to Jenny. That's when Tamara realized who her real friends were.

Tamara knew that the Bible says to "love your neighbor" (Leviticus 19:18) and "love your enemies" (Matthew 5:44), so she prayed every day for two things: that God would help Jenny get over her pain and that she herself would be able to stick with her friend during her hard time.

Got More Time?

Is there a girl at your school or church that most of the kids don't like because of the way she behaves? Ask a teacher or another adult if there's anything you can do to understand her better or to help her. Try becoming friends with her. Maybe she's just lonely and hurt and needs someone to show her God's love and kindness.

Journaling

"If god is for us, who can be against us?"
—Romans 8:31

How to Please God

Truth — *God wants you to trust Him.*

Which do you think your parents would prefer to have: a small robot that always did everything they asked it to, quickly and perfectly each time … or you, their human daughter, who may not always listen to them as she should?

Of course you know that your parents would rather have you! Sure, it would be wonderful if you always obeyed them, and that's something you can work on as you get closer to God and as He helps you to love your parents more.

But your parents know the times that you do obey and respect them happen because you have a relationship with them and you love and trust them. A robot wouldn't have those feelings (or any feelings!), so it could never *really* make your parents happy.

When you trust in God and obey Him because of your faith in Him and love for Him (and not just because you have to), that pleases Him.

DARE — Don't just obey God as a duty…. Trust Him too!

TRIPLE-DOG DARE!

1 Have you been doing your devotions just because you have to? Ask God to help you do them because you *want* to grow spiritually.

2 Write a letter to God telling Him why you believe in Him and love Him.

3 Think of two ways you will please God today. Tell your mom or a friend so she can encourage you.

ournaling — How did it go? What did you learn?

Mark 10:1-9

Together Forever

Truth god designed marriage to be forever.

If you asked all the kids in your school if their parents were married or divorced, almost half of them would probably say divorced. Maybe your own parents are divorced. With so many families (even Christian ones) having divorced parents, it might seem like it's perfectly normal for couples to get married and then split up if things don't work out.

Actually, God hates divorce. He doesn't hate the *people* who get divorced, but He hates divorce because it hurts the people in the family that's splitting up. When a couple gets married, God wants them to make a promise to love each other and stay together forever … and then *keep* that promise.

You may think you're too young to think about marriage, but it's a good idea to start praying now that God will guide you as you get older and help you make wise decisions about the man you will date and marry.

With God's help you can have a marriage that doesn't end up in divorce.

DARE Start asking God to help you prepare for your future marriage.

TRIPLE-DOG DARE!

1. Ask your grandparents or another couple who has been married for a long time to tell you how they made their marriage work.

2. Write out a promise to God that you won't start a relationship before praying for wisdom and getting advice from an adult you trust.

3. If your parents are still married, pray for their marriage as often as you can.

Journaling How did it go? What did you learn?

Look Up!

Truth

God is in heaven, so your heart and mind should be there too.

Imagine that your parents told you that you were going to Disneyland next month. You'd already be bouncing in your seat, wouldn't you? For the next few weeks, you'd think about the trip all the time. You'd tell all your friends, start planning what to pack, and ask your parents a hundred questions about what you're going to do there.

You might even have trouble paying attention in class because your mind would keep wandering to Disneyland!

As a Christian, you have an even more amazing trip to look forward to. One day, either after you die or when Jesus comes back to earth, you will go to heaven where God is and spend eternity in a place that is much, much, *much* better than Disneyland.

Wouldn't it make sense to feel more excited about God and heaven than you do about the things here on earth? Of course, you have to concentrate on your everyday life…. But your heart and mind should always be on God, too.

DARE Think about "things above"!

TRIPLE-DOG DARE!

1. Write down at least five ways that heaven is better than Disneyland. For example, "You never have to go home from heaven."

2. With a friend or sibling, spend time daydreaming about what heaven will be like.

3. If you're not sure that you'll go to heaven one day, check out the page "Want to Know More about How to Become a Christian?" at the end of this book.

Journaling How did it go? What did you learn?

Friends Rescue Friends

Truth Helping your friend stay away from sin can save her life!

Would you let your best friend jump into a pool that had no water in it? What if she wanted to play with a poisonous snake or stick her hand in a wasp nest? Would you just stand and watch as she drank a glass of bleach?

It might seem crazy to think that anyone would let her friend do such dangerous things. In fact, you would probably even warn a stranger who was about to do something so foolish.

What you might forget sometimes is that sin is the biggest danger of all because it can hurt us (or kill us) more than just physically. Sin separates us from God and puts our souls in danger.

When you warn a friend about sin (in a loving way) and help her to turn back in God's direction, that's even more heroic than saving her from a burning building!

DARE Save your friends from the dangers of sin.

TRIPLE-DOG DARE!

1. Agree with your best friend that you'll be honest with each other if either of you sees the other one taking the wrong path.

2. If you are very concerned about a friend who is struggling with a sin, pray for her first. Then ask a Christian adult for advice on how to help her.

3. Think of some ways you might be setting a bad example for friends and ask God to help you change.

Journaling How did it go? What did you learn?

Even Though ...

Truth *god deserves your thanks even when things seem to be going badly.*

When I was little, my dad had a sign up in his radio store that said, "When I do something right, no one remembers. When I do something wrong, no one forgets."

Do you ever feel like that? God probably does too!

Most people start worrying or complaining as soon as something bad happens. It could be a bad storm, a sickness, someone dying, someone losing a job … These are all difficult situations that can make us feel upset and nervous. It's natural to feel that way, but the problem is that we forget to continue to feel thankful at the same time. God's goodness doesn't disappear when hard times come our way.

No matter what's going on in our lives, we have to remember all the other things God has blessed us with, most of all His love for us, and take time to thank and praise Him.

DARE Thank God on your worst days.

TRIPLE-DOG DARE!

1 Read all of Habakkuk 3.

2 In your journal, write about the worst thing that ever happened to you. Then write down some reasons you can still thank God.

3 Ask your parents to tell you about a time when they were able to thank God even though they were going through a hard time.

ournaling How did it go? What did you learn?

Read Luke 19:28-40.

In this story, the religious leaders got upset because Jesus' followers were happily shouting about how wonderful Jesus was. They were praising Him and calling Him the King while they placed their coats on the ground in front of the donkey He was riding on.

When the Pharisees asked Jesus to tell His followers to stop, Jesus told them that even if people stopped praising Him, the stones would start!

Can you imagine how strange it would be if the rocks started their own "concert," worshipping Jesus? Of course, that's not their job.... That's *our* job.

This weekend, your dare is to make sure Jesus doesn't need a "rock" concert to glorify Him.

Choose at least one of these activities to do:

1. Play this game with a few friends. Give everyone a pen and a piece of paper. On "Go!" everyone has two minutes to write down as many things as she can think of that God deserves praise for (such as He knows everything, or He loves us even though we sin). After two minutes, everyone stops writing. Go around and have each girl read her list. If anyone has the same thing on her own list, that item gets crossed out. Go around until each list has been read. At the end, whoever had the most original ideas wins.

2. Ask everyone in your family to think of one thing they praise God for. When you go to church, do the same with as many people as you have the courage to! If they ask you why you're doing this, tell them about this weekend's devotion and Bible reading and how you want to hear people talking about how great God is.

3. Whenever someone asks, "How are you?" tell him or her about something you're thankful to God for.

Write some praises to God here!

Journaling

Every oak tree started out as an acorn.

Get Smart

Truth *If you want to become wise, you have to start with god.*

You've probably already discovered that many teachers and scientists don't believe in God, creation, or the Bible. Atheists are people who say that God doesn't exist.

It might sound harsh, but the Bible says that it is foolish not to believe in Him. Of course, that doesn't mean you should call your teacher a fool. Please don't do that!

What it does mean is that when you put your trust in God and believe that He is the Creator who has all power and knowledge, that's your first step in becoming wise. The world, life, and many other things make more sense when we believe—and obey—what God says. You also learn to make wise decisions because you know what God would want you to do and you trust that He knows what's best for the girl He created and loves so much (you!).

DARE Trust God before you trust people.

TRIPLE-DOG DARE!

1 When your teachers say things about God or the world that you aren't sure about, ask a more mature Christian to tell you what the Bible says about those things.

2 Make it a habit to read your Bible every day so that you can become wise.

3 In a small notebook, write down every new thing you learn about God. Read your notebook once in a while.

Journaling How did it go? What did you learn?

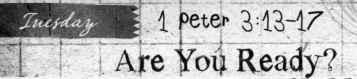

Tuesday — 1 Peter 3:13-17

Are You Ready?

Truth *god will bless you for your courage to tell others about Him.*

If someone asked you why you love your best friend, would you have to think long and hard about the answer or would you know what to say right away? What if she asked how you feel about your mom or your favorite aunt, teacher, or celebrity? What about a hobby that you really enjoy?

When you love someone or something, people can probably tell right away.… And maybe your enthusiasm gets other people interested too. It should be that way about your relationship with Jesus.

If you feel excited about knowing God and about all that He's done for you, you won't be able to hide the peace and joy and hope in your heart. So you should also be ready to share your faith when people ask about it.

If they mistreat you because of it, don't worry. God promises to bless you always for doing good.

DARE Share your faith and don't be afraid!

TRIPLE-DOG DARE!

1 Write down what you would say to someone who asks you about God. Then practice it so you can be ready.

2 Before you talk to someone about your relationship with God, quickly think about whether you've been a good example lately.

3 Every morning, take a moment to remember that Jesus is your Lord and that you want to live for *Him,* not for yourself.

Journaling How did it go? What did you learn?

The Thirst Quencher

Truth *god can quench your real thirst.*

Imagine the hottest day of summer. What is the one thing you would love to have? Ice cream? Lemonade? Watermelon? You can almost taste it before you take your first sip or bite!

Deer know what it's like to be thirsty too, especially after running away from hunters or other predators. They also know what to do when they're thirsty: look for a river or a brook. If you've never seen a thirsty deer, think of what a dog does when it's hot and thirsty, how it pants hard with its tongue hanging out.

When you love God and recognize how much He blesses you, you will experience that kind of thirst—not in your body, but in your heart. During difficult times, if the first thing you want to do is go to God for help and comfort, that's a very good sign about your relationship with Him!

DARE Get thirsty for God!

TRIPLE-DOG DARE!

1. If you don't already know it, learn the song "As the Deer" and sing it often this week as a reminder of today's truth.

2. When a friend tells you she feels discouraged, share how you turn to God when you're down.

3. Use a permanent marker to decorate two plain mugs with the words of Psalm 42:1. Give one to a friend and keep the other.

Journaling How did it go? What did you learn?

PSALM 46:10

Shhh ...

Truth *When you're quiet and calm, you can get close to God.*

Think of a famous person you admire and would love to meet. Now imagine having the chance to hang out with him or her and then spending the whole time talking about yourself, looking out the window, or doodling in your notebook. Crazy, right? You'd probably sit very still, listen to every word, and learn as much as you could about him or her.

So it makes sense that the best way to develop a relationship with God and learn about Him is to spend quiet time with Him. God wants you to make time every day to "be still"—in other words, just take a break from whatever you're doing or thinking about—and concentrate on Him.

When you do this, you'll grow in your faith, wisdom, courage, and character. In other words, you'll start to become more like Him!

DARE Make time for God every day.

TRIPLE-DOG DARE!

1. Just for today, turn off your music, the television, and anything else that keeps your mind busy. Instead, try to listen to God talking to you.

2. Write a letter to God listing ten ways you think He's awesome.

3. Next time you're in church, focus on God and not the people around you.

Journaling How did it go? What did you learn?

Keep Your Way Pure

Truth
Studying the Bible is the best way to know how God wants you to live.

What do you do before a big math test? You study your textbook, right? You might also ask your teacher to explain difficult ideas to you, or you may go over your notes and do some problems to practice. But you can't expect to do well if you never study.

Instructions, guidelines, or rules can help you with many other things, such as playing a new game, learning how to use a new camera, or performing in a drama.

You only have one life to live the right way, so wouldn't you like to know how to do that? Well, you can: by regularly reading and memorizing the Bible and—just as you're doing while working through this book—putting into practice the things you learn each day.

When you live according to the Word, God will help you keep your path pure and you will experience great joy!

DARE   Get hungry for God's Word.

TRIPLE-DOG DARE!

1 Memorize Psalm 119:9, but change "young man" and "his" to "young woman" and "her" … or to "I" and "my"!

2 Write verse 10 on a sticky note and put it on your computer screen so you can see it the next time you want to search for something on the Internet.

3 Pray verse 11 in your own words, asking God to help you obey His Word.

Journaling   How did it go? What did you learn?

Rational ...or Rash?

The entire book of Proverbs gives good advice on how to be wise and think things through before talking or acting or making decisions. In other words, how to be *rational*. When you quickly react without thinking, that's called being *rash* ... And it often leads to trouble!

Take this quiz to see whether you're rational or rash ... or somewhere in between.

1. You've told your little sister a hundred times not to poke around in your closet. When you get home one day, she's walking out of your room, and your closet door is open. You ...

   a. yell at her for sneaking into your room when you weren't there and treat her meanly for the rest of the day.

   b. don't say anything, but the next time she's not home, you go through her stuff and make a mess. It's only fair, right?

   c. calmly ask her if she needed anything and find out that she was just returning a book she had borrowed awhile ago.

2. You find out that your favorite store is having a huge 80-percent-off clearance sale. You ...

   a. drop whatever you're doing, run over there with your friends, and grab everything you like before it's gone. What a great deal! You *need* this stuff!

   b. go to the mall as soon as you can and spend an hour or two going through the store. You walk out feeling great because you got $150 worth of stuff for only $30!

   c. think about whether you need anything and decide to check it out with your mom later if you both have time. You figure that if you didn't know about the sale, you wouldn't feel like you were missing out on anything.

3. You've got a little crush on a boy at school, and your friends keep teasing you about him. One day one of your friends blurts out to him that you think he's cute. You ...

   a. run away screaming about how embarrassed you are and how you're never going to talk to her again.

   b. laugh and say things like, "What? Him? Are you crazy? No way!"

   c. blush a little and just smile before changing the subject to something less embarrassing.

Your Score

If you answered ...

- **mostly A,** you have difficulty controlling your emotions and react too quickly to things happening around you. Pray that God will help you slow down and think through a situation before you respond.

- **mostly B,** you have pretty good control of your feelings but need to develop more wisdom to react to situations in a more appropriate way. Ask God to guide you in your everyday life.

- **mostly C,** you handle situations with maturity and wisdom. Pray that God will help you to continue being calm and rational.

Got More Time?

Make up a skit or write a story about a girl who reacts rashly in every situation and how she finally learns to think first.

Get Ready for a New Week!

Don't _worry_ about it ... _Pray_ about it!

Jesus Can Help You

Truth
When you feel down and discouraged, Jesus can help you.

Who's the person you run to when you're feeling miserable or hurt or angry? Your best friend? Your mom? Your big sister? Isn't it great having someone who will just give you a hug and let you cry without giving you a lecture or advice that doesn't really help you?

You may have days, though, when even your best friend doesn't really understand what you're going through, and you feel like you have no one to turn to.

Jesus promised that anyone who is weighed down by problems can go to Him and find rest.

"Rest" doesn't mean your problems suddenly disappear. But it does mean that you can feel calm because you're trusting Jesus to be with you through your problems. When you ask Jesus to help you with whatever you're facing, you can go to sleep at night with peace in your heart.

DARE   Rest in Jesus.

TRIPLE-DOG DARE!

1. Share today's verse with a friend who is going through a hard time and tell her how much Jesus cares for her.

2. Take five minutes to lie on your bed and just focus on God's love for you.

3. Write this verse on pretty paper and leave it on your mom's pillow.

Journaling   How did it go? What did you learn?

Romans 12:10

Devoted Love

Truth *god's kind of love takes devotion.*

There's a difference between *doing* an activity and *devoting* yourself to it. You might clean up your room every day because you know your parents expect you to. Imagine the difference it would make if you enjoyed having a clean room so much that you constantly picked up after yourself and put things away … without needing reminders. That would be *devotion* (commitment) to a clean room.

Another example is a girl who takes piano lessons and practices just enough to get by … compared to a girl who uses all her spare time to practice because she really wants to do her very best.

This verse tells us to *devote* ourselves to each other in brotherly (let's say "sisterly") love. That means you love your siblings, friends, and others not because you *have* to but because you really want to make the effort. It means you think of them before you think of yourself.

DARE Honor others above yourself.

TRIPLE-DOG DARE!

1. Write a note to your sister (or brother or a friend) listing five things you appreciate about her (or him).

2. Before you watch TV or play a game today, see if anyone needs your help with something.

3. Think of someone you haven't been very nice to lately. Now do something special to make her smile and feel cared for.

Journaling How did it go? What did you learn?

"Thanks"—No Matter What

Truth *There's always something to say thanks for.*

Have you ever helped a friend or done a favor for someone and then she didn't thank you? It's kind of annoying, isn't it? Unfortunately, we all forget to show gratitude sometimes. Humans have the tendency to be selfish, and we often feel like we deserve the best treatment, the best experiences, and the best stuff.

It's no surprise, then, that God reminded us to be thankful in *all* situations—not just good ones. He didn't *suggest* giving thanks; He *commanded* it.

If you are trying to figure out what God's will is for your life or what He wants you to do, this verse is a big clue! When things go wrong and you're able to find something to be thankful for, that's spiritual maturity.… And God will bless you for it.

DARE Develop an attitude of gratitude.

TRIPLE-DOG DARE!

1. Think of something you're upset or concerned about. Thank God that you can trust Him to make something good come out of the situation.

2. Next time a cashier or server is rude to you, smile and say thank you … sincerely, not sarcastically!

3. Apologize to your parents if you have complained more than you've said thanks lately.

Journaling How did it go? What did you learn?

proverbs 4:23

Guard Your Heart

Truth
What you store in your heart is what will come out of it.

Some versions of this verse describe the heart as a "wellspring." A wellspring is the spot where a stream begins to flow, kind of like the faucet of a sink or the spout of a fountain, only much cooler because it's natural! The water may bubble or burst out of a crack in a mountainside, almost as if it's alive.

The Bible compares your heart to a wellspring because that's the source—the starting point—for your life. The feelings, attitudes, and beliefs in your heart will influence how you behave, how you think, how you treat others ... how you live.

If your heart plays such an important role in your daily life, it makes sense to protect it, doesn't it? Just as guards don't let robbers into a bank, and bodyguards protect people in high positions, you can guard your heart to make sure sinful influences don't get in.

DARE
Be careful what—or whom—you let into your heart.

TRIPLE-DOG DARE!

1. Instead of magazines that focus only on gossip and outer beauty, read something that helps you become more beautiful on the inside.

2. When you feel yourself getting a crush on a boy, ask God to help you guard your heart so that you won't do, say, or think anything He doesn't want you to.

3. Write this verse on heart-shaped paper and stick it on your mirror as a daily reminder.

Journaling
How did it go? What did you learn?

Romans 1:16

Not Ashamed

Truth
The good news about Jesus is powerful!

Imagine this: You're walking down the street one day, and you trip over a plain brown box. You start to walk on, but something makes you look inside the box. There you see a plain white envelope, which you pull out and open. On plain white paper, in small letters, someone has written a rather boring-looking paragraph.

Suddenly you realize that you're holding on to something amazing: a secret formula that can make zits, crooked teeth, and chubby legs disappear in an instant! (Okay, I know … impossible.)

What do you do? You probably try it and, when it works, go running and screaming to tell all your friends the good news, right?

The good news that Jesus died so we can be saved from our sins is more powerful and wonderful than this formula (and actually *true*). Are you excited to tell people about it?

DARE Don't be too shy to talk about Jesus.

TRIPLE-DOG DARE!

1 If you're too shy to tell a friend about Jesus, start by asking her if she has a Bible. If she doesn't, offer to get one for her (your church can probably give you a New Testament to share).

2 Invite a classmate to your youth group or a church event.

3 When a friend is going through a hard time, tell her about how Jesus has helped you.

Journaling How did it go? What did you learn?

Cross out every second letter and write the remaining letters in the spaces below to see what Proverbs 22:4 says about being humble. (The answer is at the end of the book.)

HJUFMRIYLCISTXY PAUNKDM TOHDEQ FZEBANR KOPF
LTRHAE YLUOBRED GBTREIXNEGJ WDEHABLSTWH
FARNED CHIOTNSOMR HARNPD ILKIZFRES

_ _ _ _ _ _ _   _ _ _   _ _ _   _ _ _ _

_ _   _ _ _   _ _ _ _   _ _ _ _

_ _ _ _ _   _ _ _   _ _ _ _ _   _ _ _

_ _ _ _

Someone once said, "It is the branch with the most fruit that bends the lowest." Picture an apple tree loaded with juicy, full-grown apples ready to be picked, and imagine a branch low enough that you could reach it and pick the fruit off of it.

If that branch had about twenty apples on it and you got them all, what do you think would happen to the branch? It would probably swing up higher, maybe even above your reach because the weight of the apples wouldn't be pulling it down anymore. (I'm sure you can imagine how heavy twenty big apples would be!)

That's a good picture of how Christians should be humble. When God blesses us with gifts and abilities and opportunities, instead of being proud and bragging, we should humble ourselves (just as the branch drops lower as it gets heavier) and give the honor and glory to God.

John 3:30 says, "He must become greater; I must become less." A Christian who is really growing in her faith and getting closer to God will not expect people to notice and say, "Wow, you're such a strong Christian!" Instead, she'll want God to receive all the praise because she knows how much more He deserves it than she does.

Got More Time?

Read these extra verses about humility. Write down what you want to remember.

2 Samuel 22:28
Proverbs 11:2
Proverbs 15:33
Proverbs 18:12
Zephaniah 2:3
Philippians 2:3

journaling

"If you want to feel rich, just count all the things you have that money can't buy."

—Old proverb

Cheerful Giving

Truth   *god loves a cheerful giver.*

Can you remember a time when you got a birthday present and you were secretly disappointed when you opened it? Did you ever go way out of your way to help someone and barely get a thank-you afterward?

We all know what it feels like to not be appreciated, and yet we sometimes forget to be generous and thankful toward others. God is so good to us, not only providing for all our physical needs but also giving us Jesus, hope, and help in difficult times.

If we want to be more like Him, we need to develop a character that is more grateful, generous, and unselfish.

One way to show God you're thankful is to give to Him and to those who need your help … and to do it with a happy heart that isn't thinking about what you're giving up.

DARE   Give generously and trust God to still take care of your own needs.

TRIPLE-DOG DARE!

1 Use part of your allowance to secretly bless someone else or support a good cause.

2 Whenever you find money or receive an unexpected gift, put that money aside for a special surprise gift for someone.

3 Every time you give—not just when you receive—thank God for blessing you enough that you can share with others.

Journaling   How did it go? What did you learn?

Your Body Is God's Temple

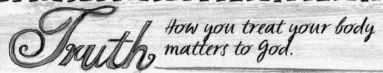

Truth   How you treat your body matters to god.

Most Christians worship in buildings called churches, not temples, so you might not know what a temple is. In the Old Testament, God instructed His children to build a temple for Him—a beautifully and richly designed building where He "lived." Only the priests could enter the temple, under strict conditions, and speak with God for the people.

Today, since we can pray directly to God through Jesus, we don't need a temple. However, if you have asked Jesus to be your Lord and Savior, He lives in you … and that makes your body His temple.

How does that make you feel about how you treat your body or what you do with it? Why not decide today to take care of your "temple" and keep it pure from sin?

DARE   Keep yourself pure—inside and out.

TRIPLE-DOG DARE!

1. Even if you don't have a weight problem, switch your "junk" snacks to nutritious ones.
2. When you get dressed, look in the mirror and make sure that your outfit honors God and is appropriate for a Christian girl. (If you're not sure, ask an older woman!)
3. Make a decision today not to experiment with drugs, alcohol, and anything else that's harmful for you.

Journaling   How did it go? What did you learn?

A Different Kind of Prize

Truth
Your training as a Christian will bring the best award.

Can you think of a competition that you had to train for? It could have been a spelling bee, a talent show, a writing contest, a basketball game, or a race. When your goal is to win a competition, you train hard so that you can do your best.

For some activities, the goal isn't to beat the competition, but instead to finish what you started … to cross the finish line, to reach the top of the hill, or to make it to the other side of the lake. But training is still important!

As a Christian, your life is a training period too. "Crossing the finish line" is being in heaven with Jesus. *That* is the best prize you could ever receive, so you should put more effort into living a life that pleases God than into anything else you do.

DARE   Train hard to be your best for God.

TRIPLE-DOG DARE!

1 Set a goal for this week, such as reading your Bible or praying for twenty minutes a day. Then do it!

2 Every morning, do ten jumping jacks while saying (one word per jump): "I am training for a crown that will last forever!"

3 Take a moment to pray before you read your Bible or go to church and ask God to make you *spiritually* strong.

Journaling   How did it go? What did you learn?

Stand Firm

Truth Nothing you do for God is for nothing.

In college, I studied chemistry, expecting to work in a lab one day. When I found it difficult to keep up with my class, I realized I needed to look for a different career!

At first I thought, *I wasted over two years taking classes I will never need!* But later, even when I became a writer, I could see how those classes helped me think more clearly than I might have without them. I didn't study chemistry for nothing!

Sometimes when we serve God, we don't see results right away. You may pray a long time for someone who doesn't seem to want to change, or you may volunteer at your church, and no one notices your hard work. Maybe your friends make fun of you for going to church every Sunday and you wonder if it's worth the hassle.

The Bible promises that, in God's eyes, what you do for Him *always* counts.

DARE Don't let anything stop you from serving God.

TRIPLE-DOG DARE!

1 Memorize today's verse, and whenever you see a large rock, stand on it and repeat the verse to yourself.

2 Write the verse on a card and find a way to give it to your pastor or youth leader this Sunday.

3 Find one *new* way to serve God this week.

Journaling How did it go? What did you learn?

1 John 1:8-10

Don't Deceive Yourself

Truth   *We've all sinned.*
But we can all be forgiven.

How many times has this happened to you? Your friend is talking super loud so you ask her to stop yelling, and she screams back, *"I'm not yelling!"* Or you ask someone why she's angry, and she snaps back, "I'm not mad!"

What about you? If your mother complained that your room is always messy, would you admit it or make excuses? What if someone pointed out one of your bad habits?

As humans, we usually don't want to admit our mistakes or faults. It's even harder for people to confess their sins. The problem is that you can never fool God by pretending not to have any sins to confess…. You can only fool yourself.

The good news is that if you *do* admit your sins and humbly go to God to confess them, you can have confidence and peace in your heart, knowing that He will forgive you … *always*. Don't miss out on that blessing!

DARE   If you've sinned … fess up!

TRIPLE-DOG DARE!

1 Whenever you catch yourself making excuses for something you did wrong, ask God to forgive you for that … *and* for what you did wrong.

2 On a piece of paper, write down any sins you haven't confessed yet. Humbly pray for forgiveness and then rip up the list!

3 Read all of 1 John 1. (It's only ten verses!)

Journaling   How did it go? What did you learn?

Read 1 Corinthians 13.

Many people call 1 Corinthians 13 "The Love Chapter," and since it talks so much about love, it's common to hear it read at weddings. But Paul didn't write this chapter for weddings. These verses about love aren't just for married couples. They're for all of us! The love described here is the love between parents and children, brothers and sisters, friends, people at church, people in a community, and so on.

The first three verses of this chapter can seem a little hard to understand—they talk about speaking in the tongues of men and angels, the gift of prophecy, fathoming mysteries, moving mountains, and surrendering your body to flames. Hmm, not the kind of stuff most preteens (or even adults!) experience in their everyday lives.

Here's an idea for bringing those verses closer to your own experience. Think of some good things *you* can do, things that might show people you love God, and then think of some ways you might forget to love people. Write down how useless those good actions are without love. I've given two examples from my own life ...

If I write devotional books that thousands of girls read, but I don't spend time with and encourage my own teenage nieces, I'm just writing a lot of meaningless words.

If I study my Bible for hours and teach Sunday school and share my faith with others, but I don't honor my parents or show kindness to my neighbor, I'm wasting my time.

Now you try.

_____

_____

_____

For verses 4–7, here's another great way to test yourself to see if you have the kind of love God wants you to have: Wherever the word *love* appears, fill in your own name.

_____ is patient, _____ is kind. _____ does not envy, _____ does not boast, _____ is not proud. _____ is not rude, _____ is not self-seeking, _____ is not easily angered, _____ keeps no record of wrongs. _____ does not delight in evil but rejoices with the truth. _____ always protects, always trusts, always hopes, always perseveres.

Read that again slowly. Is it true? Some of it might be, but most of us would struggle to make all of it true. This weekend, spend time in prayer asking God to help you grow in your love toward Him and others. Focus on one quality at a time until you've gone through them all. (There are fourteen, so you could focus on the first seven on Saturday and the last seven on Sunday.)

Also, write—or print out on your computer—the paragraph above with your name in place of the word *love,* and keep it in your Bible or planner as a regular reminder to practice those qualities in your life.

Journaling

Dear god,
"Because your love is better than
life, my lips will glorify you."
Amen.

-Psalm 63:3

Choose God

Truth
Nothing the world offers lasts forever.

On average, girls in North America can expect to live about 81 years. Did you know that the Galápagos land tortoise has an average lifespan of 193 years? An Amazon parrot might live to around 104, while a bee will live only about 1 year (except for queen bees, who can live up to 5). A little goldfish can live around 20 years (the world record is 43!).

There are all kinds of other things on earth—objects, food, relationships, experiences—that last for different lengths of time. Often it seems like fun events finish too quickly or yummy food is gone too fast, while boring activities or painful experiences last forever.

The Bible warns against loving what the world offers more than you love God. The things that tempt you will give you pleasure only for a little while, but your faithfulness to God will bring you joy forever!

DARE Choose God over the world.

TRIPLE-DOG DARE!

1 Make a list of your favorite things to do or have and about how long each one lasts. At the bottom, write, "Being with God ... forever!"

2 Say no to anything that takes you away from God, even if it doesn't seem so "bad."

3 Give up one activity today to do something special that would please God.

Journaling How did it go? What did you learn?

1 peter 4:12–16, 19
Suffering for God

Truth *suffering for god is nothing to be ashamed of.*

In North America, Christians don't yet face the difficulties that believers in many other countries have to deal with. We don't have to worry about being put in prison or beaten for going to church or for having a Bible—terrible things you might be surprised to know happen all over the world.

Still, you might face difficult situations because of your faith. For example, you may make people angry because you told the truth or refused to go along with a sin. Classmates may tease you for being a "goody-goody." Or, if your parents aren't Christians, you might not be allowed to participate in church activities the way you'd like to.

Whatever the case, remember that Jesus suffered far more than you ever will—or can even imagine—because of His love for you. He will always be with you and give you the strength you need. That's something to be glad about!

DARE Don't give up when following God makes life difficult.

TRIPLE-DOG DARE!

1. When you're teased for your faith, don't get upset. Stay calm and pray for the people bothering you.

2. If you're *not* suffering for believing in God, ask Him to send a challenge your way!

3. Write a letter to God promising to continue obeying Him, no matter what.

Journaling How did it go? What did you learn?

Don't Imitate Evil

Truth, *If you truly love God, you'll want to be like Him.*

Don't you love it when people do really good impersonations and can imitate someone else's voice, accent, and actions? We often call that *aping* because monkeys are really good at copying the behavior of humans and other animals!

It can be fun to copy—or *mimic*—others once in a while, but the Bible warns us about one kind of imitation: behaving the way evil behaves.

You might think, *I never do that!* It can be easy to do without realizing it, though, because we usually think of "evil" as really, really, really bad and terrible things. Remember that anything different from what God wants is wrong—or evil.

Mimicking the inappropriate behavior of celebrities, even just to be funny, doesn't please God. Using bad language just because "everyone else does it" doesn't please God.

God wants your actions and words to imitate His goodness. When you're close to Him, that becomes easy!

DARE Say no to evil and yes to good!

TRIPLE-DOG DARE!

1 Make sure your fashion choices aren't picked up from someone who dishonors God, which will make it look as if you admire her.

2 Study the character of a Christian you look up to and find ways to have similar good qualities in your life.

3 Refuse to laugh at dirty jokes or watch inappropriate shows and movies.

Journaling How did it go? What did you learn?

Jeremiah 29:11

God Has Good Plans

Truth — *god's plans for your life are really good!*

Don't you just love surprises? You walk into a room, and suddenly a bunch of people start yelling and making noise and singing "Happy Birthday!" You never expected a party, so the surprise makes it even more special.

Or you walk up a steep hill, and when you get to the top, you look over and are amazed by the most beautiful scenery you've ever seen.

Sometimes we can't imagine a really wonderful thing until it happens to us. And sometimes, if things aren't going that great, we actually imagine that they're just going to get worse instead of better. It's like we forget that God loves us and cares for us.

This verse is a promise to you that God knows you—your past, your present, and your future—and you can trust His plans for your life. He would never do anything to harm you; only to bless you.

DARE Trust God's plans!

TRIPLE-DOG DARE!

1 If your attitude has been negative and full of complaining lately, confess it to God and ask Him to help you trust Him.

2 Write down some dreams you have for your future. At the end, write, "God's plans are even better!" (It's true!)

3 Write this verse in a blank card and give it—along with a hug—to someone who is worried about the future.

Journaling How did it go? What did you learn?

A Clean Heart

Truth *Only God can make your heart clean.*

What's your least favorite thing to clean when it's your turn to do chores? The fridge? The toilet? The cat's litter box? How about your own room?

The longer you wait until you clean something, the harder it becomes to clean. If you don't wash dishes for a couple of days, the food gets stuck on them, and then you have to scrape it off. If you don't put your clothes away immediately, the job (and the pile) gets bigger every day.

What's worse than dirty dishes or a yucky toilet, believe it or not, is a heart full of sin. When you don't immediately admit your wrongdoing and ask for forgiveness, that sin stays there. Not only do your sins start to pile up, but like a garbage can you forgot to empty, they start to stink.

But God can wash those sins away and make your heart squeaky clean and as good as new!

DARE Ask God to purify your heart.

TRIPLE-DOG DARE!

1 Try to find and learn the song "Create in Me a Clean Heart," written by Keith Green. Ask someone at church or have your parents help you search online.

2 Make a list of the things in your heart that need to be cleaned out and then pray about them.

3 If you need to resolve a problem with someone, try to do it today.

Journaling How did it go? What did you learn?

Paddling the Wrong Way

A couple of years ago I attended a weekend youth retreat. My teenage niece Alexis and her cousin Lauren were there too, and the three of us decided to go kayaking one hot, sunny afternoon.

Alexis got in a single kayak, and I shared a double one with Lauren, with me in front. I'm not a good swimmer, but I used to teach boating at summer camp many years ago, so I was pretty confident that I could manage this without any problems.

After a few simple instructions from the waterfront staff, we set off across the lake. After a little while, we noticed that Alexis seemed to be ahead of us. I figured it was because her kayak was lighter with one person, but then I noticed that she was also paddling strongly, her paddle dipping deep into the water while mine was doing little more than scraping the top of the water. The harder I tried to paddle, the worse we seemed to do. What confused me even more was that whenever I stopped paddling, it felt like we were moving faster.

Suddenly Lauren suggested that I might be paddling the wrong way. I turned around to see what she was doing and noticed she was "pulling" the water with her paddles instead of "pushing" it.

DUH!

I reversed the direction of my paddling and we began to glide across the water beautifully. You can imagine the great laugh we all had over this!

I later realized what went wrong: I was trying to row the same way I always did when sitting in a rowboat. That's what I was used to. But in a rowboat—unlike in a kayak—you move backward, not forward.

I think there is a great lesson here!

It doesn't matter how hard you work at being good and doing the right things—just trying hard isn't enough to save you or to please God. You can be sincere, but sincerely wrong if you're moving in the wrong direction. Unless you obey God and do things His way, all your efforts will be useless. You may have been used to doing things one way before you became a Christian, but now you have to change directions.

Isaiah 48:17 says, "I am the LORD your God, who teaches you what is best for you, who directs you in the way you should go." Make sure you're putting your trust in God … and not in your own wisdom!

Your Turn

How are you rowing your "boat"? Are you moving in the right direction? Are you doing things God's way? Is anything or anyone stopping you from moving forward?

_____

_____

_____

Journaling

Get Ready for a New week!

It only seems impossible until it's done.

Nothing Compares to God

Truth
Compared to knowing god, even the best things in life are worthless.

What do you dream about accomplishing? Do you want to become rich and famous one day? Do you want to help poor people? Do you want to have a big family, own a ranch, travel around the world, write a best-selling novel, climb Mount Everest, win an Olympic medal, discover the cure for cancer, win a beauty pageant …?

Whew! Life holds more amazing possibilities than you could ever experience in your lifetime, even if you accomplished one every year.

Still, the Bible says that none of those things is as awesome as knowing Jesus as your Savior and Lord and receiving His gift of eternal life. So, if you never experience any of the wealth or success that the world says is so important, but you know Jesus, you will actually be better off than the most successful person on earth who *doesn't* know Him!

DARE Make knowing God your number one priority.

TRIPLE-DOG DARE!

1. Compare the time you spend with God to the time you spend on other things. Plan how you will make God a bigger priority in your life.

2. Give away something you really like to someone who needs it more than you do to practice letting go of "things."

3. Take five minutes to tell God all the things you love Him more than.

Journaling How did it go? What did you learn?

Forgive Them

Truth *You can forgive your enemies!*

If you've ever had anyone tell you that you should forgive your enemies just like Jesus did when He died, you might have thought, *Yeah, but He was Jesus! He was God. He could do it.... I can't.*

The story of Stephen in the book of Acts (if you want to read it all, start at Acts 6:8) shows a human being just like you who was not only treated badly but also killed because of his courage to stand up for his belief in Jesus and preach the truth. And yet Stephen's last words were, "Lord, do not hold this sin against them." Stephen felt compassion—not anger—toward his abusers. He asked God to give them another chance.

When God's Spirit lives in you, you can do amazing things like forgiving your enemies.

DARE Pray for the people who hurt you instead of hurting them back.

TRIPLE-DOG DARE!

1. Think of someone who has treated you badly and pray for God to help her (or him).
2. Think of someone who quickly forgave you for something wrong you did. Give or send a thank-you note to express how much you appreciate it.
3. Share the story of Stephen with a friend who is angry with someone else.

Journaling How did it go? What did you learn?

"Jesus Says ..."

Truth *If you listen to the voice of Jesus, you can stay safe.*

In the game Simon Says, the leader calls out different instructions—sometimes very silly ones!—that the rest of the group has to obey. The catch is that you're only supposed to obey the instructions if they begin with "Simon says ..." If you make a mistake, you're out of the game.

The Bible compares Christians to sheep that have Jesus as their shepherd. He is the best kind of shepherd; He protects and cares for His sheep.... But the sheep have to recognize and listen to His voice or they will get lost or hurt.

You will "hear" all kinds of messages and voices in life—temptations, lies, false teachings about God, and more. Get to know Jesus as well as you can; that way you can obey the "Jesus says ..." instructions and ignore the rest.

DARE Do what Jesus says!

TRIPLE-DOG DARE!

1 Quickly write down ten things you know God wants you to do and ten things you know He doesn't want you to do.

2 Draw a picture of a sheep following a shepherd and write out the words of John 10:27. Put this up where it will remind you to listen for the voice of Jesus.

3 Pray for a friend who seems to have trouble following Jesus.

Journaling How did it go? What did you learn?

John 12:26
Follow Jesus

Truth Serving Jesus means following Him.

Do you remember playing Follow the Leader when you were younger? It might have been a little scary at times if the leader made you climb high or jump around a lot or walk through dark places. But if you really trusted the leader, you probably followed even when you felt afraid because you knew that he or she would never make you do anything truly dangerous.

When you become a Christian, you make a promise to follow Jesus. Sometimes that means doing things you don't really understand—such as treating someone better than yourself or giving up something you really like. The closer you get to Jesus, though, the more you will learn to trust Him and to follow Him without being afraid.

Life may take you through dark situations, but you can find courage in knowing that Jesus, who loves you so much that He was willing to die for you, will always be with you and will help you reach the other side safely.

DARE Trust in Jesus and follow Him.

TRIPLE-DOG DARE!

1. Play Follow the Leader with your little brother or sister (or another child) and then talk about your decision to follow Jesus.

2. Using fancy letters, make a small sign that says, "I will follow Jesus!" Put it up in your school locker.

3. Every morning, pray something like, "I'm ready, Lord! How can I serve You today?"

Journaling How did it go? What did you learn?

Grow in Jesus

Truth   *god can make you grow!*

If you've ever planted flowers or vegetables, or even if you've just paid attention to a houseplant over a period of time, you probably know some of the basic things that plants need.

Good soil, the right amount of sunlight or shade, water, weeding, fertilizer, the right temperature, and even enough room to grow—all these things help plants, flowers, and trees to develop properly, stay healthy, and either bloom or produce fruit. If you ignore a plant, it will die.

As a Christian, you need special things to help you grow too. This Bible passage promises that if you add goodness, knowledge, self-control, perseverance (the willingness to stick to something even when it's hard), godliness (obeying God), kindness, and love to your life, you will grow into a wise and strong person who can serve God.

DARE   Be a good plant in God's garden!

TRIPLE-DOG DARE!

1 Write the seven things listed in these verses on a sticky note and place it on your mirror as a daily reminder of what to add to your life.

2 Get a small plant to take care of. Whenever you water it, pray that God will help you to grow more like Him.

3 Start by doing something unexpected and really *good* for someone today.

ournaling   How did it go? What did you learn?

The Best Reward

Eleven-year-old Fiona (you can read about her older sister Rachel later in this book) enjoys helping her big family share the good news about Jesus to people in the Philippines, where they live.

As you'll see, she really has the courage to serve God and others.

I enjoy serving God because of the love He has for us, the blessings that he bestows upon us, and the joy that comes when you serve Him. It is difficult sometimes but God always blesses you for every hardship you face.

I also enjoy teaching others about God and the Bible. I like to give out tracts on the street; even though sometimes it can be tiring it is really fun to know all the people you are helping.

I also enjoy serving others, especially the poor. When you see their faces when you give them something [it] is the best reward you can get. Whenever I serve God and others this is the verse that comes to mind: "He who goes out weeping, carrying seed to sow, will return with songs of joy, carrying sheaves with him" (Ps. 126:6).

In the space below, write all the different ways you can think of to serve God with your own special talents. Ask God to give you the courage to start doing some of those things.

_____

_____

_____

Find out if your church has a special ministry that reaches out to people who are needy or sick. Check with your parents first and then volunteer to help in whatever way you can.

Journaling

Get Ready for a New week!

If you see someone without a smile, give her one of yours!

Help Those Who Help

Truth
We should support each other in serving God.

If you go to church regularly, you may have heard your pastor or someone else talk about missionaries the church supports by sending money, writing letters, and praying for them. Or maybe you've seen their photos up on a bulletin board.

Your church might also support charities that help poor people, either in other countries or right in your own community.

We know that God could send those people whatever they need some other way, but He wants us all to work together and to encourage those who are dedicated to serving God. You may think your little contribution doesn't make a big difference, but it does!

When you care enough about others to support them in what they do and help however you can, that gives them strength to continue serving God.

DARE   Be an encourager!

TRIPLE-DOG DARE!

1 If a missionary your church supports has children, write them a letter. They might enjoy having a pen pal!

2 When you see an older person at church doing a job that you could manage, offer to do it so that he or she can have a break.

3 Instead of buying something you don't need this week, put some extra money in the offering plate on Sunday. Use an envelope and write a note on it asking that the money go toward mission work.

Journaling How did it go? What did you learn?

John 17:14-16
In the World

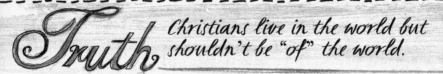

Truth — Christians live in the world but shouldn't be "of" the world.

Have you ever wondered whether fish drink water? Well, some do and some don't—depending on where they live!

Freshwater fish never drink water through their mouths, otherwise they would just swell up. But fish that live in saltwater need to drink a lot and then push the salt out through their gills.

Christians are a little like freshwater fish. We live in a world that can damage us and make us forget God. The challenge is to continue living in this environment without letting it get into our hearts and minds. Like the fish, we have to swim around in the water but not drink it!

These verses can encourage you as you think of how Jesus prayed for you over two thousand years ago. He knew it would be hard sometimes, so He asked the heavenly Father to protect you from temptation and bad influences.

DARE — Don't "drink" the world.

TRIPLE-DOG DARE!

1. Don't automatically follow fashion trends. Just because "everyone" wears tight tank tops doesn't mean you should. Be creative and appropriate.
2. Say no to music, magazines, or TV shows with messages that dishonor God.
3. Drop a goldfish cracker (or a small piece of any cracker) into a glass of water and watch what happens to it. Ask God to help you keep the influence of the world out of your life.

Journaling — How did it go? What did you learn?

I, I, I!

Truth *Pride is ugly.*

Guess what the most-used word is in the English language. Flipping through this book for clues might tell you which word is *written* the most (clue: it has three letters and, oddly enough, appears only once in this sentence). If you guessed *the,* you're right!

But did you know that one of the words we *speak* the most is *I?* It seems that when we're having conversations with people, we talk a lot about ourselves—what we're thinking, feeling, or doing.

God knows that humans think about themselves more than anything or anyone else. That's probably why He tells us in the Bible not to be conceited or proud. He wants you to do your best to live peacefully with others, without thinking that you're better than they are. He expects you to treat people who aren't as smart, rich, pretty, talented, or popular as you are just as well as you would treat your best friends … or as you would want to be treated yourself!

DARE Don't be a snob!

TRIPLE-DOG DARE!

1 Is there a girl at school you usually avoid? Make the effort today to treat her kindly.

2 Have a contest with your friends: Who can go the longest without saying the word *I?* It's hard!

3 Write a note of encouragement to someone who would be very surprised (and glad) to receive it.

Journaling How did it go? What did you learn?

Need Some Help?

Truth More mature Christians can help you understand the Bible.

"Pulchritude possesses solely cutaneous profundity." If you were reading a fashion magazine and suddenly came across that sentence, what would you do? Just skip over it? Look up the words in a dictionary? Ask your mom what it means?

Well, that sentence is actually just a silly way to say "beauty is only skin deep" by using difficult-sounding synonyms (words that mean the same thing).

When you read your Bible, you may sometimes come across verses that are difficult to understand—not because of long words, but because you're not sure what the message is. Instead of skipping over those verses, it's a good idea to ask someone who understands the Bible well to explain them to you. (If no one is around at the time, tuck a note into that page of your Bible to remind you later.)

Just like schoolwork, studying your Bible—even when it's difficult—is how you will learn.

DARE Ask for help!

TRIPLE-DOG DARE!

1. In your Bible, keep a list of questions you have about difficult verses. Whenever you have a few, ask your pastor if he can help you with them.

2. Write thank-you notes to whomever helps you understand the Bible.

3. If you don't go to a Sunday school, ask your parents if you can go to one to learn more about the Bible.

Journaling How did it go? What did you learn?

Tell Someone!

Truth
Telling someone about Jesus might change her life ... or the world!

We don't read a whole lot about Andrew, one of Jesus' twelve disciples. In fact, you'll find his name only fourteen times in the whole Bible. What we *do* know about Andrew is really cool, though.

When Andrew heard John the Baptist get excited about Jesus, he stopped what he was doing and followed Jesus! He trusted Jesus so much that the first thing he did after meeting Jesus was find his brother, Peter, and tell him about his experience. The Bible says that Andrew brought Peter to Jesus.

As you study the Bible, you will discover that Peter became a great preacher who did mighty things for God. Can you imagine what would have happened if Andrew hadn't told his brother about Jesus?

You can have that kind of influence on someone too!

DARE Get excited about sharing Jesus with others.

TRIPLE-DOG DARE!

1 If any of your siblings or cousins don't know about Jesus ... tell them!

2 Invite a friend who doesn't follow God to go to church with you this Sunday. Pray first, asking God to make her ready for your invitation.

3 If you think you're too shy to tell someone about Jesus, ask God to give you the courage you need.

Journaling How did it go? What did you learn?

When Joni Eareckson Tada was seventeen years old, she went to Chesapeake Bay in Maryland to go swimming with her sister and some friends. She dove into the water and suddenly knew that something was terribly wrong. She couldn't move!

Her sister rescued her from the water and called an ambulance, but it was too late: Joni had broken her neck and was paralyzed from the shoulders down.

Can you imagine the awful feeling of knowing that because of an accident that took just a second, you wouldn't be able to use your arms or legs for the rest of your life? Joni had grown up riding horses, hiking, playing tennis, and swimming. Now, still a teenager, she'd never be able to do those things again.

While her friends went back to school and their various activities that fall, Joni had to learn to live in a wheelchair. She went through a time of anger and depression, but she also remembered a prayer she had said before the accident. She had asked God to change her life so that she could really live the way He wanted her to. It was a bit extreme, but maybe this was God's answer to her prayer!

Joni began to grow closer to God again and used her experience to encourage other people who were disabled and suffering. She also learned how to draw and paint with her mouth (she drew the picture for this devotional!), starred in a movie about her life, got married, has written many books, and reaches thousands of people around the world through her ministry, Joni and Friends.

That diving accident happened on July 30, 1967—maybe your parents weren't even born yet. But Joni has continued to joyfully serve God and others. Now in her sixties, Joni has breast cancer, but she still thanks God for everything He has done in her life.

Joni could have stayed angry, or she might have given in to the temptation to end her life. She could have used her disability as an excuse not to serve God. Instead, she chose to trust and obey Him.

Talk about daring!

Got More Time?

- Check if your church library or Christian bookstore has a copy of the movie *Joni* that you can watch to learn more about Joni's accident and how she trusted God.

- List at least thirty things you can do with your hands and feet that you have never thanked God for. Take time today to thank Him and to ask Him to help you use your abilities to serve God and others.

Journaling

Get Ready for a New Week!

Try to learn something new every day.

He's Coming One Day

Truth

You never know when Jesus might come back, so be ready!

Okay, this would never happen (although we've heard of some very silly criminals), but imagine your parents got a letter that said:

This Saturday at 8:00 p.m. I am going to break into your house and steal all your stuff.

What do you think your parents would do that evening? Go out for dinner? Go to bed? No, they'd probably call the police and wait by the door to catch the robber! They'd be ready.

Of course, robbers don't tell you when they're going to break in. That's why good locks are important.

We know that Jesus is going to come to earth again one day, but we don't know *when,* so we always have to be ready … not to catch Him like a robber, but to meet Him with pure hearts.

DARE Get yourself ready to meet Jesus.

TRIPLE-DOG DARE!

1 If you're not sure you're ready to meet Jesus, ask Him to forgive your sins and to help you live for Him.

2 Make yourself a bookmark with the words of verse 44 and use it in your planner or Bible as a reminder to be prepared for Jesus' return.

3 Ask an older Christian to tell you how he or she stays "ready" to meet Jesus.

Journaling How did it go? What did you learn?

Matthew 23:25-26

Inside and Out

Truth *It's not enough to be clean only on the outside.*

What would happen if you always ate ice cream in the same bowl … but only wiped the outside of it with a cloth each time? Dried-up ice cream in your bowl would be bad enough the first time, but can you imagine how gross it would be a month or two later?

Although crusty dishes are disgusting, they're not nearly as bad as a human heart that is full of sin. No matter how hard you try (or pretend!) to be kind and sweet on the outside, if you are walking around feeling angry or jealous or proud, if you are thinking thoughts that are not pure, if you wish you could disobey your parents and get away with it … your outside goodness doesn't count for much.

The Bible warns us not to be hypocrites but to be completely pure … inside and out!

DARE Keep your heart pure!

TRIPLE-DOG DARE!

1 Whenever you rinse out your cup or bowl, take a moment to ask God to forgive you for any sins you haven't confessed yet.

2 Do the same thing whenever you take a shower or wash your hands!

3 Look up the definition of *hypocrite* and write it on a piece of paper. Tuck it into your Bible on the page of these verses as a reminder.

Journaling How did it go? What did you learn?

Pass the Salt!

Truth
God can use you to make His truth "tasty" to others.

Did you know that salt has many uses besides making your fries yummy?

Salt can put out grease fires (never pour water on one!), soothe a bee sting (if you wet it and then put salt on top), comfort mouth sores (if you rinse with salty water), melt ice on slippery roads and sidewalks, and a lot more! Have you ever noticed that salt also makes you thirsty?

The Bible says that, as a Christian, you are like salt to the people around you. Although the verse doesn't quite explain why, it's easy to think of ways you can be as useful as salt. For example, when you live the way God wants you to, you can make people "thirsty" to know God too.

Can you think of other ways you can be the "salt of the earth"?

DARE   Be salty!

TRIPLE-DOG DARE!

1. Keep a little packet of salt (the ones you get from fast-food restaurants) in your wallet to remind you to be "salty" for God.

2. Do some research about salt and think of more ways a Christian can be like salt.

3. Using fancy letters, design a small sign with the words of this verse and stick it up on your fridge. Add a drawing of a saltshaker for fun!

Journaling   How did it go? What did you learn?

God Knows What You Need

Truth *When you have God, you have everything!*

It's natural to want to have great stuff. Television commercials and big billboards constantly tell us about the latest and greatest gadgets, toys, clothes, DVDs, and more. If your friends always seem to have new things, you might even feel a little jealous. Of course, "stuff" requires money, and that can make you wish your family had more of *that*.

Kids who become greedy for money usually grow up to become even greedier adults, which can lead to all kinds of problems: working so hard to earn money that family life suffers, gambling and losing money, stealing, and never being happy because of always wanting more.

You can avoid all that by trusting in God's promises. When you are happy with what you have, you're … well, happy! You may not get everything you *want* in life, but God will always provide what you *need*.

DARE Be happy with what you have.

TRIPLE-DOG DARE!

1. On a piece of paper, start listing everything you own, even the little things. You may be surprised by how much you have. Thank God for all of it.

2. Instead of comparing yourself to girls who have more than you do, compare yourself to girls around the world who have almost nothing.

3. When you have extra money, ask God for wisdom to know what to do with it.

Journaling How did it go? What did you learn?

Serve Others Gladly

Truth — *Loving others should be a top priority.*

We live in a world that encourages young people to think about themselves before others and to do whatever they need to do to feel good, have fun, and get the things they want. Of course, everyone admires someone who is kind and generous, but deep inside, most people would rather be selfish and greedy.

God wants His children to stand out from the crowd by joyfully serving others and loving them even when it's difficult. When your parents invite another family over for dinner—maybe that family with the annoying little boy who always touches your stuff—you might feel tempted to think, *Ugh … not again!* But God wants you to be ready to make them feel welcome and to help cheerfully.

He also wants you to use your talents for the good of others—not just yourself.

DARE — Give service with a smile!

TRIPLE-DOG DARE!

1 At school, look for kids who seem lonely and find ways to put smiles on their faces.

2 When you have company over, don't wait for your mom to ask you to help. Just jump in and do whatever you know needs to be done.

3 If you're not sure how you can use your talents to serve God and others, ask your parents or your Sunday school teacher for ideas.

Journaling — How did it go? What did you learn?

Karina is a teenage girl from São Paulo, Brazil, who loves serving God.

When she was fifteen years old, a missionary came to her church and started some projects to reach out to poor children. One Bible verse that always meant a lot to Karina is 1 Corinthians 15:58.

Therefore, my dear brothers, stand firm. Let nothing move you. Always give yourselves fully to the work of the Lord, because you know that your labor in the Lord is not in vain.

So she was eager to learn more about the projects.

Traffic Lights

The first one involved helping poor children—sometimes as young as seven years old—who are forced by their parents to stand at street corners with traffic lights and to ask people who stop in their cars for money. Sadly, the money that many of them take home isn't spent on food for the children but, instead, on drugs.

Karina helped to prepare small packages that included a can of milk, some cookies and candy, and a colorful booklet that talked about God's love and how Jesus came to save us from our sins. People in Karina's church could buy these packages for a dollar and keep them in their cars to give out to the children they met at traffic lights.

Karina hoped that many children would come to her church, but when they didn't, she remembered 1 Corinthians 15:58 and the promise that her "labor in the Lord is not in vain," which means that just because she couldn't see results it didn't mean that her work for God was wasted. "We can never know the future results," she says.

Favelas

The second project Karina got involved with was visiting *favelas,* poor neighborhoods where many people live in tiny shacks. These shacks are just one room, sometimes with no bathroom, with as many as ten people living together! A lot of these neighborhoods are controlled by drug dealers, so they can be dangerous areas to go into.

Karina and the missionary got permission to visit favelas and share Bible stories with the children there. Before they went home each time, they always left activity papers and encouraged the children to work on them and memorize Bible verses. Karina says it was scary sometimes if she saw people with guns or a lot of police officers, but she is really happy that she got to see some of those children accept Jesus as their Savior and start going to church.

- Look up *favela* in an encyclopedia or on the Internet (ask your parents first!) to get a better idea of the types of areas Karina was serving God in. If you can find some aerial photos (photos taken from the air) of favelas in São Paulo, you'll see the big difference between the favelas and the rich neighborhoods or tall city buildings they are right next to.

- Pray for teenagers like Karina who courageously serve God in countries around the world where life is not as easy as it is in North America.

- Ask God to give you a heart that wants to help others who don't know Jesus. Talk to your parents and Sunday school teacher or pastor to come up with some ways you can serve God now.

Journaling

*Don't waste time. It's the one thing
in life you'll never get back.*

Watch Your Step

Truth
God wants you to be humble so you can see where you're going.

In Aesop's fable "The Tortoise and the Hare," a rabbit and a turtle agree to have a race. Knowing that rabbits run fast and that turtles just sort of crawl along, the rabbit decides to take a nap and get up near the end of the race. He's very confident that it'll take him just a moment to speed ahead of the slowpoke turtle and win the race.

What the rabbit didn't count on was oversleeping. When he woke up, the turtle had already won the race! Can you imagine how silly the rabbit felt, especially when he had made fun of the turtle earlier for being so slow?

Sometimes you may feel like that proud rabbit. You may think you know everything … and then mess up because you were too confident to be careful.

Follow God's advice and fight the temptation to feel too confident about yourself.

DARE Don't trip over your pride!

TRIPLE-DOG DARE!

1 Break the habit of saying "I know!" whenever a parent tells you something.

2 When you feel like you've studied enough, do one more review, just to be sure.

3 Think of someone you've made fun of or acted proud around and apologize to her (or him).

Journaling How did it go? What did you learn?

Fake Member or Real?

Truth
You can call yourself a Christian only if you do what Christ says.

If you joined the "Girls Who Ride Purple Bikes Every Day Club," what do you think you'd be expected to do? Easy: Ride a purple bike every day, right?

What if you went to the club meetings and talked about how much you love purple bicycles and how you really want to ride one every day for the rest of your life … and then went home on your green scooter? What if people outside the club asked you if you liked purple bikes, and because you were afraid of them making fun of you, you answered, "I guess they're okay, but you know … It's not like I ride one every single day."

You wouldn't be a true club member, would you?

It's kind of the same problem when you say you love God but don't do the things He teaches. It's only when you live like Jesus that you can say you're following Him.

DARE   Walk like Jesus!

TRIPLE-DOG DARE!

1. List three ways you can change to be more like a true follower of Jesus. Ask God to help you make those changes.

2. Pray for a Christian friend who seems to have difficulty following Jesus. (Make sure you feel love and not pride in your heart.)

3. Ask a more mature Christian to pray for your spiritual growth.

Journaling   How did it go? What did you learn?

Get Out of the Darkness

Truth
If you don't love, you're in the dark.

Imagine you were trapped in a cold, dark room for a long, long time with a blindfold over your eyes, and then someone came and rescued you, removing the blindfold and taking you out into the lovely sunshine.

If you kept your eyes tightly shut but smiled and said, "Oh, I love it out here," wouldn't that be foolish? Would you really be in the light again, or would you still be stuck in darkness? As long as your eyes are shut and you can't see the light around you, you might as well be in a dark room!

In the same way, if you say that you're a Christian and that you follow God (the Light of the World), but you keep your spiritual eyes shut tight and don't love the people around you, you're actually still in the darkness caused by sin.

Ask God to help you walk in His light and in His love.

DARE Walk in the light.

TRIPLE-DOG DARE!

1 Think of someone you're angry with. Ask God to forgive you for not loving him or her the way you should.

2 Try walking around your room in complete darkness (spin around twice first). Think about how much worse it is to walk in spiritual darkness.

3 Write the first half of verse 10 on a sticky note and place it by your light switch as a reminder.

Journaling How did it go? What did you learn?

Philemon 1:6

Share Your Faith

Truth *sharing your faith will make it grow.*

When your mom asks you to share a favorite dessert with your little sister or to let someone else use your stuff, it might feel like you're losing out because you're giving something away either forever or for a short time. You know that sharing is good, but you might not always *feel* good about it.

The neat thing about "sharing" your faith—or telling others about your relationship with Jesus and what you believe the Bible teaches—is that it doesn't make you have less faith. It actually increases your faith and makes it stronger.

You could compare it to the tiny planarian worm that, if cut in half, becomes two separate worms! Instead of dying, it actually increases.

When you actively share your faith (that means you look for opportunities to do it—you don't just sit around waiting for opportunities), you will understand what you believe better and better.

DARE Share your faith!

TRIPLE-DOG DARE!

1. Find out if there's an outreach or evangelism project at your church that you could get involved with or be trained for, and then sign up.
2. Practice talking about your faith with your little sister or a friend. Work on the points you're not sure about.
3. Ask a friend if there's anything she'd like you to pray about for her.

Journaling How did it go? What did you learn?

Dead Flies

Truth

It takes only a little foolishness to ruin something good.

If someone handed you a glass of lemonade and said, "By the way, I accidentally spilled a drop of deadly poison into your glass…. But don't worry, it was just a drop," would you drink the lemonade? Hopefully not! Even that one drop would make the lemonade very dangerous.

What if you saw your Sunday school teacher at the mall and overheard her telling an inappropriate joke to a friend? Would you think, *Well, it's just one joke,* or would you lose some of your respect for her?

The Bible warns that even a small act of foolishness can quickly ruin all your hard work at developing a good reputation. If people know you as an honest and respectful girl, make sure you don't spoil that by talking back to your parents, dressing in a way that's not modest, or using language that doesn't honor God, or they will quickly forget the good things.

DARE Watch your reputation!

TRIPLE-DOG DARE!

1 Before you tell a joke, ask yourself if you would tell it to Jesus.

2 If you catch yourself saying, "Once won't matter," think twice about doing or saying whatever you had in mind.

3 Draw a picture of a dead fly in a perfume bottle and tuck it into your pencil case as a reminder of this verse. Draw the same picture on this page if you have time!

Journaling How did it go? What did you learn?

True Obedience

Read Genesis 19:12-26.

About a dozen of the weekend devotionals in *Truth and Dare* are true stories about girls who have had the courage to live out their faith in daring ways. This isn't one of them.

The story of Lot's wife shows us a good example of someone who didn't have faith. Or maybe we should say it's a *bad* example of faith!

God had sent angels to warn Lot and his family to leave their city because He was going to destroy it with fire. The people there had completely rejected God and dishonored Him by doing terrible, sinful things. But Lot's family believed in God, so the angels went to lead them to a safer place.

They actually had to run out of there, which meant they probably didn't have time to pack up all their nice stuff. They just had to get out—and fast! The angels warned them not to stop along the way and, most of all, not to look back.

But Lot's wife looked back. Maybe she was thinking about the nice home they had left behind. Maybe she was leaving some friends she went shopping with. Maybe she was sad that her vegetable garden was going to be burned up. Even though she knew they were leaving a sinful place, a little part of her probably wished they could have stayed.

The punishment for Lot's wife's disobedience was very serious: She lost her life.

This weekend, think about these questions:

1. If you only half obey God, like Lot's wife did (she left the city, but she looked back), are you really being obedient … or are you being disobedient? Explain.

2. When you obey God because you have to and not because you really want to, is that true obedience? Explain.

3. If you love God but also enjoy some activities that don't honor Him, can you really say you love Him? Explain.

4. What behaviors or attitudes do you think God wants you to leave behind? Are you willing to completely obey Him?

Write your answers to the questions here.

Journaling

The best way to _receive_ a hug is to _give_ a hug.

Make Things Right First

Truth — *You can't truly worship God when you feel angry.*

You can probably think of times when you pretended you were happy even though you felt angry or sad inside, or times when you treated someone nicely but only because you *had* to and not because you *wanted* to. If you're talented in acting, you can probably hide your real feelings very well and make people believe you're fine when you're not.

Don't ever forget, though, that you cannot hide your true feelings from God. When you go to church and sing and smile but, at the same time, think mean thoughts about that girl who made fun of you or feel angry because your parents won't let you go to a party next weekend … God knows.

It's impossible to focus on God and worship Him with a pure heart when your thoughts and feelings are wrapped up in a situation with someone else. That's why the Bible says to resolve problems right away—*before* going to church.

DARE   Make things right … right away!

TRIPLE-DOG DARE!

1 If you go to church before fixing a problem with someone, ask God to forgive you and to help you make things right before next Sunday.

2 When you've hurt someone, ask for forgiveness right away. It's easier (and less painful) than doing it later!

3 If you're angry about something that doesn't really matter, be quick to forgive.

Journaling — How did it go? What did you learn?

Luke 9:23-25

Don't Lose Your Life

Truth — *To receive the greatest gift, you have to let go of what you're holding on to.*

Imagine you're holding a bucket full of coins adding up to fifty dollars. Someone comes to you and offers you a bigger bucket full of coins adding up to two thousand dollars. The only way you can take that bucket is to put yours down.

How silly would it be not to take the big gift because you don't want to give up the little bit that you have?

Believe it or not, people do this with life. They say no to God's gift of eternal life in heaven because they don't want to give up the not-so-great stuff the world offers them.

Unless you're willing to give up the things you love more than God, you won't experience the amazing plans God has for you.

DARE — Give your whole life to Jesus.

TRIPLE-DOG DARE!

1 Get rid of any magazines that have messages that don't agree with what God says.

2 Give up a favorite activity today to do something you believe God has been asking you to do for a while.

3 Make two lists: (a) what God has given you, and (b) what God asks of you. You will probably be inspired to do more for Him than you have before!

Journaling — How did it go? What did you learn?

Don't Be a Caterpillar Christian

Truth
Knowing Jesus changes you from the inside out.

Caterpillars and tadpoles have something interesting in common: They don't stay caterpillars and tadpoles. Creepy crawly caterpillars, after spending time rolled up in a cocoon, turn into beautiful butterflies. Swimming tadpoles, as they mature, change their form and turn into hopping frogs.

Imagine if a butterfly thought, *I'm not going to fly among flowers and enjoy their nectar or show people my beauty. I'm going to crawl through dirt like I did when I was a caterpillar.* Wouldn't that be sad? It would still *look* like a butterfly, but it wouldn't be living the life of a butterfly and probably wouldn't survive.

As a Christian, you are also a new creature. The verses in Titus give examples of how Christians should behave, such as respecting and obeying authority, not speaking badly of others, and showing humility.

If you behave like someone who doesn't know Jesus, that's like a butterfly not being a butterfly!

DARE Do what God created you to do!

TRIPLE-DOG DARE!

1. Have you talked behind someone's back lately? Ask God for forgiveness and promise to stop.

2. Write down how you've changed since becoming a Christian. Then list changes you still need to make and ask God to help you.

3. Make a poster with the words of 2 Corinthians 5:17 and a butterfly image.

Journaling How did it go? What did you learn?

What Is He Worth?

Truth
God deserves the best of our worship—not just some of it.

Have you ever won an award? Maybe you came in first in a race or got top prize in an art contest or a talent show. Didn't it feel good to have your talent and hard work recognized?

Even if you've never won an award, you've probably had people thank you for helping them or tell you what a great job you did on a project.

Imagine you had done something really amazing, such as rescuing a drowning child or raising hundreds of dollars for cancer research, and no one noticed, or you just got a simple card saying, "Good job." How would you feel?

Now imagine how God feels as He watches His children—including you—go to church every week. Do you think He gets the worship and honor that He actually deserves or just the little bit that makes people feel like they've done their Christian duty?

God deserves more than a few songs and prayers. He deserves our passionate adoration and a lot more of our time and gifts.

DARE   Worship God the way He deserves.

TRIPLE-DOG DARE!

1 Write a letter to God describing how you think He deserves to be worshipped.

2 Read today's verses before church each Sunday to remind you to worship God sincerely.

3 Are you using your money, time, and talents to worship God? If not, start doing it!

Journaling   How did it go? What did you learn?

The One Inside You

Truth
God is more powerful than the temptations you face.

If your dad or another family member has served in the military, or if you've ever watched a movie or TV show about war, you might have a pretty good idea of what a soldier's uniform looks like. However, one of the most important things that soldiers and even police officers wear is not always visible: a bulletproof vest.

When an enemy attacks, that vest protects some of the most important parts of the body, especially the heart.

You've probably already learned that, as a Christian, you have an invisible Enemy (the Devil) who attacks you with temptations and doubts. It can be discouraging if you feel like you're always being tempted to do things you know you shouldn't do or if you're confused about God and what the Bible teaches.

God's Holy Spirit is like a bulletproof vest—on the *inside*—but so much more than that too! You can trust God because He is stronger than your Enemy ... *and* He loves you enough to help you in hard times!

DARE Don't fear the Enemy!

TRIPLE-DOG DARE!

❶ Start each day by thanking God for watching over you and asking for His protection.

❷ When you're tempted, remember that you don't *have* to give in. Pray for the courage to say no.

❸ Make a bookmark for your planner with the words of this verse. Decorate it with hearts.

Journaling How did it go? What did you learn?

Read Ephesians 6:10-14.

For the next six weekends, we'll be looking at the different pieces of armor that God provides us with. The first one is the "belt of truth."

What do you use a belt for? Nowadays most people wear belts to hold up their pants or, especially for girls, as a fashion accessory. But in Bible times, a soldier's belt was an important part of his armor, or his protective gear.

A soldier's belt protected his middle section, but it also kept his clothing near his body so that it didn't flap around and get in his way while he was fighting. It probably also kept his breastplate (which we'll look at next weekend) in place and gave him a place to keep his weapon.

As a Christian, when you know God's truth (by studying the Bible) and keep it close to you in your heart, you won't "flap" around in confusion when you hear different messages about God. The truth will support you and make you strong in your beliefs.

Most of us would never see an armadillo except at the zoo, unless you live in the southcentral part of the United States (for example, Texas), where one type of armadillo lives, or in Central or South America, where there are twenty kinds of armadillos … including one that's called a pink fairy!

Did you know that armadillo means "little armored one" in Spanish? What a perfect name for a small animal that is covered by a protective shell.

This weekend, take some time to read up about armadillos. You'll learn all kinds of interesting facts about them.… And you might find them kind of cute, too!

Why are we talking about armadillos? Because their protective shells can help us think about the "armor of God" that we can wear as Christians to protect us from the Enemy's attacks. The armadillo never removes its armor.… And neither should you!

When you do your *Truth and Dare* devotions every morning, you're starting off your day by putting on the belt of truth! Just make sure you don't take it off later by taking your mind off what God has taught you. You don't want to leave yourself unprotected against the Enemy's lies.

How is wearing a seat belt also a good example of putting on the "belt of truth"? Write your thoughts in the journaling section.

Tip: Whenever you buckle up in a car or put on a belt, try to remember this lesson and ask God to help you put on the belt of truth.

Journaling

Get Ready for a New Week!

Happiness isn't about doing what you like, but about liking what you do.

Love Others, Love God

Truth You can't say you love god if you don't love others.

Do you think of yourself as a liar?

Like anyone else, you've probably told at least a few lies in your life.… But unless you have the bad habit of lying many times a day, you probably wouldn't call yourself a *liar*.

Now think about whether there is anyone—it could be your brother, someone at church, or even a teacher—you secretly hate or, to put it another way, really don't love at all.

These verses remind us of a very hard truth: If you say you love God but have unloving feelings and thoughts about someone … God sees you as a liar. Why? Because God *is* love, and when He lives in us, He fills our hearts with love for Him and for others.

If you're not feeling that love, it could be a big clue that there's something not right in your relationship with God. Take time to pray about it today.

DARE Love the way God does.

TRIPLE-DOG DARE!

1 Honestly tell God about anyone you're having trouble loving and ask for His help to start loving her (or him).

2 Think of a friend you haven't been nice to lately. Write her a card saying that you appreciate her … and that you love her.

3 Read 1 John 4:7–21 slowly and thoughtfully.

Journaling How did it go? What did you learn?

Trust Your Creator

Truth *god knew what He was doing when He made you.*

If you're like most girls, you've looked in the mirror more than once and wished you could change something about yourself—your hair color, your height, your skin color, your teeth, your toes, or your clothes. Maybe you've wished that you could sing beautifully or run faster, that your family were richer, or that your sister didn't laugh so loud.

Humans have never been completely satisfied with the way God created them or the situations He allowed them to be born into.

Although "everyone does it," this sort of wishing doesn't please God.

It's like planning the most amazing birthday party for your best friend with the prettiest decorations, lots of gifts, her favorite cake, great music, her best friends, and really fun activities … and when she arrives she asks, "Why did you buy pink napkins instead of purple? And why is the party so early? I wanted to sleep in today!"

If you would feel hurt by her ungratefulness, imagine how God feels when you question the way He created you.

DARE Thank God for making you you.

TRIPLE-DOG DARE!

1. Write the words of Isaiah 64:8 inside a thank-you card. Tuck it into your school locker as a reminder to thank God for creating you the way you are.

2. Tell your mom she's beautiful! (Moms sometimes worry about how they look too.)

3. Ask God to forgive you for the times you've grumbled about your life.

Journaling How did it go? What did you learn?

Payback Time

Truth
god has a different way of paying back.

"I owe you one." You may hear someone say that to a friend who did a favor or helped out in some way. It seems fair, doesn't it, that if someone does something nice for you, you do something nice back? For example, if a friend gives you a birthday gift, you'll probably give her one on her birthday.

But what do you do when someone does something *bad* toward you? If a friend hits you, do you hit right back? Or if someone at school makes fun of you, aren't you tempted to make fun of her too?

The Bible teaches that we need to have a different attitude. When someone treats you badly, your reaction should not be to treat him or her just as badly. Instead, you should find a way to be a blessing in that person's life and show God's love.

Not only will that stop the fighting right away (it always takes two!), but God will also bless you for obeying Him.

DARE   Repay evil with good.

TRIPLE-DOG DARE!

1 When a friend hurts you, take five seconds to ask God to help you react with love.

2 Pray for someone who always seems mean. He or she probably needs to experience God's love.

3 If a friend asks why you're repaying evil with good, explain how God set the example by dying on the cross for our sins.

Journaling   How did it go? What did you learn?

1 Peter 5:8

Watch Out for the Lion

Truth *The Devil never takes a break!*

What's your favorite animal at the zoo? A lot of girls enjoy seeing cute or funny animals such as pandas, penguins, giraffes, zebras, and monkeys.

What about lions? They're very beautiful animals that are great to watch … when you feel safe outside their cage. Male lions, with their fluffy manes, look soft and cuddly, but everyone knows that they're not called "king of the jungle" for nothing. Powerful, fast, and very dangerous when they're hungry, wild lions would not make great pets!

The Bible compares the Devil to a hungry and ferocious lion that is wandering around the wilderness looking for its next meal. Just as a zebra has to constantly watch out to make sure it doesn't become the lion's next victim, you have to be careful to stay far away from the Devil and the temptations he will send your way.

Ask God to give you the self-control and wisdom that you need.

DARE Watch out for the Enemy.

TRIPLE-DOG DARE!

1 Write down and memorize this verse and repeat it to yourself during the week.

2 After today's devotion, take five minutes to ask God to help you tell the difference between good and evil and to protect you from temptation.

3 Share this verse with a friend who is struggling to make good decisions and encourage her to pray as you did.

Journaling How did it go? What did you learn?

Choose the Better Thing

Truth *A good thing might not always be the best thing.*

You probably do many good things each day, such as make your bed, set the dinner table, help your mom wash dishes, play with your baby sister, and do your homework before watching TV.

It doesn't take a lot of wisdom to know that all those things are better than stealing, disobeying your mom, being rude, and telling lies.

The choice between good and bad is usually simple, but the choice between good and *best* can be more difficult and yet still important. Mary and Martha show us a good example of how they both did *good* things—there was nothing wrong with Martha wanting to serve Jesus—but only one of them chose the *best* thing, which was to spend time with Jesus and learn from Him.

You may not be doing your very best for God if you think it's enough to just make a small effort. Time to change that!

DARE Give God your 100 percent effort.

TRIPLE-DOG DARE!

1 Don't just *attend* church on Sunday. Connect with God by paying attention and worshipping Him with your heart.

2 When you can choose between two chores, do the one that will be most helpful for your family—not the one that's easier for *you*.

3 Ask God to help you be more like Mary and choose the *best* things.

Journaling How did it go? What did you learn?

Read Ephesians 6:14 and 1 Samuel 24.

King Saul had been jealous of David for a long time and kept trying to find ways to get rid of him or kill him. Saul was stubborn and disobedient to God, while David honored God. So when David had a chance to kill Saul, don't you think it would have been fair for him to do it? His friends thought so!

But David didn't do what would have made his own life safer. Because he loved God, David wanted to do what was *right* and not what was *easy*. When Saul realized how close he had been to dying and how David put God's will before his own, he was touched and his respect for David grew. He thanked David for sparing his life and then blessed him.

David's righteousness protected him, and that takes us back to the spiritual armor of God that we need to put on every day. When we make righteousness—doing the right thing in God's eyes—our priority, it's like putting on a breastplate that protects our heart and all the important organs in our middle area. We become more able to resist the Devil's temptations to sin.

Got More Time?

With your family or a few friends, make up a story that shows how righteousness can protect a Christian. Find a small audience and act out the story as a play (or just do it for fun without an audience). Go all out with costumes and props! If you're really daring, ask your Sunday school teacher if you can present your play during class one day. After you do the play, share the lesson from today's devotional.

journaling

Dear god, this week help me not to love anything more than 1 love you. Amen

Putting Up with Put-Downs

Truth

Others may laugh at your faith, but God will bless you for it.

No one likes being made fun of or insulted, especially when you've done nothing wrong. It's one thing to have classmates laugh at you because the teacher caught you passing notes to a friend—you kind of deserve that, don't you?—but it feels different when they make fun of you for going to church every Sunday or praying before you eat your lunch.

Don't be discouraged (or surprised!) when you're trying to live for God and people give you a hard time. Instead, thank God for giving you the strength to remain faithful to Him.

The Bible says not to worry about being insulted for being a Christian. God will see your faith and courage and bless you for it. You may not see that reward right away, or even ever, because sometimes God's blessings are not obvious, but you can trust God to keep His promises!

DARE
Stand up for Jesus, even when you're insulted.

TRIPLE-DOG DARE!

1. When you're eating in public, close your eyes and bow your head to pray first, no matter who's around.
2. When someone makes fun of you for going to church, invite her to go with you to check it out for herself.
3. Look up the lyrics of "I Stand for You" by the Christian group Tree63. Can you make that your prayer?

Journaling
How did it go? What did you learn?

Trying to Fit In?

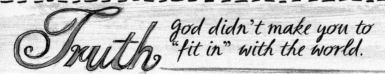

Truth — god didn't make you to "fit in" with the world.

Have you ever tried to eat ice cream with a toothbrush? Do you use your Christmas tree as a bed? Would you swim wearing a fluffy dog costume?

Silly questions? Yes! It's ridiculous to try to use things in ways they weren't designed to be used. Not only does it make you look foolish, but it also doesn't accomplish anything. In fact, as in the example of swimming with a dog costume on, it can even be dangerous.

You may be tempted to try to fit in with the world around you. Peer pressure can be very strong. You may feel like you should dress like other girls, listen to the same music, say the same words, and do the same things. But the Bible warns that we shouldn't "conform" (try to fit in) to the pattern of the world.

Instead, we should ask God to change our hearts and minds so that the things we want are the same as the things He wants for us … *good* things.

DARE — Let God change you.

TRIPLE-DOG DARE!

1. Stop comparing yourself with others. Instead, thank God for His special plan for your life.
2. Avoid listening to non-Christian music. Instead, fill your mind with worship and praise songs.
3. When you shop, look for clothes that will help people respect you … not just what's trendy.

Journaling — How did it go? What did you learn?

Holy Hands

Truth
god wants you to have holy spiritual "hands."

If you were going to visit the president of the United States, the Queen of England, or someone else you really admire and respect, would you go with beat-up running shoes, a stained shirt, and dirty fingernails? Probably not!

If you happened to be in a bad mood that day, would you let this special person see it? Would you be so distracted by whatever was bothering you that you didn't pay attention to the celebrity you were with? I didn't think so.

Strangely, people often go to church to worship God—to *meet* with Him—without preparing themselves. If you think about it, God not only sees what we look and act like on the outside, but He also sees our hearts so we should put more thought into our preparations for church than anything else.

When this verse talks about "holy hands," it doesn't mean the hands you wash in the sink. It means that however you worship God, you should do it with a clean heart and without any anger toward others.

DARE   Get ready for worship.

TRIPLE-DOG DARE!

1 Before going to church, confess any angry or distracting thoughts to God and ask Him to help you focus on Him.

2 During worship, don't look around at your friends. Pay attention to the words and sing the songs like a prayer.

3 Make a habit of saying a quick prayer—about anything!—whenever you wash your hands.

Journaling   How did it go? What did you learn?

So You're Young ...

Truth *You're never too young to set a good example for others.*

When you think of your role models, are they usually people who are older than you? Whom do you look up to as a good example of someone who follows Christ? Your Sunday school teacher, youth leader, pastor, mom ...?

It's normal (and wise) to follow the example of those who are more mature, but you have probably met or heard of kids younger than you who have made you think, *Wow! That's impressive. I wish I was that brave (or creative or kind or smart).*

You may not realize it but you, too, can set an example for others ... not just younger children but even older teens and adults. When you make a commitment to obey and follow God, people will notice and respect your maturity. Even adults who have lost some of their passion for God may think, *Hey, that's impressive. I wish I was that brave in my faith!*

You don't need to wait until you've grown up to be a good influence.

DARE Set a good example!

TRIPLE-DOG DARE!

1 Instead of playing computer or board games with your friends, do Bible quizzes to encourage each other to learn more about the Bible.

2 Write thank-you notes to your Christian role models and ask them to pray for you to be a good example too.

3 Offer to read a Bible story to your little sister or brother, or to a child at your church.

Journaling How did it go? What did you learn?

Contentment

Truth
Happiness comes from being close to god ... not owning stuff.

Flip through just about any magazine and you will come across advertisements about all the things you "need" to make your life better. Those designer shoes will turn you into the coolest girl at school, this toothpaste will give you a prettier smile, and those gel pens will change the way you write!

You may say you don't believe all that, but honestly, don't most of us give in to the influences around us to buy buy buy, get get get, have have have? And are we really happier because we have more stuff or more money or more popularity? Not really.

The Bible teaches that when we focus on being godly—more and more like God in our character—and are satisfied with what we have, that's when we start to feel truly wealthy and happy. That's when we realize that when we have God, we have everything, but when we don't have God, we have nothing!

DARE   To be happy, be godly.

TRIPLE-DOG DARE!

1 Next time your friends want to go shopping, suggest that you do random acts of kindness instead.

2 Ask your parents if you can subscribe to a Christian magazine or buy some Christian books.

3 Ask your mom to help you go through your stuff and choose good items that you can give away to a charity for people who need them more than you do.

Journaling   How did it go? What did you learn?

Read Ephesians 6:15.

Say the word *shoes* and most girls (and older women) will suddenly become very interested in what you're talking about. Girls really like shoes! And it's not just the "girlie girls"—whether you're sporty, artistic, a bookworm, or a nature lover, you're probably at least a little picky about what kinds of shoes you wear.

Shoes can tell people a lot about us and what we're interested or involved in. But besides making fashion statements, shoes serve a purpose! We wear different kinds of shoes for different activities and in different situations. For example:

Would you wear sandals during a snowstorm?

Would you wear cowboy boots while swimming?

Would you wear ballet shoes while playing basketball?

Would you wear bright yellow rain boots at a wedding?

Would you wear flippers while tap dancing?

The right shoes at the right time not only protect our feet, but they also help us do an activity properly.

In the Bible's description of the spiritual armor a Christian needs to wear, it talks about our feet and says they should be wearing "readiness." What does that mean?

Just as a soldier's combat boots protect his feet and help him to march on rough ground, the gospel (the good news about Jesus that we read about in the Bible) gives us peace, which helps us to stand firm even in tough spiritual battles. It also gives us the confidence to reach out to others with the truth about Jesus and His love for them.

When your spiritual "feet" are standing firm on God's Word, you'll be ready to face the Enemy's attacks!

Tip: Whenever you put on your shoes, try to remember this lesson and ask God to help your spiritual feet to be ready for battle.

Got More Time?

In your journal, draw a line down the middle of the page. On the left side, list some ways the Devil sometimes tempts you or tries to discourage you in your Christian life. Then, next to each one, in the right column, write how standing firm on God's Word can help you be ready the next time you face the same attack.

Journaling

It's better to be hated for doing the right thing than liked for doing the wrong thing.

Created to Do Good Works

Truth

God created you with a special purpose: to do good works for Him.

If you enjoy crafts, inventing, or cooking, you probably know ahead of time—or at least before you finish—what your creation is for. If you sew a tote bag, it's to hold your stuff. If you make a kite, it's to fly it on a windy day. If you bake cookies, it's to have a yummy treat.

It wouldn't make any sense—and it would be a big waste!—to randomly glue objects together with no plan. You might end up with something that looks interesting, but it probably wouldn't be useful at all.

When God created you, He had a plan and a purpose for your life. He designed you to have a relationship with Him and to share His love with others. When you do what you were created to do, that's when you experience true joy!

DARE Do good works!

TRIPLE-DOG DARE!

1 Every morning, ask God to help you live according to His purpose for you and to show you good works you can do.

2 Make a habit of asking your family if you can help with anything. Even chores can be good works!

3 Ask your parents to help you look up "random acts of kindness" on the Internet for lots of ideas of how you can do good for others.

Journaling How did it go? What did you learn?

1 Thessalonians 2:2

Dare to Tell the Gospel

Truth *God can give you the courage to tell others about His love.*

If you live in the United States or Canada, you don't really have to feel afraid of telling others that you're a Christian. Sure, you may have friends—or even teachers—who don't respect your faith and either make fun of you or try to convince you that what you believe is wrong.

However, many of the first Christians in Bible times suffered because of their beliefs. And there are Christians all around the world today who live in fear because if they're caught having a Bible or praying or going to church, they can be tortured, sent to prison, or even killed. But that doesn't stop them from standing up for their beliefs!

When you put your trust completely in God, you'll find the courage to tell others about Jesus and how He died so that they can be saved from their sins. In other words, you'll care about them so much that you'll be willing to take some risks!

DARE Tell others the good news about Jesus!

TRIPLE-DOG DARE!

1 Check if there are any mission, evangelism, or outreach projects (or training) at your church that you can participate in.

2 Practice talking about your faith with a Christian friend or one of your parents.

3 If your church has brochures or invitations, give them to a few classmates. Or make your own invitations!

Journaling How did it go? What did you learn?

Stop Grumbling!

Truth   *Complaining hurts God.*

Guess what one of God's pet peeves is. Lying? Cheating? Stealing? He does hate all those sins, but there's something else the Bible warns us about … something most of us do a lot but don't think of as terrible.

Have you ever muttered something under your breath when your mom asked you to turn off the TV and clean your room or do your homework? Have you ever whined, "It's not *fair!*" when someone got something you wanted? Have you ever been in trouble and said, "*She* started it"? Have you ever sat down at the table and wrinkled your nose because you had to eat something you didn't like?

When we complain and whine and grumble, God is not happy. In the Old Testament, many people were punished harshly for complaining.

Grumbling tells God we're not thankful. It says that we think we deserve better than what we have when, actually, none of us deserve all the good things God blesses us with.

DARE   Break the habit of complaining.

TRIPLE-DOG DARE!

1 The next time you're tempted to grumble, come up with something positive or funny about the situation instead.

2 For each time that you catch yourself complaining, find two things to thank someone for.

3 Instead of complaining about a situation, think of a good way to solve the problem.

Journaling   How did it go? What did you learn?

Treat Your Parents Right

Truth — Your parents deserve your respect.

Parents! Sometimes you love them so much you can't imagine life without them. Other times … Well, we all know what those other times feel like.

The cool thing about this challenge from God is that it comes with a reward if you obey it. The Bible teaches us that God promises to bless us for honoring our parents. That's how important this commandment is!

You may not always like what your parents do or say—that's normal. But God wants you to treat them with respect, to obey them, and to love them, even when it's hard. And He wants you to do it from your heart! That means—remember yesterday's dare?—no grumbling, not even on the inside.

No matter what your relationship with your parents is like, God can help you to make it better.

DARE — Wow your parents with your love!

TRIPLE-DOG DARE!

1. When you see your mom or dad after school or when they get home from work, ask them how their day was before you talk about yours … and really *listen!*
2. Do something you know your parents expect you to do … *before* they have to remind you.
3. Give your dad or mom a big hug and thank him or her for at least three things.

Journaling — How did it go? What did you learn?

_____
_____
_____
_____
_____
_____
_____
_____

You're Not the Only One

Truth

Even your worst temptation is something others have faced.

You may be tempted by things that make you think, *What is* wrong *with me? Why do I feel curious about trying that? If anyone knew, they'd think I was horrible!*

Believe it or not, *everyone* has felt that way. The Devil knows how to make you feel so ashamed of the things you're tempted by that it keeps you from asking someone you trust to pray for you or to help you fight that temptation.

Whether you're tempted to steal, cheat on a test, starve yourself to be thinner, or look at sexual material on the Internet (yes, even girls are tempted by that), don't feel like you're alone.

The temptations might be strong and awful, but God promised that He will help you overcome them if you ask Him. He's there for you … and so are the people who love you.

DARE   Turn to God when you're tempted.

TRIPLE-DOG DARE!

1 Talk to your mom or a Christian adult you trust about a temptation you're struggling with. Keeping it a secret will only make it worse.

2 Memorize today's verse and repeat it to yourself throughout the day.

3 List all the things that tempt you. Confess them to God and ask Him for help to say no the next time you face these same struggles.

Journaling   How did it go? What did you learn?

Read Ephesians 6:16.

How much do you know about turtles … besides the fact … that they … are very… very … very … s … l … o … w …?

Did you know that …

- turtles that live on land are called tortoises?
- there are many types of turtles, divided into twelve main biological "families"?
- some freshwater turtles have soft shells that are more like leather?
- large leatherback turtles that live in the sea can weigh over one thousand pounds?
- some turtles can live over one hundred years?
- catching sea turtles is against the law?
- only one out of every thousand baby sea turtles lives to be an adult turtle?
- turtles have beaks instead of teeth?
- a turtle's shell is part of its skeleton?
- a turtle's shell is not one piece but is made up of around sixty bones covered by "plates" called *scutes?*

Turtle shells are a bit like your fingernails. They're hard enough to protect what's under them, but a turtle can still feel pressure put on its shell. A turtle's shell protects it from many dangers: predators (enemies), falling branches, and anything else that the turtle wouldn't be able to hurry away from because of how slow it moves.

Sometimes, as Jesus' followers, we may not be able to think fast or move fast when our Enemy, the Devil, attacks us with temptations, difficulties, and confusing thoughts. That's why we need the shield of faith as part of our spiritual armor. Just as a turtle knows that its shell can protect it, you can have the confidence that when you are God's child and trust Him with your life, He will protect you.

What are some ways the Devil may attack you? (We've included a few suggestions.)

Telling you God doesn't love you.

Tempting you to disobey your parents.

Distracting you during church so that you stop listening.

_____

_____

_____

_____

_____

This weekend, make sure you carry your "shield of faith" wherever you go. Whenever you feel an attack coming your way, remember that your faith is in God. And 1 John 4:4 tells us that "the one who is in you [God] is greater than the one who is in the world." In other words, as long as you're on the right side of your shield, the Enemy can't hurt you!

Got More Time?

Ask your parents if you can visit a pet store that sells turtles so that you can have a close-up look at their shells. If the store owner lets you, gently touch a turtle's shell to see what it feels like. (Be sure to wash your hands afterward!)

People won't care how much you know
until they know how much you care.

1 John 3:16-18

Do Love

Truth — *Love is an action ... not just a feeling.*

When you hear the word *love,* what's the first thing you think of? Hearts, kisses, flowers?

Many people think of love as something you feel toward someone else—warm fuzziness deep inside, admiration, appreciation, or happiness whenever you think of her or him.

It's easy to forget that *love* isn't just a noun. It's also a verb ... just like *support, encourage, help,* and *protect* are. Jesus gave us the best example of how to love when He gave up His life so that we could be saved from our sins. He showed us that true love is putting aside your own wants and comforts for the good of someone else.

Like Jesus, if we say that we love someone, we should be able to prove that it's true.

DARE — Show the love you feel through what you do.

TRIPLE-DOG DARE!

1 Today, do a chore that would take some pressure off your parents. Thank God for them while you do your work.

2 Give up your favorite TV show to play with your little brother or to call your grandmother just to see how she's doing.

3 Get up fifteen minutes early tomorrow and spend that extra time reading all of 1 John 3. Ask God to help you put your love into action.

Journaling — How did it go? What did you learn?

No Idol

Truth *Nothing and no one should have a higher place than God in your life.*

Some of the most popular TV shows are talent competitions that sometimes turn ordinary kids and adults into celebrities. These performers can suddenly have thousands of fans who look up to them and actually go a little crazy over them!

It shouldn't surprise anyone that a few of these shows have the word *idol* in their titles because celebrities are very often worshipped by the people who admire them.

Maybe you're not the type to idolize another person. What else do you think girls worship—or give too much priority to—these days? What about clothes and shoes, cell phones and other gadgets, TV and movies, hanging out with friends, or talking about boys?

If any of these things take more of your attention than God does, you might have a problem with idols.

DARE Make God number one in your life.

TRIPLE-DOG DARE!

1 List the ten most important things or people in your life. If God isn't at the top (be honest!), plan how you can change that.

2 Whatever your favorite activity is, try to give it up for one day (or longer) and use that time to do something that honors God.

3 Get rid of anything you have that you know God wouldn't be pleased with.

Journaling How did it go? What did you learn?

Say No to Temptation

Truth — *Fighting is good ... when it's against temptation.*

Remember when you were little and you imagined monsters lived in your closet or under your bed? Did you put cookies and milk out for them ... or did you turn on the light really fast so they would disappear?

Temptations are kind of like little monsters. They bug your mind and try to get you to do things you know are wrong. When you don't ask God right away to help you say no to those temptations but instead think about them and wonder if they're really so bad, it's as if you're feeding them. What do you think would happen to a little monster if you fed it? Right! It would grow.

When you resist (say no to) temptation, you can live the good life God wants you to live. And your life can be a great influence on the people around you, helping them to see God's love and power.

DARE Starve those temptation-monsters!

TRIPLE-DOG DARE!

1. Write down your temptations and then, while asking God for help, rip the paper into tiny pieces. This can help you remember that you don't *want* to sin!
2. When you feel tempted, call someone just to chat to help you forget about the temptation.
3. Try saying "NO!" out loud when you're tempted (if no one else is around, of course).

Journaling — How did it go? What did you learn?

1 peter 3:3-4

Beautiful You

Truth
Inner beauty is worth more—and lasts longer—than outward beauty.

Long hair, straight hair, wavy hair, hairy legs, chubby legs, skinny legs, clear skin, dry skin, freckles … *ack!* We girls obsess a little when we look in the mirror, don't we?

Some of us wish we looked different, maybe like someone we admire. We think people would like us better if we had softer hair or bigger eyes or straighter teeth.

The truth is that most people you meet are really interested in your *inner* beauty. Your kindness, your cheerful attitude, and your honesty are just a few examples of loveliness that will always shine through no matter how you look on the outside!

Know what else? Unlike all the beauty products many girls spend money on, what makes you beautiful on the inside—God's love for you and the love you have for others—is free, and it works on every girl, every time!

DARE
Work on being more beautiful on the inside instead of on the outside for one day.

TRIPLE-DOG DARE!

1. Instead of telling your friend you like her new top, tell her what makes her special on the inside.

2. Get rid of whatever makes you think too much about how you look, such as celebrity magazines.

3. Don't buy that lip gloss or necklace you don't really need. Use the money you saved to surprise your mom with a little gift.

Journaling
How did it go? What did you learn?

Why Lie?

Truth god wants you to be truthful ... all the time.

Think of a time you told a lie. Was it because you did something wrong and were afraid of being punished? Or was it because you were being bullied and you just said whatever you knew would make the other person stop bothering you?

Sometimes we don't exactly *lie,* but we might try to hide the truth. For example, you may feel shy about telling your friends that you go to church, or you might not admit to your parents when you disobey them. Maybe you don't speak up when someone misbehaves because you don't want to be a tattletale. Telling half the truth is a lot like telling half a lie.... It's still dishonest.

God wants you to trust Him and have the courage to always say what's true and right. There may be consequences you don't like sometimes, but God will be with you and He'll bless you for being honest.

DARE   Tell the truth!

TRIPLE-DOG DARE!

1 Make a list of lies you've told lately. Ask God to forgive you for each one and then promise to be more truthful from now on.

2 If a friend asks you to lie for her so she won't get into trouble, tell her about your promise to God.

3 The next time you do something that would make your parents angry, tell them right away instead of hoping they won't find out.

ourNaling How did it go? What did you learn?

Don't Forget Your Helmet!

Read Ephesians 6:17.

For how many of the helmets above can you identify its purpose (or what it was used for in the past)? (The answers are at the end of the book.)

Why do people wear helmets in so many different jobs and sports and other activities? Our heads need protection because a lot of our important functions happen up there! Not only do we use our heads to see, smell, hear, eat, breathe, and talk, but that's where our brains are…. And our brains are like the computers of our bodies, or the control centers. If our heads are injured, we can face many problems and difficulties.

Even sun hats and wooly caps protect us from the hot sun and from chilly winter weather.

As Christians, we face a spiritual Enemy who wants to attack our "heads" … our minds. The Devil will try to confuse you with lies about God, lies about yourself, and lies about heaven and hell. He doesn't want you to have a relationship with God or to be saved, so depending on what your weaknesses and fears are, he'll try to convince you that these *false messages* are true …

- God doesn't love you.
- You're good enough the way you are and don't need to be a Christian.
- You could never be good enough to go to heaven, so you shouldn't even try.
- All religions are pretty much the same in the end, so it doesn't matter what you believe.
- No one should tell you how to live your life, not even your parents.
- You can't really believe the Bible because it's an old book written by some religious nuts.

That's why the Bible tells us to put on the "helmet of salvation." When you study God's Word and know it well, it's like wearing a helmet that protects you from doubting what you know about God.

Tip: Whenever you put on your bicycle helmet or any kind of hat, try to remember this lesson and ask God to help you put on the helmet of salvation.

Journaling

Wishing you were someone else is
a waste of who you are.

1 peter 5:7

You Can Trust Him

Truth *You can trust God with all your problems.*

Have you ever played that trusting game where someone stands behind you with her arms stretched forward and you have to let yourself fall backward and trust that she will catch you? If the person is standing not too far from you, it's easy to believe that she can catch you.... But it's a little scarier if she's standing farther back. You might stumble a bit, feeling unsure that the other person will actually catch you.

It also makes a big difference who the "catcher" is. If it's your dad, you might not worry at all—not only because he's big and strong, but because you trust that he'd never let you get hurt. But if it's a young friend, you might feel more nervous.

In today's verse, God promises that you can trust Him. He's bigger and stronger than your dad, and He loves you more than you can even imagine.

DARE Give all your worries to Jesus.

TRIPLE-DOG DARE!

1 List everything that you're worried about right now. Ask God for peace as you trust Him to take care of everything.

2 Play the trusting game with a friend or someone in your family and then share today's verse and lesson.

3 Write a cheery note or card to someone who's discouraged and add today's verse in colorful letters.

Journaling How did it go? What did you learn?

Don't Stop Praying

Truth *God wants you to talk with Him all day long.*

A long time ago, girls could only chat with their friends whenever they saw each other in person. Then along came telephones, email, chat rooms, Facebook, text messages, Skype, and so many other ways to communicate that you can talk with your friends all day, almost wherever you are.

So it shouldn't surprise us that we can connect with God all day too—and we don't have to worry about technical problems or phone bills!

If you're a Christian, that means you have a relationship with God. Relationships need communication, which is why God wants you to talk to Him every chance you get. If you talk to God only for a minute or two every day, how are you going to grow closer to Him?

God loves you and cares about what's bothering you, and He also wants to hear how much you love and appreciate Him. Remember: You can tell Him anything!

DARE Put God at the top of your friends list!

TRIPLE-DOG DARE!

1. Before you call your best friend for a long chat, pray. Spend time telling God about your day, asking for forgiveness, and thanking Him for blessing you.
2. Whenever you're standing in line, pray for the person in front of you.
3. Every time something makes you smile, thank God for it.

Journaling How did it go? What did you learn?

Pray for People in Authority

Truth *God wants you to pray for your leaders.*

You probably don't spend a whole lot of time thinking about the president (or prime minister or king) of your country. Politics can seem complicated and boring, and even a lot of adults don't like to get involved.

It's important to remember, however, that the leaders of your country, your city, your school, and so on make a lot of important decisions that affect your everyday life. If they make bad decisions, you might lose the peace or safety or comfort that you live in.

That's why it's important to pray for your leaders. God allowed them to be in the positions they're in, and He wants you to be thankful for the work they do and to pray for their needs. If we all supported our leaders in that way, they probably would do an even better job!

DARE Ask God to be with the leaders in your life.

TRIPLE-DOG DARE!

1 This week, make a point of praying for the principal of your school.

2 Ask God to touch the hearts of the leaders of countries where Christians are treated badly.

3 Send a thank-you card to your mayor for the work he or she does and say that you're praying for him or her. (Don't forget to pray!)

Journaling How did it go? What did you learn?

What Are You Wearing?

Truth *You can please God with your clothes.*

Isn't it great when summer finally comes around and you can spend more time outdoors?

One problem with summertime, though, is what to wear. Because it's hot, a lot of girls and women start pulling out their shorts, tank tops, short skirts, and sundresses. Suddenly we start to see a lot of skin, and sometimes it's embarrassing!

The Bible teaches us, as Christian girls, to be modest. That means our clothing should not attract too much attention to us, especially the *wrong* kind of attention where people are tempted to look at our bodies instead of our faces. (Remember that too-tight clothes can be inappropriate too, so think of modesty all year round.)

When you dress in a way that's stylish but modest, it shows that you honor God and that you respect others enough to think about how your outfits make them feel.

DARE Dress with care.

TRIPLE-DOG DARE!

1. As you get dressed, think of everyone who will see you during the day. Are you showing more than they should see? If so, cover up!

2. At church, make sure your clothes don't distract people from worshipping. Church isn't about you.… It's about God.

3. Do you think more about how you look than about your relationship with God? Start changing that today. The closer you get to God, the wiser you'll become about how to dress.

Journaling How did it go? What did you learn?

Stay Away!

Truth
You need to stay far away from bad influences.

Although the New Testament was written nearly two thousand years ago, it describes the world we live in today so accurately you'd think you were reading a new book.

The Bible warns us that, as time goes on, most people—even the religious ones—will become more and more selfish and disrespectful. People might pretend to love God or give the impression that they are good, but deep inside they will be looking out only for themselves.

It might seem like a harsh thing to say, but the apostle Paul told Timothy, a younger believer, to have *nothing* to do with such people. He didn't mean that Timothy should hate unbelievers or not share God's love with them but that Timothy had to guard himself from being influenced by the evil around him.

God wants you, too, to be careful about whom you spend your time with.

DARE
Try to be different from the non-Christians instead of trying to be like them.

TRIPLE-DOG DARE!

1 Walk away from situations you know Jesus wouldn't want you to be in, even if it will make you seem "uncool."

2 Don't watch movies that make sin look like it's not a big deal.

3 If you have friends who dishonor God and the Bible's teachings through their words and behavior, ask God to help you end those relationships.

Journaling
How did it go? What did you learn?

Read Ephesians 6:17-18.

Have you ever participated in a sword drill at Sunday school or camp? It's a fun competition that tests your knowledge of Bible verses. Why is it called a *sword drill?* That name comes from this weekend's Bible reading, which tells us that the final piece of spiritual armor that God gives us is His Word. This piece of armor isn't armor, actually.... It's a weapon!

Earlier in this book we talked about how Jesus fought against the Devil's temptations (in Luke 4) by remembering Bible verses that destroyed the lies the Devil tried to use. God's Word became like a sword for Jesus! (Hey, notice how "word" and "sword" are different only by one letter? That can help you remember that your *sword* is God's *Word*.) And the truth of the Bible can be your sword too when you have to fight the Enemy's attacks.

Your Turn

This weekend, instead of playing a board game or computer game, get your family or friends to try out this sword drill with you. If you can't find anyone to play with you, you can do it on your own using a watch or clock to time yourself. It won't be as easy, so use your creativity to make it fun.

If you play this as a group, keep score by giving a point to whomever finds each verse the fastest.

Each person needs his or her own Bible to play. Everyone has to hold the Bible up in the air between turns, holding it from the spine. No one is allowed to start looking up a verse until you yell "Go!" When someone finds a verse he or she has to stand up right away and start reading it loud and clear.

Here are ten Bible verses you can use for the first round of your game (all of them are from devotionals in this book).

Luke 12:25	John 14:6
James 1:17	Proverbs 1:7
Micah 6:8	Romans 6:23
Psalm 118:1	Matthew 11:28
John 12:26	1 John 4:4

Got More Time?

If you play alone, test yourself three or four times during the weekend. Every time you do it, you should be finding the verses faster, which means you're getting to know your Bible better. You may even be able to remember what each verse says before finding it!

If you played as a group, play one or two more rounds but, instead of using the verses in the list, open this book to a random page and read out the Bible passage on that day. Keep playing for as long as everyone wants to. Think of a funny prize or reward for the winner.

Journaling

No one can ruin your day
without your permission.

Finish What You Started

Truth — *It's easy to get distracted from following Jesus.*

Did you ever start a fun craft project but then get bored before you finished? Have you ever stopped reading a book after a few chapters? When you clean up your room, do you always leave one thing out instead of putting it in its place?

A lot of people have what's called *good intentions* to do things. But somewhere along the way they give up or get distracted by something else.

This bad habit, if it's not worked on, can creep into our lives as Christians too. You may plan to read your Bible every morning but then stop after a week. You may promise God to be more obedient, to pray more, or to tell your friends about Him … but then forget all about it.

With God's help, you can finish the things that He wants you to do!

DARE Keep your promises to God.

TRIPLE-DOG DARE!

1. The next time it's your turn to do the dishes, take the time to put them all away.
2. Read Hebrews 10:35–39. If you've broken any promises you made to God, ask Him to forgive you.
3. Make a list of five important things (or people) you think you should pray for and see how many days you can go without forgetting to pray for them.

Journaling — How did it go? What did you learn?

Daniel 1:3-17

Dare to Be Different

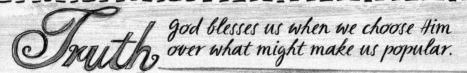 **Truth** *God blesses us when we choose Him over what might make us popular.*

Some people think only wimps become Christians, but Daniel's story is just one example in the Bible—and in our present time—of very courageous young people who trust in God!

It's much easier to go along with the crowd than to stand for your own beliefs, so a lot of kids dress, talk, and behave like their friends. Some disobey their parents and teachers or do things they know are wrong because they're afraid of being laughed at.

The truth is that doing what's right in *God's* eyes, especially when it's really hard, will get people's attention … in a good way! Not only will they respect you, but you may even help them get to know God.

DARE Say no to negative peer pressure!

TRIPLE-DOG DARE!

1. When your friends make fun of another girl, remind them that if you're all really better than she is, you can prove it by being friendly to her.

2. Even if your parents would never find out, don't watch movies or TV shows at your friend's house that you aren't allowed to.

3. Obey safety rules even if other kids start laughing. But act confident—not embarrassed!

Journaling How did it go? What did you learn?

The Heart Transplant

Truth When you trust Him, God gives you a new heart!

Every year, about 3,500 people have operations to receive a new heart.... But there are actually about 800,000 people who need transplants because of serious heart disease. Sadly, there aren't enough healthy new hearts to go around. (Transplanted hearts come from people who recently died, if they had signed an agreement beforehand.)

Now let's talk about our *spiritual* hearts—our spirits, or who we are on the inside. All humans are born with spiritual heart disease because of sin, and that leads to spiritual death. That's when someone is separated from God, here on earth and also in hell after he or she dies.

The good thing is that there is a cure.... And no one has to wait for an organ donor! When you ask Jesus to forgive your sins and come into your life, He gives you a brand-new heart that will live forever.

DARE Let Jesus change your heart.

TRIPLE-DOG DARE!

1 In your journal, draw a big heart on a piece of paper. Inside the heart, write some of your sins that you're sorry for. Then cut a bigger heart out of colored paper and tape it over the first heart as a reminder of the new heart Jesus has given you.

2 What changes do you need to make in your life? Ask God to help you.

3 Do you have a friend who doesn't want to follow Jesus? Pray that God will "soften" her heart.

Journaling How did it go? What did you learn?

Galatians 5:16

Live by the Spirit

Truth *When you let God give you power, you can say no to temptation.*

What do these things have in common?

flashlight	*digital watch*	*camera*	*MP3 player*
cell phone	*calculator*	*electric toothbrush*	*remote control*
car	*portable radio*		

All the things listed above need batteries to run. Without batteries, they won't have any electrical power and can't be used.

Here's another question for you: Do all the items above use the same kind of batteries? Could you use a watch battery (sometimes called a button cell) in a camera? How about a car battery in a flashlight? No, of course not! Each type of electronic equipment will work only if the batteries designed for it are put inside.

Humans are designed to run on a God-sized "battery." To put it another way, the only way we can live the way God wants us to and have the power to resist temptation is to live by the Spirit or, in other words, to ask Jesus to come into our lives and be in control.

DARE Live by the Spirit!

TRIPLE-DOG DARE!

1 Memorize today's verse.

2 List five things you'd like to do today. Then list five things you think God would like you to do. Try to get God's list done before yours!

3 Think of a temptation you struggle with a lot. Take time today to talk to God about it and ask Him to help you "live by the Spirit" so that you can have the strength not to give in.

Journaling How did it go? What did you learn?

Not Heavy!

Truth — When god's family loves each other, it's easy to help out.

There's an old story about two brothers who were walking home together from a long distance away. After a while, the younger brother became so tired that he could hardly walk anymore, so the older brother lifted him up and carried him. Along the way, someone saw the two boys and said to the older one, "Wow! He must be really heavy!"

The boy answered, "He's not heavy. He's my brother!"

Of course, the weight of the little boy would have been the same no matter who was carrying him, but because his brother loved him, he didn't feel like he had a burden in his arms.

That's how it should always be in families … and in God's family of believers, too. We should be ready to help out whenever someone is going through a hard time, without thinking about the weight we might have to carry.

DARE Help others carry their loads.

TRIPLE-DOG DARE!

1. Ask your mom what you can do today to give her a bit of a break from all her work.

2. Do you have a friend going through a hard time? Pray for her today and then write her a cheery note letting her know how much you care.

3. Are there people in your family or at church who are always there for you? Give or send them thank-you cards expressing your appreciation for their support.

ournaling — How did it go? What did you learn?

Thirteen-year-old Rachel is one of eight children in her family! (You read about her younger sister Fiona earlier in this book.) Along with her parents, her grandmother, her three sisters, and her four brothers, Rachel enjoys doing missionary work in the Philippines.

Check out how this "daring" girl lives out her faith in Jesus!

I really enjoy Christian outreach because it is very fulfilling and fun even though sometimes it is quite hard here in the Philippines, as it is very hot and outreach may sometimes be quite slow. But no matter what happens, God always has His perfect will with everything.

Right now, I am in a Christian outreach competition with a worldwide group of teenagers, and it is very fulfilling. I am very happy about it, and I am having a lot of fun. I really enjoy doing Christian outreach, and even though I am not super good at it yet, I am getting a lot of experience from it.

I do sometimes have my ups and downs, even sometimes to the point of where I don't really feel like doing it (I must admit), but I just pray and ask God that He will help me and I am always able to bounce back quite quickly.

I also enjoy doing humanitarian aid projects for poor school children. Just to see all these little kids who have so little really helps me to be thankful for what God has given me.

I think missionary life is very fulfilling, fun, and interesting, and I am able to learn a lot. I wouldn't trade this life for anything. This is the verse that I have always really liked and that helps me in Christian outreach: "Go into all the world and preach the good news to all creation" (Mark 16:15).

- Find out if anyone in your church is going on a mission trip or is involved in evangelism. Encourage them by writing a note that says you're praying for them. Put a sticky note somewhere obvious to remind you of your promise to pray.

- Chat with your parents, Sunday school teacher, youth leader, or pastor to come up with one or two ways *you* can "preach the good news to all creation."

journaling

*You already have everything
you need to be happy.*

More than Milk

Truth
We need solid spiritual food ... not just the baby stuff.

Everyone knows that milk is good for babies, but have you ever wondered what would happen to a child if he or she had *nothing* but milk? A lot of people enjoy milk even as adults, but it's certainly not the only thing they eat or drink!

Just as a baby needs to learn to eat solid food—even if that means eating gross-looking mashed peas and carrots for a while—Christians need to grow up from spiritual "baby food" to solid teaching.

Young Christians need time to learn the basics of what the Bible teaches. That's spiritual "milk," and it's very important! But don't get stuck on easy things. Dig deeper into God's Word as you grow in your faith.

Reading *Truth and Dare* will also help you move beyond "milk"!

DARE Learn something new from the Bible every day.

TRIPLE-DOG DARE!

1. Slowly read through the book of James over the next month or so. Whenever you learn a new lesson, spend that day thinking and praying about it.

2. Take a notebook to Sunday school or church and write down what you learn.

3. Memorize one Bible verse a week. Choose from one of the *Truth and Dare* devotionals for that week.

Journaling How did it go? What did you learn?

hebrews 12:2-3

Focus on Jesus

Truth *Jesus is the best example.*

Most girls—and probably most adults, too!—have role models they look up to. It's good to find people who have good characters, especially mature Christians, whom you can learn from.

But it's also important to remember that people are, well ... human! That means even the wisest and most honest person won't be a perfect example 100 percent of the time.

Jesus, however, showed us exactly how to live unselfish, God-honoring, courageous lives. Even when He faced dying on the cross for sins He never committed, He didn't think about His own suffering. Instead, He found joy in knowing that His sacrifice would make a way for you and me to be saved.

When you focus your mind on how Jesus did the right thing even in the hardest situations, you can find the courage and strength to obey God in your daily life too.

DARE Follow Jesus instead of the crowd.

TRIPLE-DOG DARE!

1 When you have to do something you don't like to do, list the good things that will come out of doing it. Then focus on the positives as you complete the task.

2 Do the right thing, even if all your friends think you're crazy for it.

3 Read Hebrews 12:1–6 and *thank* God for your struggles.

Journaling How did it go? What did you learn?

Aim for Holiness

Truth *you need to be holy to see god.*

How many times have your parents or teachers told you to "do your best"? They probably say it to encourage you when you have to do something challenging and you're not sure whether you'll succeed. They may remind you that as long as you do *your* best, it doesn't matter if you're *the* best.

The other question is this: Do you always do your very best, or do you sometimes make half an effort?

The Bible tells us to do our very best to live in peace with others and to be holy. "Holy" means being like Jesus as much as we can: pure, honest, and obedient to God. You can't say you're a Christian and then go through life behaving just like everyone else.

God wants you to be *different* and to honor Him with all that you do and say.

DARE Make holiness a top priority in your life.

TRIPLE-DOG DARE!

1 Refuse to get into fights and arguments even when you know you're right. Making peace honors God; showing someone else she's wrong doesn't.

2 When your friends act silly and flirty with boys, don't participate. People will respect you for behaving more appropriately. (And God will be pleased!)

3 If you have any habits you wouldn't do in front of Jesus, ask Him to help you stop.

Journaling How did it go? What did you learn?

Obey Your Leaders

Truth *Leaders deserve your respect.*

Who are some of the leaders in your life? Of course, there are your parents and your teachers, but you probably have other authority figures around you too. Pastors, youth-group leaders, police officers, babysitters, coaches, lifeguards, and bus drivers are some examples of people who have the responsibility of teaching you, protecting you, or helping you.

God expects you to treat leaders with respect, even if there are times you don't like what they do or say. He has allowed them to be an important part of your life, and when you honor them, it's like you're honoring God. When you *don't* honor them, it shows disrespect for God.

Sure, leaders can make mistakes or do a bad job of leading. There may be times when you need to talk to someone you trust about a problem you're having with a leader. But remember that leaders often face bad attitudes from the people they are trying to help, so think of how you can be a blessing in your leaders' lives by respecting them.

DARE Honor your leaders ... even when you don't feel like it.

TRIPLE-DOG DARE!

1 Thank one of your teachers today for what he or she does.

2 When someone asks you to do something, don't wait to be asked a second time.

3 Pray for a leader in your life whom you have difficulty liking.

Journaling How did it go? What did you learn?

Soar Like an Eagle

Truth
When you trust God, He gives you all the strength you need.

Did you know that …

- an eagle has about seven thousand feathers?
- it's illegal to have an eagle feather without a permit?
- an eagle's eyes are four times sharper than perfect human vision?
- an eagle can see as far as a mile away?
- eagle nests can be as wide as ten feet and weigh up to one ton?
- half of the world's bald eagles live in Alaska?

If you're American, you know that the symbol of the eagle is important to the United States. But the Bible mentioned eagles thousands of years ago!

Today's verses promise that God watches over you. He knows when you're discouraged or feel weak and tired. Sometimes it's not easy to follow Him. But when you put your hope in Him and believe in His love and care, He will give you strength. Not just a little bit of strength but the kind of strength that makes eagles soar high in the air!

DARE Put your hope in God.

TRIPLE-DOG DARE!

1 Are you feeling down about something? Write about it in a prayer to God and ask Him to give you strength and peace.

2 Do you know someone else who needs encouragement? Send him or her a card with today's verses and a joyful message.

3 Quiz your friends on the eagle trivia above…. And then share today's lesson with them.

Journaling How did it go? What did you learn?

Read Genesis 1.

The first chapter of the Bible not only gives us lots of information about how the world we live in was created but it also shows us what an amazing God we have. He has the power to just speak and make planets and stars and oceans and lions and turtles appear! Not only that, but He has the creativity to make millions of types of trees and flowers and animals and insects and precious stones and … Well, you get the idea.

As if all of that isn't incredible enough, verse 27 tells us some exciting news: When God created humans, He made us in His image. That means that we have many qualities similar to God's. We have the ability to feel, to love, to choose, and even to create.

This weekend, your challenge is to use the gift of creativity that God gave you. If you're thinking, *But I'm not artistic!* … don't worry. We've listed a variety of ideas to choose from that even a non-artsy girl could enjoy.

Choose at least one of these activities to do this weekend:

1. With your parents' permission, redecorate your room. We don't mean paint the walls or change your curtains. Just rearrange the furniture in a fun new way and organize your stuff to make your room look less cluttered. Get your mom or a friend to help you if you're not sure what to do.

2. Write a poem or a song about your favorite things that God created.

3. Take photos of things that make you smile, get the photos printed, and use a small notebook to create a "happy" scrapbook you can carry around with you.

4. Organize a fun party just for your family with the theme "Creation." Think of unusual decorations, snacks, and games that go with the theme.

5. Design a coloring page about creation for the younger children at your church. Make sure the pictures for coloring in are large and simple. Make some copies (ask your parents how many to make) to take with you the next time you go to church.

6. Come up with another way to celebrate your creativity!

your Turn

Brainstorm your ideas here!

Journaling

What you see depends a lot on what you look for.

Count to Ten

Truth
A quick temper displeases God.

"Think twice, speak once" is a common saying that many people know but very few actually follow! You may have even heard a parent or teacher say that since God gave us two ears and only one mouth, we should talk half as much as we listen.

Unfortunately, a lot of people (at any age!) blurt out what they're thinking before they consider how their words will make others feel.

James, the brother of Jesus, gave this advice about two thousand years ago when he said we should be "quick to listen" and "slow to speak." He also warned that we should be slow to anger.

It takes a lot of maturity, wisdom, and patience not to blurt something out when you're upset or when you disagree with someone. But maturity, wisdom, and patience are qualities God wants you to develop. Speaking before thinking can get you into trouble or make you regret saying something.

DARE
When you're angry, don't say the first thing that comes to your mind.

TRIPLE-DOG DARE!

1 Whenever you feel angry, count to ten—slowly!—before saying anything. While you count, ask God to help you say the right thing.

2 The next time you chat with a friend, let her talk more than you do … and really *listen* to what she's saying.

3 If you catch yourself talking back to your parents, apologize right away and then pay attention more respectfully.

Journaling
How did it go? What did you learn?

What You *Don't* Do Matters Too

Truth *Not doing something good is just as wrong as doing something bad.*

When you hear the word *sin*, what do you think of? Lying, stealing, swearing, cheating, murdering …? Many sins are easy to spot because they involve bad behavior. Some people call these sins of "commission" (because you're *committing* a sin).

But did you know that it can be a sin to *not* do something? This is the sin of "omission" (you're *omitting* something you should be doing). Some examples:

- Punching someone is a sin of *commission*, but not helping someone who has been hurt is a sin of *omission*.
- Watching a TV show you're not allowed to is a sin of *commission*, but not praying is a sin of *omission*.
- Disobeying your parents is a sin of *commission*, but not apologizing and asking for forgiveness is a sin of *omission*.

Get it?

Make sure you don't feel comfortable in thinking that you're good because you don't do terrible sins.… Because there are probably things you should be doing that you're not. Right?

DARE Always do the right thing.

TRIPLE-DOG DARE!

1 Ask God to show you something special He wants you to do today … and to give you the courage to do it!

2 Today, do that chore or assignment that you've been avoiding for a while.

3 Say "thank you" to someone who deserves your appreciation but hasn't received it.

Journaling How did it go? What did you learn?

The Ticket to Eternal Life

Truth
Believing in Jesus is the only way to get to heaven.

In this puzzle, can you find nine words that have something in common? (Tip: One of the words is actually two words together.) The answers are at the end of the book.

Q	U	E	E	P	R	C	R	T	P	L
M	F	A	V	G	B	J	Z	M	L	D
U	Y	M	U	J	U	P	I	C	A	G
S	P	O	R	T	S	E	V	E	N	T
E	H	V	T	E	I	R	B	C	E	R
U	A	I	T	H	E	A	T	E	R	A
M	R	E	N	S	K	F	Y	X	B	I
C	H	Q	U	I	G	F	I	U	K	N
A	E	B	I	C	O	L	U	B	G	Y
Z	C	C	O	N	C	E	R	T	N	S
E	I	D	C	G	T	C	S	D	R	B

Each of the words above describes something that you usually need a ticket for. Tickets allow you to enjoy an event or go somewhere you want to be. Some of those tickets cost a lot, while others are not expensive.

How much do you think a ticket to heaven would cost? Do you think you could afford it if God made you pay for it? The Bible says that none of us could ever do anything or pay anything that would be enough to spend eternity with God in heaven because we're all born with sin.

But Jesus, who never sinned, loved you so much that *He* paid the price for your ticket to heaven. You only need to believe in Him and follow Him.

DARE
Make sure you have your ticket to heaven.

TRIPLE-DOG DARE!

1 If you've never asked Jesus to save you from your sins, do that today.

2 The next time you go to an event with friends, ask them if they have their ticket to heaven. Use the opportunity to tell them about Jesus.

3 Throughout the day, pray for people you know who don't believe in Jesus.

Journaling
How did it go? What did you learn?

Wonderful, Prickly Love

Truth *Sometimes loving someone else takes sacrifice.*

There once were two porcupines that lived in Alaska. Wanting to get warm, they moved close to each other, but when they did that, their needles poked each other. It hurt too much, so they moved away from each other. But then they were cold, so they tried huddling together again.

No matter what the porcupines did, they were going to feel either cold ... or pain.

This is a good example of how relationships—at home, at school, with our friends, or at church—take work. Sometimes relationships hurt because humans are not perfect. But if we're not willing to take a little bit of pain now and then and give up some of our comfort, we'll just end up alone and cold inside.

Jesus showed us how to love unselfishly when He died on the cross to take the punishment for our sins. He was willing to suffer because He loved us.

Are you willing to love someone, even if it hurts sometimes?

DARE Love ... even when it hurts!

TRIPLE-DOG DARE!

1. Are you avoiding a friend who hurt you lately? With God's help, humble yourself and make peace with her as soon as possible.

2. Do you sometimes have trouble loving someone in your family? Surprise him or her today by doing something super nice!

3. Memorize today's Bible verses.

Journaling How did it go? What did you learn?

Strong and Brave

Truth — *God wants you to have courage. And He can give it to you!*

Some people don't seem to be afraid of anything. They can sing in front of a huge crowd, dive in the deep end of a pool, or walk through the woods at night without thinking twice. They're not scared, so it's easy for them to do whatever they're doing.

You might think, *I wish I were that brave!*

But being brave doesn't mean not feeling afraid. It means doing something *even though* it scares you! For example, a little girl who tries petting a dog even though she's scared of it is much braver than a professional lion tamer who knows what to expect. Or you may have the courage to tell the truth about something even though you know you will get in trouble.

God knows that there are times when you'll feel afraid. You don't need to feel bad for being scared, but you *can* feel good by remembering that God will give you the strength to go through whatever difficulty you're facing.

DARE   Do the right thing, even if it's scary.

TRIPLE-DOG DARE!

1 Tell someone you trust what you're afraid of and ask her to pray for you.

2 Make a plan for how you will face one of your fears this week. Start with something simple.

3 Ask your parents to tell you about fears they have overcome … and how.

Journaling — How did it go? What did you learn?

In John 15:13, Jesus said that the greatest proof of love is willingness to sacrifice your life for someone else ... just like He did!

Take this quiz to see how loving *you* are.

1. Your best friend trips on her way to the table and her all-dressed burger lands on your favorite white T-shirt. You ...

    a. start screaming about how she's ruined your top and owes you a new one. You don't talk to her for a week after that.
    b. get upset and then rush to the bathroom to see if you can wash out most of the stain.
    c. ask her if she's okay and then try to think up some fun ways you can match the rest of the T-shirt to the stains made by the burger.

2. You've been invited to the birthday party of one of the coolest girls at school, but it's on a Sunday morning and you can't go because of church. You ...

    a. argue with your parents for days and whine about how unfair they are. On Sunday you cry and complain the whole way to church and back.
    b. feel upset but obey your parents and politely turn down the invitation. On Sunday you sit through the service feeling sorry for yourself.
    c. tell your parents that you'd rather go to church anyway. On Sunday you enjoy the worship time and happily think about the gift you will give the birthday girl when you see her at school.

3. You're babysitting your little brother and he asks you to read to him just when your favorite TV show starts. You ...

    a. tell him to leave you alone. When he continues to ask you, you raise the TV volume and ignore him.
    b. promise you'll read to him during the commercials and then you give him a few cookies to keep him busy while you watch your show.
    c. turn the TV off, snuggle on the couch with your brother, and read the story to him, making him laugh by using funny voices for each character.

If you answered ...

- **mostly A,** you have difficulty loving. Read 1 John 4:10–11. Thank God for loving you and giving His life for you. Then ask Him to forgive you for being unloving and to help you love others more.

- **mostly B,** you know how to treat people kindly but not always out of love. Ask God to show you how to love from your heart and not just through your actions.

- **mostly C,** God's love is in you and you're sharing it with others. Great job! Pray every day that God will fill your heart with love.

journaling

Get Ready for a New week!

You matter more than you think you do!

Joshua 24:1–15

Whom Will You Serve?

Truth — *It's up to you to choose to serve god.*

In this story, Joshua reminded the people of Israel of all the ways that God had been good to them, even when they disobeyed Him and worshipped other gods. Then he challenged them to make a decision: Were they going to serve God or not? Joshua and his family had decided to follow God, and he was not ashamed to tell everyone about it.

You might not remember a specific time you decided to follow God. Maybe you've done it just because that's what you learned to do as you grew up, and you haven't given it much thought.

God doesn't want you to serve Him just because your parents do—it's not your good deeds that He wants from you. It's your love and devotion. He wants you to follow Him because *you* want to do it.

DARE — If you've never made up your own mind about serving God before, do it today!

TRIPLE-DOG DARE!

1. Write a letter to God telling Him why you want to follow and serve Him. Then ask Him to give you the courage to do it.

2. Ask a friend if she believes in God … and then tell her about *your* faith in Him.

3. If your friends want to do things that don't honor God, ask yourself whom you will follow: them or God?

Journaling — How did it go? What did you learn?

Luke 10:25-37

Your Turn

Truth
God expects you to live what you learn.

Many people have grown up going to church and reading the Bible. If that describes your experience, you may know a lot of important verses and stories in the Bible. You may even feel proud that you know the Bible better than other kids your age do.

The parable of the good Samaritan is a well-known story, but a lot of people miss the point. Jesus wasn't simply teaching us to be a good neighbor, although that is definitely a strong theme here.

The point is that it's not enough to know what the Bible says. We have to put it into practice, or our knowledge becomes useless, just as in the examples of the priest and the Levite who were religious but didn't show God's love to the man who needed their help.

Jesus told His listeners—and that includes you and me—to "go and do likewise."

DARE Use your Bible knowledge to be gutsy for God.

TRIPLE-DOG DARE!

1 Think of the scariest thing God might ask you to do. Then pray for the courage to obey Him no matter what.

2 Surprise a stranger by being unexpectedly kind and helpful.

3 Ask your mom or youth leader to honestly tell you about an area of your Christian life that you might need to work on.

Journaling How did it go? What did you learn?

Why Worry?

Truth *Worrying doesn't accomplish anything.*

Worry is like a rocking chair: It gives you something to do, but it doesn't get you anywhere.

This well-known saying reminds me of a funny story of a woman who had trouble sleeping at night because she was always afraid that burglars would break into the house.

One night, her husband heard a loud noise downstairs so he went to investigate. Sure enough, there was a burglar in the living room! The husband went to the robber and said, "Good evening, sir. I'm so glad to see you. Would you please come upstairs and meet my wife? She's been waiting for you for ten years!"

Although that story is just a joke, it gives a good picture of how we often worry about things that never happen.… Or they don't happen the way we expected. And even if they *do* happen, worrying about them obviously doesn't change anything! Not only do we waste time when we worry, but it also shows that we don't trust God to take care of us.

DARE Stop worrying!

TRIPLE-DOG DARE!

1. Do you know someone who worries a lot? Share today's verse and the rocking chair quote with her in a pretty note or card.
2. In your journal, list the things you worry about. Then pray about each thing, asking God to help you trust Him with it.
3. When you're tempted to worry, think of something positive you could be doing instead of wasting your time.

Journaling How did it go? What did you learn?

Innocent Faith

Truth *Our faith needs to be simple, like a child's.*

Whether you still think of yourself as a young girl or you feel all grown up, this is a great verse to remember!

Little kids usually believe anything you tell them. Santa Claus, the tooth fairy, the Easter bunny … children are happy to believe in them. They trust grown-ups, and if something makes sense to them, they'll go along with it.

Of course, most kids outgrow their belief in things that aren't real. But when it comes to believing in God and what the Bible teaches about Jesus, young children seem to know deep in their hearts that it's all true. They have the perfect kind of faith that makes them love God and want to obey Him.

Unfortunately, adults sometimes let go of that innocent faith and let knowledge about the world confuse their beliefs about God. You are at the perfect age—young but becoming mature—to make your faith in God strong and lasting.

DARE Stay humble and innocent.

TRIPLE-DOG DARE!

1. When you get confused about what you believe, explain it to yourself like you would to a five-year-old.

2. Ask a couple of small children at your church (or in your family) why they love God. The answers may inspire you!

3. This week, pray every day for a child you know who isn't a Christian.

Journaling How did it go? What did you learn?

The Best Gift Exchange

Truth *Jesus gave His life for you.*

Do you look forward to Christmas? Does your family or your class at school do a gift exchange?

Over two thousand years ago, Jesus gave you the best gift you could ever receive: His life.

When He came to earth as a baby in Bethlehem, He gave up His wonderful home in heaven and became a human. He had to face temptation and hunger and pain just like you do. He even died on the cross, taking the punishment for your sins because He loved you so much.

Jesus gave you the gift of His life. Now you can give Him *your* life in return. That doesn't mean dying physically; it means giving Him your heart and promising to follow and obey Him from now on.

The neat thing about this gift exchange is that the more of your life you give to Jesus, the more of it He gives back to you. He gives you a life that's full of joy!

DARE Give your life to Jesus.

TRIPLE-DOG DARE!

1. If you've never done this gift exchange with Jesus, do it today! Believe that He died for you and accept His forgiveness for your sins. Then give Him the rest of your life.
2. If you haven't already, memorize today's verse. Encourage your younger siblings or a friend to learn it too.
3. In your planner, write "John 3:16" in the space for December 25. On Christmas Day, see if you can remember what that verse means.

Journaling How did it go? What did you learn?

As you move from elementary school to middle school to high school, you'll notice more and more people asking you questions like, "So, what do you want to be when you grow up?" or "What are your goals in life?"

You might have already decided that you're going to be a photographer or a pastry chef or an architect. Maybe you want to be a missionary or a pro tennis player or a pilot.

Then again, maybe you have no idea what you want to do because you're still trying to figure out what you like and what's important to you.

It's okay not to have specific goals for your far-away future just yet, but it's never too early to think about what your priorities are. Not only will setting your priorities now help you in the future, but it will allow you to grow as a Christian and to develop good character traits that will help you in every area of your life.

Take this quiz to see how your priorities line up with what the Bible teaches.

1. You were planning to sleep in on Saturday and spend a lazy day watching cartoons, but you just found out that your church is having a fund-raiser that morning and they need volunteers … *and* that one of your school friends is having a pool party. You …

    a. pretend you didn't hear about either event and still sleep in on Saturday.
    b. go to the pool party. You're not going to miss out on the fun!
    c. get up early and go help out at church, letting your friend know that you'll try to make it if you finish early.

2. When you daydream, you …

    a. think about how much freedom you'll finally have when you're older.
    b. think about that cute boy whose locker is across the hall from yours.
    c. wonder what heaven will be like.

3. What qualities do you look for in your friends?

    a. They like to have fun and hang out and chat.
    b. They're stylish and popular.
    c. They challenge you to be your best and cheer you up when you're down.

4. Your favorite thing about church is …

    a. having cookies and juice after the service.
    b. catching up with your friends.
    c. learning something new from the Bible.

If you answered …

- **mostly A,** you have a pretty laid-back attitude about life. That can become a problem if you never take anything seriously or have no motivation to get involved in activities. Ask God to help you focus less on having fun and more on developing good qualities.

- **mostly B,** your friends are important to you, which is great, but you might be focusing on them more than you do on God. Ask God to help you not put your friends before Him.

- **mostly C,** you care about things that really matter in life and are growing spiritually. Ask God to help you keep Him as your first priority.

Got More Time?

Read these verses:

Matthew 16:24–27
Matthew 19:16–22
Proverbs 4:25–27
Mark 12:28–34

Get Ready for a New week!

This week, give someone a second chance.

Let's Go Fishing!

Truth
Jesus' followers should lead others to Him.

Imagine that your uncle came to your house carrying a fishing rod and a tackle box and wearing rubber boots and a fishing hat. If he said, "Come on, let's go!" would you think he was taking you skating, to a concert, or to the mall? No, you'd probably know right away that he was taking you fishing.

One of the best ways to catch a fish is to lure it with bait. That means you offer the fish something it likes or finds attractive (such as live worms). Different kinds of fish need different kinds of bait.

Many of Jesus' disciples were fishermen, so they understood when Jesus told them they'd become "fishers of men." From then on, they were going to "catch" people for Jesus by telling them about His love and the gift of eternal life in heaven.

As a Christian, you can also make the good news about Jesus attractive to your friends. When they see the joy and love in your life, they will want to experience that too. But you have to tell them about Jesus. Having the right gear isn't enough…. You actually have to go fishing!

DARE   Go fishing for Jesus!

TRIPLE-DOG DARE!

1 Do people see Jesus in your life? Ask God to help you be a better "fisher of men."

2 Plan at least one way you will share the good news about Jesus with someone today.

3 Ask your parents if you can keep a goldfish as a reminder of today's lesson.

Journaling   How did it go? What did you learn?

Lots of Leftovers!

Truth
Even if you have only a little to give to God, He can make a lot out of it!

I really like leftovers, even if they dry up a bit from being warmed up again the next day. Rice, fish, chicken, pasta … Bring it on! And it makes me happy that I'm not wasting the food by throwing it out.

In today's Bible story, Jesus performed an unforgettable miracle that ended with lots and lots *and lots* of leftovers. And it all started with an unselfish young boy who was willing to give up his lunch so that others could have some food. Imagine you were that child and you watched as Jesus took your fish and bread, prayed that God would bless it, and then started passing it around.

I don't know about you, but my mouth would probably drop open in amazement as I watched the food mysteriously multiply.

I like to imagine that this boy grew up to follow Jesus after he saw how God blessed his small act of trust. What a great example to help you believe that God will bless everything you do to honor Him.

DARE Give all you have to God!

TRIPLE-DOG DARE!

1 Do you struggle to put your money in the offering plate at church? Pray that God will help you give generously, like the boy in today's story.

2 The next time your family has leftovers, talk about Jesus' miracle with the bread and fish.

3 With a friend, come up with a modern version of this story.

Journaling How did it go? What did you learn?

A Lesson in Humility

Truth   *We depend on god for everything.*

After God rescued the people of Israel from Egypt, where they had been badly treated as slaves, He started to lead them to a wonderful land He had promised them. But it didn't take long for the Israelites to start grumbling and complaining and disobeying God. They created so many problems for themselves that, instead of completing the journey in one or two months, it took them forty years!

God was patient with His people but also had to teach them some tough lessons. When they complained that they missed the food they ate in Egypt—forgetting how much they suffered there!—God let them go hungry for a while. The only thing they had to eat was strange snowy stuff (manna) that appeared on the ground every day. They weren't allowed to save it for the next day. They could just eat what they needed each day.

God wanted to teach the people that they depended on Him for everything, but they still would not humble themselves. They suffered because of their own stubbornness.

DARE   Ask God to feed your heart ... not just your body.

TRIPLE-DOG DARE!

1 Read Exodus 16 to learn more about the manna the Israelites ate.

2 Besides these devotions, what do you do to grow spiritually every day? Make extra time for God today.

3 Challenge your family to repeat Matthew 4:4 whenever someone says the word *bread* today (for example, during meals).

Journaling   How did it go? What did you learn?

Love the Unlovable

Truth _god wants you to love your enemies._

You can probably quickly list the people you love: your parents, grandparents, siblings, best friend, favorite teacher, and maybe even that little old lady at church who still pinches your cheeks every week.

The people you *love* are usually the people you *like* … the people who are nice to you.

But what about the girl who embarrassed you in front of the whole class or the boy who keeps picking fights with your little brother?

Jesus said we have to love our enemies just as much as we love others. He also set an example for us by forgiving the people who were mean to Him and killed Him. Remembering that Jesus suffered much more than we ever will can help us feel less angry toward those who are not nice to us … and maybe even love them.

DARE Don't hold any grudges.

TRIPLE-DOG DARE!

1. Ask God to bless your enemies. If you can honestly pray for their good, that's a huge step in the right direction!

2. Secretly put a kind note in the locker or desk of a girl you don't get along with. For example, "God made you special!"

3. Spread good "gossip" about your enemy by pointing out her positive qualities to other people. Then smile at her reaction when she hears people saying nice things about her!

Journaling How did it go? What did you learn?

No One Else

Truth *Jesus is the only way to god.*

If someone asked you to list all the religions of the world, how many would you be able to name? The well-known ones, besides Christianity, are Judaism, Islam, Buddhism, and Hinduism. You may also have heard of Mormonism, Jehovah's Witnesses, and New Age.

Actually, there are more than forty "big" religions—including atheism (the belief that God doesn't exist)—and many more small ones that are basically a mix of other religions. It's not surprising that many people are confused about which religion is right!

But only one way is true.

The Bible says that Jesus is the only way to God and salvation. True Christianity is not actually a *religion* like the others are; it's a *relationship* with God. Jesus, our Lord and Savior, reached out to us in love when He died on the cross. No other religion offers such a precious gift!

DARE Don't let anyone or anything turn your attention away from Jesus.

TRIPLE-DOG DARE!

1 Pray for your friends who follow other religions and ask God to help you show them the truth.

2 Read Acts 4:1–12 to get a better understanding of today's verse.

3 Draw a maze puzzle where the correct path will lead the player to "Jesus." Write this verse at the bottom and share the puzzle with a friend.

ournaling How did it go? What did you learn?

When Amelia was seven years old, she and her family were watching a TV show about people who go a little crazy decorating their houses for Christmas. The point of the show was for one of the families to win an award for the tackiest Christmas house. Some people on that show were willing to spend thousands and thousands and *a lot more thousands* of dollars to win this contest.

As she watched, Amelia asked her mom, "Mommy, why do people spend all that time and money on lights and Christmas decorations when they can give the money to missionaries and people that are starving?" Good question, Amelia!

So her family decided that, instead of putting money into their own Christmas decorations, they would put the money toward helping missionaries and people in need. They shared their plan with friends and challenged other Christians not to buy any new decorations that year and, instead, to put that money toward helping a missionary or buying gospel tracts or anything that could help Christians in other countries share the good news about Jesus with others.

Amelia says, *"I got the idea from Mommy and Daddy. Mommy talks to us about missionaries and we pray for them every day. We also learn about those who have less than us and how we should help by sharing our blessings given to us by God. Our family has bought a bicycle, a Jesus Well, and other things for missionaries, and we also bought some animals for people in India. We also sponsor a girl from India who is close to my age. I get to write her letters and draw pictures for her. I like it when we get a letter in the mail from Aalisha because she colors pictures for us!*

"It's important to me because I want to make God happy! It's more important for missionaries (and the people missionaries reach out to) to have food and clothes than it is for us to have Christmas decorations. It's okay to have some decorations as long as people don't overdo it. People and their souls are more important! We won't be taking our Christmas decorations to heaven!"

Amelia's family has a bottle in their kitchen in which they put money to save for bicycles for missionaries. Amelia and her little sister love to put their own money into the bottle. Then they order items from a mission organization's Christmas catalog. These items are sent to needy families.

A Bible verse that reminds Amelia to serve and obey God is 1 John 3:16–18, which says, "This is how we know what love is: Jesus Christ laid down his life for us. And we ought to lay down our lives for our brothers. If anyone has material possessions and sees his brother in need but has no pity on him, how can the love of God be in him? Dear children, let us not love with words or tongue but with actions and in truth."

- Think about some of your family Christmas traditions. What could you do differently this year to bless others instead of spending money on things you don't need? Write your ideas here:

_____

_____

_____

- Share your ideas with your family and come up with a plan together, just like Amelia and her family did. Write about your discussion and how you feel about it here:

_____

_____

_____

Journaling

"Learn from yesterday. Live for today. Hope for tomorrow."

–Albert Einstein

It's Not Yours, Anyway

Truth

All the stuff we have belongs to God, so we shouldn't get too attached to it.

Having a lot of stuff can make us feel important … and a little greedy. Sometimes we forget to share with others or to be thankful, and we may buy things without thinking because we feel we deserve what we want.

The truth is that everything we have, even if we worked for it, is a gift from God. Not only does the earth He created for our enjoyment belong to Him, but so do all our belongings.

Girls, especially in North America, buy and own more stuff now than ever before in history. You may have your own spending money or know that you can just ask your mom or dad for whatever you need. But many girls around the world survive on much, *much* less than what we have, so let's remember that we don't always *need* what we *want.*

DARE
Fight the temptation to be greedy by doing something amazingly generous today!

TRIPLE-DOG DARE!

1. For your next birthday party, have a gift exchange where everyone gets one gift instead of you getting all of them, and focus on having fun together!

2. When you find money on the ground, secretly give it to someone who needs it more than you do.

3. If someone accidentally breaks or ruins something that's special to you, be quick to forgive and remind yourself it's just a "thing."

Journaling — How did it go? What did you learn?

Matthew 6:25-34

Don't Worry about Tomorrow

Truth
You can't change tomorrow by worrying about it today.

We know that some animals, such as ants and squirrels, store food away for the winter. They've been created with an instinct to do this, so they probably don't have to put a lot of thought into it. As humans, we do have to be wise and plan ahead, but the Bible says we should be as calm as the birds that happily look for the food they need each day without stressing about the next day.

Maybe you don't worry about your food very much, since your parents or someone else who takes care of you probably feeds you. However, you *might* worry about your clothes. Girls can be preoccupied with what they're going to wear and with having the "right" clothes.

These verses remind us that if God cares enough to give flowers such beautiful "clothes," He will take care of us, too.

DARE
Think about people more than you do about "stuff."

TRIPLE-DOG DARE!

1. If you feel worried about the future, take five minutes to thank God for ways He has taken care of you in the past.

2. The next time you want to buy a top or accessory you don't really need, think of a way you can use that money to bless someone else.

3. List twenty things God created that you find beautiful. Then thank Him for making *you* beautiful too.

Journaling
How did it go? What did you learn?

The Problem with Judging

Truth
You can't judge others if you aren't ready to be judged yourself.

Have you ever had a friend accuse you of something small and thought to yourself, *What is she talking about? What about what* she *did? It was so much worse!* How would you feel if someone who cheated on all her exams called you a thief because you accidentally took the teacher's pen home with you? What if someone who swore all the time said you were rude because you forgot to say "please"?

Most people seem to like pointing fingers at others who have done something wrong. But how many of us like it when we have to face our own mistakes or sins?

The Bible warns us that we will be judged the same way we judge others, so we should either make sure our lives are pure and right ... or stop looking for the faults of others!

DARE
Make things right in yourself; don't judge others.

TRIPLE-DOG DARE!

1 Make a list of any of your recent bad attitudes, words, or actions for which you haven't asked forgiveness yet. Be honest!

2 Make things right with God or the people you hurt by apologizing and promising to change.

3 When a friend does something wrong, ask God to help you resist the urge to point it out to her.

Journaling
How did it go? What did you learn?

Excellent Thought!

Truth *Your mind should be focused on good things.*

Every day, your brain is hit by thousands of messages from television, radio, magazines, the Internet, billboards, advertisements, store windows, friends, teachers, strangers, and more. It can be easy to get mixed up about what's true and false, what's good and bad, what pleases God and what doesn't, what's healthy and what's not.

God knows that our minds influence our feelings, our actions, and our attitudes. What we allow to stay in our brains eventually influences our attitudes and feelings and comes out in the way we talk or behave.... And sometimes it's not good stuff!

Think of how you use a digital camera: Whatever you take pictures of is what you're going to upload to your computer. You can't take pictures of trash and end up with pictures of pretty flowers.

Keep your mind on things that are pure and good, and the results will be wonderful!

DARE Delete all the bad thoughts in your mind. And then click on "Empty Trash"!

TRIPLE-DOG DARE!

1 When you have extra reading time, make the Bible your first choice.

2 Listen carefully to the words of the songs you listen to. If they don't have positive messages, switch to gospel or worship music.

3 Avoid movies and TV programs that have cursing, inappropriate situations, and violence. Stick to shows that honor God.

Journaling How did it go? What did you learn?

You Can Do Everything

Truth Jesus can give you the strength to do everything you need to do.

Have you ever sat down to do your homework or practice the piano and thought to yourself, *It's too hard! I can't do it!* What about the time your friend hurt your feelings and then apologized, but you found it hard to forgive her?

Life is full of problems and pressures that might make you feel like giving up. You might wonder where you're going to find the strength or courage or time or creativity to finish the project you're working on or solve the problem you're facing.

The Bible says that you can do *all things* with the help of Jesus, who will give you the strength you need.

"All things" doesn't mean flying like a bird, passing a test you didn't study for, or suddenly growing two inches.… But it does mean all the things He knows you need to do but feel discouraged about.

DARE Don't get stuck. Get Jesus.

TRIPLE-DOG DARE!

1. Face the hardest thing you have to do today by asking Jesus to help you. Then just dive in and, instead of thinking about how you *can't* do it, trust that God *can.*

2. Tell a non-Christian friend that God loves her. You can do it!

3. Choose an activity you're involved in and try to reach the next level of difficulty.

Journaling How did it go? What did you learn?

Read Matthew 25:14–30. Then take this quiz to see how well you are using the talents and gifts God gave you.

1. You've always been really good at math and can solve difficult questions quickly. You ...

   a. volunteer to help kids at church who are struggling in math, for half an hour after each Sunday service.

   b. participate as a tutor in your school and earn a bit of spending money every week.

   c. continue getting good grades on your tests and don't worry about other students.

2. Your parents are wealthy, so you get a bigger allowance each week than most of your friends do. You ...

   a. put half of it in the offering plate every Sunday.

   b. spend a little of it on your friends or family, spend most of it on yourself, and then save the rest.

   c. keep it all for yourself. It is *yours,* after all.

3. You're very organized with your schoolwork and chores, so you usually end up having quite a bit of free time. You ...

   a. get involved with an outreach or volunteer program in your church or neighborhood.

   b. work on your hobbies, go for nature walks, write letters, and read books.

   c. hang out at the mall, watch TV, and play on the computer.

4. Little children quickly feel comfortable around you, and you have a special way of making them listen and participate in activities. You ...

   a. volunteer to be a teacher's assistant in Sunday school or to help in the church nursery.

   b. offer babysitting services in your neighborhood.

   c. think you do enough just looking after your little brother.

your Score

If you answered ...

- **mostly A,** you are using your gifts in a way that honors God! You appreciate all that God has given you, and you want to give some of it back by using your talents, time, and money to serve Him and others. Keep up the good work, always praying that God will guide you.

- **mostly B,** you are using your talents well instead of wasting them. Ask God to show you how you can do more to use your gifts in a way that really helps others and not just yourself or those close to you.

- **mostly C,** you are wasting your talents and, in a way, telling God that you don't feel thankful for all that He's given you. Take time to pray about this over the weekend and ask God to help you use your gifts in a way that pleases Him.

Got More Time?

In the chart below, write down what you think some of your talents are and then come up with some plans for how you will use them according to what you learned this weekend. (Then do it!)

MY TALENT	HOW I WILL USE IT

Get Ready for a New Week!

Every day is special because once it's gone, you can't get it back. (Just like a flower!)

Lose the Lazies!

Truth
God wants you to use your time in good ways.

No matter how old, how smart, how rich, or how popular we are, we all get the same twenty-four hours each day that we're alive. Those hours and minutes are precious gifts from God, and He expects us to do our best with them!

That doesn't mean we can never rest or play or have a vacation, but it does mean that we have to try not to *waste* time by being lazy and just goofing off when we could be doing something more useful, like reading, helping our parents, or praying for a friend. Sometimes we waste time by doing things much more slowly than we need to—like taking too long getting dressed or fixing our hair.

Imagine that God planned your schedule for each day. Would it be very different from what it is now?

When you are wise and generous with your time, it's like you're giving a gift back to God!

DARE   Use your time to honor God.

TRIPLE-DOG DARE!

1 Skip playing on the computer today and write a letter to God thanking Him for everything He's given you.

2 After you finish your homework, clean up the messiest part of your room.

3 If there's a chore your parents ask you to do every day, do it *before* they ask you!

Journaling   How did it go? What did you learn?

Proverbs 12:15

Advice for the Wise

Truth
If you want to be wise, listen to advice.

Have you noticed that the kids who go around boasting about how smart they are often end up doing foolish things? And it seems like the *really* smart kids are the ones who don't talk about themselves. They're willing to ask questions and listen, which is how they learn and become smart!

Well, that makes sense, doesn't it? If you ask wise people for advice and actually listen to them, you're going to learn important things that can help you in life. But if you say, "I know!" every time your mom or your teacher tells you something, how will you ever become wise?

King Solomon was the wisest man who ever lived, so you might want to take his advice about taking advice!

DARE
Be humble enough to learn from people who know more than you do.

TRIPLE-DOG DARE!

1 Ask your mom or dad, "If you could give me one piece of advice about life, what would it be?" And then pay close attention to the answer!

2 When someone explains how to do something you already know, just listen instead of interrupting.

3 Read through the book of Proverbs—maybe a few verses a day—and, in a small notebook, write down all the good advice you want to remember.

Journaling
How did it go? What did you learn?

 PSALM 90:12

Your Days Are Numbered

- -

Truth *You're not going to live forever, so make the most of each day God gives you.*

When you're only eight, ten, or fourteen years old, it's pretty hard to imagine yourself as an eighty-year-old. That just seems so far away! You might think there's so much you can do in life before it's time to start worrying about old age and death.

It's important to remember, however, that you don't actually know how many days you will live. Babies die, young children die, and adults die at any age.

Of course, you can't go through life worrying about when you're going to die—and you don't *need* to worry when you've given your life to Jesus—but God can give you the wisdom to look at each day as a precious gift and spend it in the best possible way.

Think about this, too: You can never get back the time you wasted or spent doing things that don't please God.

DARE Spend each day wisely.

TRIPLE-DOG DARE!

1 Spend at least half an hour every day this week doing something that will bring joy to someone else.

2 Think of one way you waste time, and find a positive activity to replace it with.

3 Every morning, thank God for the new day and ask for His help to use it wisely.

Journaling How did it go? What did you learn?

Thanks!

Truth *god deserves your gratitude.*

In the list on the left side, you'll find "Thanks" written in ten different languages. Can you match the words with their languages in the list on the right? (The answers are at the end of the book.)

Shenorhagal em	Greek
Gracias	Japanese
Mahalo	Portuguese
Efharisto	Tagalog (Philippines)
Wa-do	Armenian
Obrigada (or Obrigado for males)	French
Arigato	Hawaiian
Merci	German
Salamat	Spanish
Danke	Cherokee (United States)

How did you feel when you read the story about the ten men Jesus healed? Did you think it wasn't fair that nine of the men never came back to thank Jesus for what He did for them?

Unfortunately, it's very common for people to forget to say thank you when someone does something kind for them. It has probably happened to you, too! If you know what it feels like not to be appreciated, can you imagine how God feels? He has blessed us with so much more than our brains can even understand, yet instead of thanking Him, most people go through life complaining and always wanting more.

Today you can decide to be like the nine ungrateful men ... or the one who was thankful.

DARE Thank God!

TRIPLE-DOG DARE!

1. Give your parents a thank-you card listing at least five reasons you appreciate them.
2. Whenever someone thanks you, smile and say "You're welcome" so she'll know her thanks mattered to you.
3. Challenge your friends to see who can list, in five minutes, the most things to thank God for.

Journaling How did it go? What did you learn?

Hot or Cold?

Truth
God doesn't like "lukewarm" Christians.

Do you like potatoes? I do! I like them mashed, boiled, roasted in the oven, or made into french fries. In Quebec, where I come from, a popular food is *poutine*. That's basically french fries loaded up with cheese curds and then covered with gravy. Yeah … not exactly health food!

There's one kind of potato that no one likes, though, and that's a *couch potato*. A couch potato is someone who pretty much sits on the couch and watches TV all day while pigging out on junk food (or is lazy in some other way). She's not dead. But she isn't really *living* either.

Christians can be like that sometimes. They might go to church every week, but they don't really put their hearts into it. They spend very little time reading their Bibles or praying and hardly ever serve at church or help others.

God calls those Christians "lukewarm" because they're not cold (dead) but they're not hot (living) either. They're just kind of useless because they don't care.

Is that how God's followers should be?

DARE   Stop being lukewarm.

TRIPLE-DOG DARE!

1 If your mind wanders during church, bring a small notebook and take notes about the songs, the prayer requests, and the sermon.

2 Give up some of your free time today to pray, read your Bible, or tell a friend about Jesus.

3 Do you and your friends talk about everything except Jesus? Start changing that today!

Journaling   How did it go? What did you learn?

Read Ecclesiastes 12:13 and Matthew 25:21.

It's hard to believe this is our last weekend devotional together. If you've completed all the devotions in *Truth and Dare*—not just the readings, but the dares, too—I'm sure that God would say to you, "Well done, good and faithful servant!"

But the end of this book is not really THE END. After you finish these devotions, I hope you'll continue to read God's *truth* in the Bible and then *dare* to live out what He teaches you.

This weekend, take some time to think back on all that God has taught you and how much you've grown this past year by daring to trust and obey Him. Flip through the book to read some of the notes you wrote.

Journal about it here (or use your own journal if you need more space).

_____

_____

_____

_____

_____

_____

Write out a prayer asking God to help you to continue being daring for Him in the year ahead.

_____

_____

_____

Journaling

Want to Know More about How to Become a Christian?

The Truth

God created everything in this universe: the planets, the stars, the sun and moon, the world we live in, the animals, and, best of all, human beings. God created everything perfect, and He loved the people He made very much.

Sadly, the first humans who existed (Adam and Eve) rebelled against God and sinned. Since then, humans have always been born with a sinful nature that separates us from God and heaven. The Bible says that the punishment for sin is death (hell). But there's good news!

About two thousand years ago, God came to earth in the form of a human named Jesus (that's what we celebrate at Christmas). Jesus was God, but He loved us so much that He was willing to come to earth to help us find God. He was also willing to die on a cross to take the punishment we deserved for our sins and make a way for us to live forever in heaven with Him. There's even more good news: Because Jesus rose from the dead three days after He was killed (which is what we celebrate at Easter), we know that we can also have eternal life after we die!

The Bible says, "For God so loved the world that he gave his one and only Son, that whoever believes in him shall not perish but have eternal life" (John 3:16).

The A-B-C-Dare

1. Admit that you are a sinner.

2. Believe that Jesus died on the cross and came back to life three days later.

3. Confess your sins to God and ask Him to forgive you.

4. Dedicate your life to Him and promise to love and obey Him.

You don't need to go through a complicated ceremony to become a Christian. Simply believing in the truth about Jesus and asking God to come into your heart will get you started on your new life and your new relationship with Him. After that, three things will help you grow stronger in your faith:

1. Studying your Bible
2. Praying
3. Going to church to worship God with Christian friends who can encourage and support you

If you still have questions, talk to a pastor, Sunday school teacher, or youth-group leader (or your parents, if they're Christians). You can also write to me at truthanddare@annhovsepian.com.

Answers to Puzzles and Quizzes

1. Make Peace

James 5:16
1 Peter 4:8
Colossians 2:6–7
Proverbs 19:11
2 Samuel 3:12
Philippians 2:3
Psalm 119:34
Colossians 3:12
Proverbs 12:26
Psalm 130:4

```
            P R A Y E R
      L O V E
            T H A N K F U L N E S S
  P A T I E N C E
      A G R E E M E N T
            H U M I L I T Y
U N D E R S T A N D I N G
            K I N D N E S S
      F R I E N D S H I P
      F O R G I V E N E S S
```

2. Persecuted but Not Abandoned

"Everyone who wants to live a godly life in Christ Jesus will be persecuted."

3. No More Idols

"You shall not make for yourself an idol."

4. Thank God for Parents!

1. Jacob—Isaac—Rebekah, 2. Solomon—David—Bathsheba, 3. Isaac—Abraham—Sarah, 4. Joseph—Jacob—Rachel, 5. Obed—Boaz—Ruth, 6. Cain—Adam—Eve, 7. John the Baptist—Zechariah—Elizabeth, 8. Benjamin—Jacob—Rachel, 9. Abel—Adam—Eve, 10. Esau—Isaac—Rebekah

5. The Heaviest Branches

"Humility and the fear of the Lord bring wealth and honor and life."

6. Don't Forget Your Helmet!

1. fireman, 2. construction worker, 3. medieval soldier, 4. motorcycle, 5. bicycle, 6. Roman soldier, 7. hockey, 8. baseball, 9. welder, 10. football, 11. Viking, 12. modern soldier

7. The Ticket to Eternal Life

bus, train, plane, movie, sports event, museum, raffle, concert, theater

8. Thanks!

1. *Shenorhagal em*: Armenian, 2. *Gracias*: Spanish, 3. *Mahalo*: Hawaiian, 4. *Efharisto*: Greek, 5. *Wa-do*: Cherokee (United States), 6. *Obrigada*: Portuguese, 7. *Arigato*: Japanese, 8. *Merci*: French, 9. *Salamat*: Tagalog (Philippines), 10. *Danke*: German

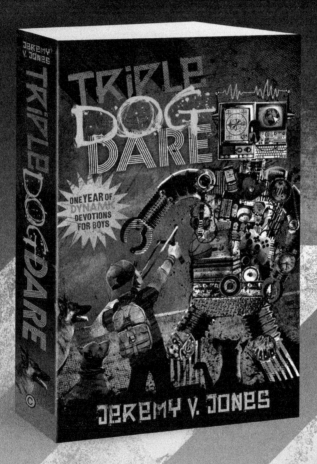